Confronting
AIDS

Update
1988

Institute of Medicine
National Academy of Sciences

NATIONAL ACADEMY PRESS
Washington, D.C. 1988

National Academy Press ● **2101 Constitution Avenue, NW** ● **Washington, DC 20418**

NOTICE: The project that is the subject of this report was approved by the Governing Board of the National Research Council, whose members are drawn from the councils of the National Academy of Sciences, the National Academy of Engineering, and the Institute of Medicine. The members of the committee responsible for the report were chosen for their special competences and with regard for appropriate balance.

This report has been reviewed by a group other than the authors according to procedures approved by a Report Review Committee consisting of members of the National Academy of Sciences, the National Academy of Engineering, and the Institute of Medicine.

The National Academy of Sciences was established in 1863 by Act of Congress as a private, nonprofit, self-governing membership corporation for the furtherance of science and technology, required to advise the federal government upon request within its fields of competence. Under its corporate charter the Academy established the National Research Council in 1916 and the National Academy of Engineering in 1964.

The Institute of Medicine was chartered in 1970 by the National Academy of Sciences to enlist distinguished members of the appropriate professions in the examination of policy matters pertaining to the health of the public. In this, the Institute acts under both the Academy's 1863 congressional charter responsibility to be an adviser to the federal government and its own initiative in identifying issues of medical care, research, and education.

Support for this project was provided in part by the National Research Council (NRC) Fund, a pool of private, discretionary, nonfederal funds that is used to support a program of Academy-initiated studies of national issues in which science and technology figure significantly. The NRC Fund consists of contributions from several sources: a consortium of private foundations, including the Carnegie Corporation of New York, the Charles E. Culpeper Foundation, the William and Flora Hewlett Foundation, the John D. and Catherine T. MacArthur Foundation, the Andrew W. Mellon Foundation, the Rockefeller Foundation, and the Alfred P. Sloan Foundation; the Academy Industry Program, which seeks annual contributions from companies that are concerned with the health of U.S. science and technology and with public policy issues with technological content; and the National Academy of Sciences and the National Academy of Engineering endowments. Additional funds were provided by The Merck Company Foundation and by the U.S. Public Health Service and Health Care Financing Administration (contract number ASU-000001–07-S).

Library of Congress Catalogue Card Number 88-61558

ISBN 0-309-03879-0

First Printing, June 1988
Second Printing, November 1988

Committee for the Oversight of AIDS Activities

THEODORE COOPER (*Chair*), The Upjohn Company, Kalamazoo, Michigan
STUART ALTMAN, Brandeis University, Waltham, Massachusetts
DAVID BALTIMORE, Whitehead Institute for Biomedical Research and
  Massachusetts Institute of Technology, Cambridge
KRISTINE GEBBIE, Oregon Health Division, Portland
DONALD R. HOPKINS, The Carter Presidential Center, Atlanta
KENNETH PREWITT, The Rockefeller Foundation, New York
HOWARD M. TEMIN, University of Wisconsin School of Medicine, Madison
PAUL VOLBERDING, San Francisco General Hospital

STAFF

ROBIN WEISS, Project Director and Director, AIDS Activities
LESLIE HARDY, Project Officer
MARY JANE POTASH, Project Officer
GAIL SPEARS, Administrative Assistant
KATHLEEN ACHOR, Senior Secretary
HOLLY DAWKINS, Secretary
JOANNE INNIS, Secretary
APRIL POWERS, Secretary

CONSULTANTS

MARK FEINBERG, Whitehead Institute for Biomedical Research, Cambridge,
  Massachusetts
LYNN I. LEVIN, Institute of Medicine
LEAH MAZADE, National Academy Press
JEFF STRYKER, University of Michigan School of Public Health, Ann Arbor
ROY WIDDUS, Global Programme on AIDS, World Health Organization

Preface

Twenty months ago, in October 1986, the Institute of Medicine/National Academy of Sciences (IOM/ NAS) issued *Confronting AIDS: Directions for Public Health, Health Care, and Research*. That report described what was known then about the acquired immune deficiency syndrome (AIDS). It contained the information on which the IOM/ NAS Committee on a National Strategy for AIDS based its conclusions and recommendations. Appendix A in this volume is the summary and recommendations from that report.

In March 1987, IOM/ NAS created a new committee, the AIDS Activities Oversight Committee, and charged it to monitor and assess the nation's response to the problems raised by AIDS in matters of public health, health care, and research. The committee was also asked to coordinate and oversee studies and activities concerning AIDS throughout the National Academy of Sciences complex.

One of the committee's first undertakings was to review *Confronting AIDS*, a year and a half later, with an eye toward assessing the nation's progress against AIDS and appraising the quality and extent of its responses. To supplement its expertise, the committee identified approximately 60 correspondents; these included experts in the fields of molecular biology, immunology, virology, drug and vaccine development, clinical medicine, epidemiology, public health, international health, infectious diseases, ethics, law, education, social sciences, the history of science, and other disciplines, as well as administrators of the major federal agencies concerned with AIDS and some state and local officials. These correspondents were asked to prepare papers for the committee describing progress and events in their fields since the fall of 1986. Appendix C is a list of the correspondents from whom material was received.

This report presents the committee's findings and the recommendations that arose from them. It should be viewed as an update of and a supplement to *Confronting AIDS;* it makes no attempt to duplicate the breadth and depth of information available in the original report. The preponderance of the factual material in *Confronting AIDS* remains accurate as of May 1988. For a basic understanding of the scientific knowledge that underlies both recent advances and the current recommendations, the committee refers the reader to that volume.

This update highlights new information or events that have given rise to the need for new directions; it also focuses on recommendations from the earlier report that deserve reemphasis. Chapters tend to vary in length and in the depth of their analysis, reflecting the reality that more or less progress has occurred in different areas and also the committee's intent to provide useful information to a varied audience of laypersons, scientists, and policymakers. The committee plans to address some areas more fully in the future; the U.S. role in combating the global epidemic, for example, awaits further study.

It is now clear that the "AIDS epidemic" is really an epidemic of HIV infection, and when referring to the epidemic in general, we use the terms interchangeably. When we discuss target populations for intervention, however, we distinguish among asymptomatic infected persons, symptomatic individuals, or people with AIDS as defined for surveillance purposes by the Centers for Disease Control (see Appendix B). As is true for any new disease, we expect that terminology will continue to evolve as our understanding increases.

Finally, like its predecessor body, the AIDS Oversight Committee was continually aware that it was assessing a "moving target." As new developments occur and new knowledge is acquired, the committee will pause again for reflection and evaluation.

ACKNOWLEDGMENTS

The committee wishes to thank the many persons who took time from their activities to assess the current status of their fields for the purposes of this report. Thanks are also due to the members of the AIDS Oversight Committee, all of whom made exceptional efforts to fulfill the requirements of the update. Finally, I wish to acknowledge the remarkable contribution and tireless assistance of the IOM/ NAS staff headed by Robin Weiss.

THEODORE COOPER
*Chairman of the Board and
Chief Executive Officer*
The Upjohn Company

Contents

Confronting
AIDS

Update
1988

Executive Summary

INTRODUCTION

The past four decades have witnessed unprecedented success in controlling infectious diseases, an achievement that has created great confidence in medicine's ability to conquer sickness. Yet in only a few years, the epidemic of human immunodeficiency virus (HIV) and acquired immune deficiency syndrome (AIDS) has shaken this confidence and revived fears at least as old as the medieval plagues.

Indeed, the plagues and more recent pestilences offer parallels to the AIDS epidemic. Both the bubonic plague and, in a period closer to our own, syphilis have evoked many of the same questions we now grapple with: tensions between individual liberties and the public good, the responsibilities of physicians toward their patients, the attribution of moral meaning to biological phenomena, the quest for a "magic bullet" cure, and controversy about the proper educational approach to changing the behavior that spreads the infection.

Epidemics of fatal infectious diseases are not unique in human history, but each is a unique event in its own time. Furthermore, there are important differences between AIDS and past epidemics, and between AIDS and other diseases of our own time that exact a heavy human toll. **The committee believes** that AIDS is a special case among current diseases. It is a fatal, infectious disease for which there is now no cure, and its sufferers appear to remain infectious for life. HIV infection and AIDS strike primarily the most productive group of society—young

1

adults. Attempts to control the disease by traditional public health measures are complicated by the fact that AIDS first occurred in already stigmatized groups—homosexual men and intravenous (IV) drug abusers—and the social response to the disease has been confounded by moralistic assignments of blame. A further compelling reason to direct special attention toward AIDS is that it is preventable by modifying the behavior that brings people into contact with the virus.

Coping with AIDS highlights many of the deficiencies in our social, biomedical, and health care systems. Just as the results of our experiences with other diseases have equipped us to address the challenge of HIV infection and AIDS, so will the solutions to the AIDS crisis produce benefits in diverse and possibly unforeseen areas that may well be applicable to other illnesses.

HIV INFECTION AND ITS EPIDEMIOLOGY

New information about HIV infection and its epidemiology has emerged either to confirm or alter earlier impressions of the disease. One question that has been resolved is the causative agent of AIDS. HIV and AIDS have been so thoroughly linked in time, place, and population group as to eliminate doubt that the virus produces the disease. **The committee believes** that the evidence that HIV causes AIDS is scientifically conclusive.

The observation of HIV-infected persons over longer periods of time has revealed that a larger and larger proportion of them develops AIDS. Current information suggests that the vast majority of persons who are seropositive—that is, carrying antibodies—for HIV will eventually progress to AIDS if no treatment is found to slow or halt the progression of the infection. A group of homosexual men in San Francisco has been studied longest because samples of their blood were available from earlier hepatitis vaccine research. After 8½ years, more than 40 percent of the HIV-infected members of the group have developed AIDS. Some analysts believe that virtually all infected persons will eventually develop AIDS.

The Spectrum of HIV Infection

HIV infection manifests itself in a variety of conditions, which complicates efforts to define the disease. Yet a definition is crucial to fighting a disease, beginning with the need simply to monitor its spread. The federal Centers for Disease Control (CDC) formulated an initial definition of AIDS in 1982 for surveillance purposes that relied on the presence of opportunistic infections and malignancies. In 1987 the definition was revised to incorporate two other syndromes: dementia and wasting syndrome. It has long been apparent, however, that many HIV-infected persons suffer from clinical syndromes and laboratory test abnormalities that signal the presence of disease but do not meet CDC criteria for AIDS. Earlier in the epidemic, certain clusters of symptoms were said to belong to an AIDS-related complex (ARC), which was incorporated in a CDC definition (but never used for case reporting). By now, however, **the committee believes** that the term ARC is no longer useful, either from a clinical or a public health perspective, and that HIV infection itself should be considered a disease.

Viewing HIV infection as a disease is important because it may eventually be amenable to treatment and patients will need to be diagnosed and treated as early as possible. Clinically, it is more accurate to describe HIV infection as a continuum of conditions associated with immune dysfunction. From a public health perspective the important event is infection rather than full-blown disease because even asymptomatic infected persons are capable of infecting others.

Modes and Efficiencies of HIV Transmission

Evidence continues to build that HIV transmission occurs only through sexual contact, the use of contaminated needles or syringes, exposure to infected blood or blood products, and transplanted tissue or organs from an infected donor. The virus may also be transmitted from mother to child either across the placenta or during delivery.

The virus can be transmitted in either direction between men and women. Heterosexual spread in the United States thus far has largely occurred when one partner was infected by a nonsexual route, usually by contaminated drug injection equipment. Heterosexual transmission of HIV has not shown the rapid increases that once were predicted, but the possibilities of such increases remain. In parts of Africa, heterosexual HIV transmission is great enough to sustain the disease in an epidemic status.

The modes of HIV transmission are well documented. What is not as clear is how easily or how "efficiently" the virus is transmitted by the various routes if a person is exposed. Comparisons are difficult because the denominators are so different—the risk of infection for each act of homosexual intercourse, for each use of a contaminated needle or syringe, for each blood transfusion, and so forth. However, it can be concluded that perinatal transmission and transfusion of infected blood are highly efficient vehicles for HIV spread. Studies of infected IV drug abusers also report high rates of infection for this group, suggesting that sharing contaminated needles and syringes, combined with frequent injections, carries a high risk of infection. Sexual partners of IV drug abusers appear to have a greater risk of becoming infected than the sexual partners of persons infected by other routes; what is not known is whether these sexual partners are infected by heterosexual transmission of the virus or by the unacknowledged sharing of contaminated needles and syringes. Sexual partners of persons infected by routes other than IV drug abuse have much lower risks of infection, as do health care workers who receive an accidental needle puncture.

Prevalence and Incidence of Infection in the United States

A report by CDC in November 1987 indicated that HIV infection remains highest in those risk groups that account for the majority of reported AIDS cases. Among homosexual and bisexual men, most prevalence estimates fall between 20 and 50 percent. However, these figures probably overestimate the true HIV prevalence in this group because they are based on surveys that used self-selected samples (i.e., the survey respondents were either seeking medical attention for sexually transmitted diseases or were concerned that their past or present sexual behavior had placed them at risk). The prevalence of HIV infection was high (50 to 60 percent) among IV drug abusers in New York City and northern New Jersey but much lower (less than 5 percent) in other areas of the country. Hemophiliacs who received blood clotting factor before 1985 show a prevalence of infection of 15 to 90 percent, depending on the type of hemophilia they have and the amount of clotting factor they received.

Data on the incidence of new infections are more difficult to obtain than are prevalence data, but they are crucial for longer term projections of the epidemic's course. Group studies of homosexual men indicate a lower HIV incidence rate during 1985–1987 than in the earlier part of the decade. Tightened procedures for blood donation and screening have greatly reduced new infections among hemophiliacs and transfusion recipients since 1985. In contrast, HIV incidence seems to be rising among New York City and San Francisco IV drug abusers.

CDC has scaled back somewhat its estimate of the number of infected people in the United States. In 1986 the estimate was 1 to 1.5 million; in late 1987 it was 945,000 to 1.4 million—a change occasioned by new information on the size of the groups that were known to be infected and new seroprevalence data for these groups.

By mid-May 1988, the AIDS cases reported to CDC totaled 62,200, a cumulative total more than two-and-a-half times that of September 1986. The demography of AIDS includes its rise to become the leading cause of death in New York City among men aged 25 to 44 and women aged 25 to

34. In 1986, New York City and San Francisco accounted for about 40 percent of all AIDS cases in the nation; by 1991 it is estimated that they will account for only 20 percent, suggesting that other localities may soon be forced to cope with the epidemic's burdens.

Epidemiological studies yielded many of the estimates described above, but the imprecision of those figures and others about prevalence, incidence, modes and efficiencies of transmission, and other crucial information bespeaks the need for more facts. **The committee therefore strongly urges** continued epidemiological research in support of appropriate prevention and control measures.

UNDERSTANDING THE EPIDEMIC'S COURSE

To alter the course of the HIV epidemic, planners must estimate, as early and as precisely as possible, how it will progress. Such predictions, like any forecasts, have to be based on the data that are available, however incomplete they may be. The techniques used to bridge the gaps in information are forms of mathematical modeling. Models project the prevalence and incidence of HIV infection and of AIDS in specific regions or populations, assess the possible consequences of interventions aimed at modifying sexual behavior and drug abuse, help plan care for AIDS patients, and extract the most information from existing data on myriad other features of the epidemic. However, existing data are sorely insufficient for definitive projections. Among the greatest needs are better information about seroprevalence in particular risk groups, sexual behavior, the size of the IV drug-abusing population, and the efficiencies of HIV transmission. **The committee strongly supports** continued research efforts to develop better ways to refine predictions about the future course of the AIDS epidemic and to evaluate potential intervention strategies.

The paucity of information on the social science aspects of AIDS has led the National Research Council to establish a committee to study what is known about the behavior that sustains the epidemic. Its first report is due to be released this fall.

ALTERING THE EPIDEMIC'S COURSE

AIDS and the HIV epidemic present a fundamental challenge to the guardians of public health in that certain properties of the HIV epidemic, which distinguish it from other dread diseases, evoke special concerns in fashioning a public health response. One factor is the lifelong infectiousness of virus carriers; another is that private, consensual behavior such as sexual intercourse and IV drug abuse are integral to the disease. A third factor is that the groups at greatest risk for infection were already vulnerable to social stigma and prejudice.

Public health efforts to combat the spread of HIV should not be limited to programs with "AIDS" in their titles. Appropriate venues for education, testing, and counseling about HIV include sexually transmitted disease clinics, drug abuse treatment centers, physicians' offices, hospitals, and health care clinics. Many of the programs designed to combat venereal diseases and drug abuse have a direct bearing on AIDS. If they lose funds to AIDS programs, the public health could be further imperiled. **The committee believes** that the HIV epidemic should prompt a reexamination of the fiscal and institutional barriers that impede effective public health efforts in all program areas related to the control of HIV infection.

Antidiscrimination Protections

A growing body of evidence bolsters our certainty that persons with HIV infection pose no danger to other persons through casual contact in the workplace, in housing, or in customary social interchanges. Therefore, there is no valid basis for discriminating against persons infected with HIV for fear they pose a health risk to others.

The committee believes that the fear of discrimination is a major constraint to the wide acceptance of many potentially effective public health measures. Public health programs will be most effective if they are accompanied by clear, strict sanctions to prevent unwarranted discrimination against those who are HIV-infected or at risk for infection.

There is no information with which to determine whether AIDS-related discrimination has paralleled the rise in AIDS cases, but numerous anecdotal accounts portray the difficulties faced by persons with AIDS or even by persons who are members of a risk group. A number of court cases have been filed involving victims of AIDS-related discrimination in a variety of settings (e.g., whether children or teachers with HIV infection should be allowed to remain in school), and complaints have been docketed with state and local human rights commissions. **The committee supports** the enactment of a federal statute specifically designed to prevent discrimination on the basis of HIV infection or AIDS.

Education

Educational efforts to foster and sustain behavioral change are the only means now available to stem the spread of HIV infection. In the past 2 years, programs initiated at the local, state, and federal levels have sought to educate the public in general and high-risk groups in particular.

Nevertheless, formidable obstacles remain to effective AIDS education. The committee believes that the urgency of the HIV epidemic warrants a multiplicity of educational efforts, including the use of paid advertising on television and in other media. A number of federal government entities, including the military, the postal service, Amtrak, and the U.S. mint, currently spend more than $300 million yearly for advertising. Administrative restrictions from the Department of Health and Human Services now preclude CDC from paying for advertising; yet public service advertisements alone are inadequate to the task. **The committee believes** that the gravity of the HIV epidemic is such that CDC, like other government entities, should be allowed to purchase advertising time and space and should be supplied with the funds to do so. Any administrative regulations that preclude such actions should be withdrawn immediately.

The implementation of AIDS education programs has continued to founder over questions involving the content of the programs' message. Information about the modes of HIV transmission must be conveyed in an understandable, yet scientifically accurate form. The message of AIDS education programs must also address sexual behavior and drug abuse. Those matters are regarded by some as immoral and not suitable for description in public health campaigns. Others, however, believe that candid presentations, including explicit language about sex, are necessary to get the message across. **The committee believes** that government at all levels, as well as private sources, should continue to fund effective, factual educational programs designed to foster behavioral change. An amendment to a health appropriations bill passed by Congress last year precluded the use of CDC funds for educational programs whose frank approach could be regarded as promoting homosexual activities. Explicit information on the risks associated with gay sex and the way those risks can be minimized does not "promote or encourage" homosexual activities. Its sole function is to help homosexuals avoid an illness that endangers their lives and those of their sexual partners and costs the nation billions of dollars.

AIDS education programs in schools, once a highly inflammatory issue, are being adopted more widely. By early 1987 half of the nation's largest school districts had begun some kind of HIV education program, but disputes continue about curricula and about who should control their content. **The committee believes** that school-based educational programs are an essential part of efforts to increase awareness of the risk of HIV and to combat the spread of infection. This education should begin at a young age and have a level of detail and explicitness appropriate for the age group. College and university education programs can take into account the possibility that the target audience may be sexually active or abusing drugs.

The public has become more knowledgeable about AIDS over the past few years, but serious misunderstandings persist. A quarter of the general public believes incorrectly that infection can be acquired by donating blood; more than a third incorrectly thinks that mosquitoes can transmit HIV. A fifth believes that they run the risk of becoming infected merely by working near someone with AIDS. **The committee believes** that more studies are needed to determine the effects of various types of educational campaigns on specific populations. For example, there have been few systematic assessments of the effect of AIDS education programs or media presentations on the behavior of heterosexuals (as opposed to the impact on their beliefs or understanding about the disease). Educational efforts aimed at persons at risk within minority communities are also critical: the prevalence of AIDS in the black and Hispanic communities is substantially higher than that among whites, and recent data suggest that the virus is spreading more rapidly among blacks and Hispanics at risk than among other population groups, especially in Northeastern cities.

Homosexual and bisexual men have responded encouragingly to education programs in San Francisco and New York, the U.S. cities hardest hit by the epidemic. That note of reassurance pales, however, beside the estimate that as much as half the male homosexual population in those cities may already be infected with HIV. Some hope lies in the possibility that those who are not infected can still be protected through vigorous educational efforts. **The committee also believes** it is essential to develop effective methods for reaching youth who are just becoming homosexually active.

Condoms are a generally effective means of preventing the spread of many sexually transmitted diseases, including HIV infection. Manufacturers and regulators of condoms have moved to ensure against product failure, but a greater likelihood of disease exposure lies in "user failure." Health care professionals should advise patients in detail about proper condom use and its importance in both heterosexual and homosexual intercourse. One obstacle to more effective AIDS education has been the long-standing refusal of the media to accept commercial condom advertising. **The committee believes** that there must be continued attention to the development of policies to foster the use of condoms.

Screening and Testing for HIV Antibody

Many public health objectives can be achieved through HIV antibody screening (of populations) and testing (of persons), including ensuring the safety of donated blood, tissues, and organs; ascertaining the spread of infection by demographic and geographic surveillance data; diagnosing patients so they can receive medical care; encouraging individual behavioral change (e.g., refraining from high-risk practices, making reproductive decisions on the basis of test status); facilitating the notification of sexual partners of infected individuals; and improving infection control in hospitals. Yet even as proposals are made to widen the scope of testing, other considerations also come into play. Test results can have psychological and social ramifications; inaccurate results can be devastating; testing and especially counseling are labor intensive and thus expensive; and test results must be protected against disclosure.

The accuracy of currently available HIV antibody tests compares favorably with other medical diagnostic tests. Nevertheless, some false results are inevitable, especially when tests are applied in populations that are at low risk for infection. **The committee believes** the federal government should give more attention to establishing standards for laboratory proficiency in HIV antibody testing, setting criteria for interpreting assays, and instituting quality assurance procedures.

Testing implies that the subject knows the test is being conducted and why, and that the results will be kept confidential so as to avoid all possibility of stigmatization. However, precautions are unlikely to be completely observed unless they are formalized. Thus, **the committee believes** that laws and regulations with strict sanctions to prohibit willful or negligent unauthorized disclosure of HIV antibody test results are an essential component of the public health effort. Confidentiality encourages subjects to volunteer for testing, which is a major tenet of public health programs. Laws and regulations to ensure confidentiality must be matched by conscientious medical recordkeeping to avoid inadvertent disclosure. **The committee believes** that, in addition to reviewing statutory protections of medical confidentiality, it will also be necessary at the local level for hospitals and other medical care institutions to review their recordkeeping policies and apprise their staff of their responsibilities to protect patient privacy.

The belief that a person's knowledge of his or her HIV test results encourages more healthful behavior is a driving force behind much public health policy related to AIDS. The committee believes that tests for HIV infection will play an increasingly useful role in the battle against its spread. **The committee recommends** expanded voluntary testing combined with counseling of all those whose behavior may have put them at risk for exposure to HIV. Those who test positive have a moral obligation to inform and protect their sexual or needle-sharing partners. In addition, **the committee believes** further studies to assess the behavioral impact of testing are essential. Most studies to determine the effects of HIV test results on behavior have enrolled homosexual men in large cities. Virtually nothing is known about such men in rural settings, about teens only beginning homosexual activity, about women facing family planning decisions, and about other test subjects.

The prospect of mandatory screening raises a number of problems, including the concern that if it is directed toward low-risk groups, it could waste resources that are needed for more effective public health programs. The committee considered the issue of mandatory screening in a variety of contexts and reached the following conclusions.

• **The committee believes** that, at this time, the only mandatory screening appropriate for public health purposes involves blood, tissue, and organ donation.

• Mandatory screening of patients entering the hospital is a questionable practice for purposes of infection control. Instead, **the committee encourages** hospitals and other health care facilities to implement the "universal precautions" recommended by CDC and the American Hospital Association. Nevertheless, for many individuals, being admitted to the hospital is a rare encounter with the health care system. **The committee believes** that, although mandatory screening of all hospital patients is inappropriate, the current situation warrants more widespread use of HIV antibody tests in the hospital setting on a voluntary, informed basis.

• **The committee reaffirms** the position adopted originally in *Confronting AIDS,* that testing marriage license applicants is inadvisable. The committee does, however, support the approach that requires potential applicants for marriage licenses to be informed of the risks of HIV transmission.

• Female prostitutes are frequent targets of proposals for mandatory testing. By engaging in multiple sexual encounters, they tend to contract more venereal diseases than the general public, but the biggest risk factor for prostitutes in the HIV context appears to be IV drug abuse. **The committee believes** that mandatory testing of prostitutes at the time of arrest or as a condition of release is not warranted at this time. **The committee supports** further seroprevalence studies to assess risk in this group and for the larger heterosexual community. Vigorous counseling efforts and the promotion of voluntary testing are necessary to encourage behavioral change among prostitutes.

The committee did not address the related question of mandatory testing of prisoners; however, it believes the issue warrants further study.

Home test kits for HIV antibody have been designed but are not yet on the market for lack of government approval. In addition, serious questions about accuracy, confidentiality, and counseling must be settled prior to their widespread use. However, **the committee believes** that home test kits and their associated questions warrant careful review. There may well be persons who are wary of encounters with the health care system or who fear being seen at a test site. For these people, home-based testing may become an appropriate alternative.

Other Public Health Measures

The law has traditionally recognized an exception to the requirement for confidentiality in situations in which third parties may be at risk. Case law on the books in many states spells out the duties of physicians to warn specific individuals of foreseeable dangers, including the risk of infection. Arguments against applying the duty to warn to persons with AIDS or to asymptomatic seropositive individuals hold that the failure to respect professional confidentiality obligations would deter patients from seeking care and would drive the disease underground. The American Medical Association has put forth guidelines about a physician's duty to warn third parties who may be at risk for infection, but questions of legal liability remain. Provisions of the AIDS Federal Policy Bill of 1987 allow physicians to use their discretion in warning third parties. Although the bill does not impose a duty on physicians one way or another, it does protect them from liability in the event of breached confidentiality in such circumstances.

Contact notification is a classic measure in venereal disease programs, but even in states in which laws demand that health officials ask for the identities of the sexual partners of an infected person (i.e., the "index case"), infected individuals are not compelled to disclose that information. The use of contact notification has been defended in venereal disease programs on the grounds that finding contacts in cases of syphilis or gonorrhea can lead to successful treatment—which is not yet true in HIV infection. Confidentiality is a major concern, although the record of public health officials in maintaining the confidentiality of information is remarkably good. On balance, **the committee believes** that voluntary contact notification programs can be useful in preventing the spread of HIV infection.

Reporting by health officers of seropositive persons is required in a dozen states. Although some arguments for mandatory reporting have merit, the committee has concluded that the costs far outweigh the benefits, especially if mandatory reporting discourages individuals from seeking voluntary testing. **The committee believes** that mandatory reporting of seropositive test results with identifiers should not be required at this time.

Isolating or otherwise restricting the freedom of infected carriers who refuse to protect others from infection historically has been a common means to prevent the spread of infection in other diseases. **The committee**

believes that there may be rare instances in which the state should act to restrict the personal liberties of some infected individuals, and states should review their statutes to ensure that such authority exists. Legal measures to restrict personal liberty should be used only when the following conditions have been met: (1) the person is infected, (2) the person is putting others at risk, (3) voluntary efforts to prevent such exposure have failed, and (4) the restrictive measure used is the least forceful appropriate to the task. Furthermore, restrictive measures should also entail the provision of intensive counseling, job training, and other supportive actions to induce behavioral change. The period involved should be short and clearly limited.

AIDS and IV Drug Abuse

Since the publication of *Confronting AIDS,* there has been widening recognition of the peril that HIV poses for the IV drug abuser, his or her sexual or needle-sharing partners, and their offspring. IV drug abusers are the second largest group of AIDS sufferers, and they are the most likely to transmit HIV to heterosexual partners. **The committee believes** that the gross inadequacy of federal efforts to reduce HIV transmission among IV drug abusers, when considered in relation to the scope and implications of such transmission, is now the most serious deficiency in current efforts to control HIV infection in the United States. The waiting lists for entry into treatment programs are a clear indication that the caliber of the ammunition in the war on drugs needs to be increased. **The committee urges** a greater commitment on the part of federal, state, and local governments to the rapid, large-scale expansion of drug abuse treatment slots, both in residential drug-free treatment centers and in methadone maintenance facilities, to offer immediate access to all addicts who request treatment.

Currently, no more than 20 percent of IV drug abusers attend treatment programs in any given year. To reach those who are not in treatment, innovative intervention programs are appearing in some localities. **The committee supports** the increased use of former IV drug abusers as community health workers to provide ''one-on-one'' risk reduction counseling and materials to drug abusers who are not in treatment, including instruction in the use of bleach to sterilize injection equipment. Our predecessor committee called for experimental programs to distribute sterile needles and syringes. **The present committee continues to believe** that evaluation of the effectiveness of providing sterile needles and injection equipment to drug abusers in certain circumstances is an essential part of planning a prevention strategy. In addition, **the committee supports** the immediate extension of serologic testing and counseling for HIV infection to all appropriate settings in which IV drug abusers are seen. Programs should also be developed to promote self-help support groups of former and current drug abusers as a means of education about AIDS and drug abuse in at-risk groups. Among long-term strategies that deserve more attention, the committee favors greater efforts to educate teens and preteens in high-risk populations about the dangers of drug abuse. Research and evaluation are necessary to determine which interventions work best.

Resources for Public Health Measures

The variety of funding sources for public health campaigns against HIV makes it difficult to determine if substantial progress is being made toward one of the goals in *Confronting AIDS:* providing by 1990 "newly available funds" totaling $1 billion a year for public health and education. Federal, state, and local governments, together with private sector sources, have made heartening contributions to the effort. Nevertheless, it is becoming apparent that present funding is insufficient for public health approaches to stem the epidemic. Perhaps the single greatest concern is the lack of availability of treatment facilities for IV drug abusers and the lack of support for programs to eliminate or reduce drug abuse or to mitigate the danger of shared injection equipment. **The committee believes** that a substantial sum of money will have to be spent for these purposes, well beyond the $1 billion originally proposed for AIDS public health and education measures. In addition, funds are needed to support expanded counseling programs linked to HIV-antibody testing and increased educational and outreach efforts among minority groups.

CARE OF PERSONS INFECTED WITH HIV

The relatively sudden appearance of large numbers of patients with a disease notable for its medical complexities and thorny social and ethical issues has highlighted inadequacies in current medical practice and the health care system. In the past 2 years, some progress has been made in improving care for patients with HIV infection and AIDS, but many of the recommendations in *Confronting AIDS* have not been addressed.

Care Needs of Special Patients

Almost by definition, AIDS patients are special patients. Their optimal care would be delivered by a multidisciplinary team of providers in facilities specializing in AIDS treatment, with effective discharge planning services to ensure the continuity of care. However, particular subgroups of AIDS patients deserve special consideration.

IV drug abusers without HIV infection pose substantial problems for the health care system because they are likely to be poor, in generally bad health, and homeless. Adding AIDS to these difficulties makes the provision of care more complicated. Even when community agencies have the resources to provide care for IV drug abusers with AIDS, they may not be eager to extend services to them or to their families. **The committee believes** that more long-term residential facilities or group homes are needed for AIDS patients who are IV drug abusers. Those patients with ongoing substance abuse or mental illness, or both, in addition to AIDS, have a special need for these facilities.

Infants and children with AIDS are a growing problem. Most of them have been infected by their mothers either before or at birth, and the mothers often are too sick to care for their children. Pediatric AIDS further disrupts families that may be already weakened as a result of parental drug abuse or HIV infection. Consequently, with few resources and social supports, pediatric AIDS patients remain hospitalized for prolonged periods. **The committee urges** that foster care, community-based residential care, and hospice care programs be developed or expanded to meet the needs of pediatric AIDS patients and their families so that hospitals are no longer the "home of last resort."

Patients with dementia or other neurologic disorders often require custodial care more than treatment, and extended care facilities are generally the setting of choice. However, such institutions do not exist in many areas, and when they do, their proprietors may be reluctant to take AIDS cases. **The committee recommends** that skilled nursing facilities or nursing homes providing inpatient long-term or hospice care be made available to AIDS patients who require these services—for example, through the construction of AIDS-dedicated facilities or by offering incentive payments to facilities that are willing to accept AIDS patients.

Health Care Providers

Although health care professionals continue to enter the field of AIDS patient care, they are not being recruited at a rate commensurate with the epidemic's growth. For one thing, providers have had to reexamine some of the tenets of their professions concerning the care of patients who may expose them to some risk of infection. Although the probability that a health care worker will acquire HIV infection on the job is low, it is not zero. Agencies such as CDC and the Department of Health and Human Services, together with the Occupational Safety and Health Administration (Department of Labor), have established guidelines for infection control that encourage greater vigilance in the handling of every patient, whether or not HIV infection is known or surmised.

Emergency care personnel and surgeons, who presumably are more likely to be exposed to HIV, are among those health care providers expressing heightened concern about infection and questioning their ethical obligation to treat HIV-infected patients. Reactions such as these have led professional groups (e.g., the American Medical Association and the American Nurses' Association) to issue policy statements against prejudicial approaches to ethics and duty. **The committee believes** that the health professions have a compact with society to treat patients with all forms of illness, including HIV infection and AIDS. To deny or compromise treatment to any patient on the grounds that a medical risk is posed to the provider breaks the fundamental trust between patient and caregiver. However, health care personnel also deserve to know the occupational risks they face in caring for infected patients. **The committee recommends** that assessments of the risk of occupational transmission of HIV continue and that new data be disseminated as widely as possible. Techniques to further reduce the risk of occupational HIV transmission should also be explored.

There have been no reported cases of the infection of a patient by a seropositive caregiver in the course of treatment. Nonetheless, a theoretical risk of such infection exists, and it has raised the issue of whether or not health care personnel should be screened for HIV antibodies. **The committee recommends** that the Institute of Medicine convene a conference on the ramifications of routine testing for HIV antibodies in health care workers.

The care of AIDS patients is sufficiently complex as to require personnel of many different skills, all trained in the context of the HIV-caused disease. Such training is being expanded, but the personnel supply lags far behind the demand. **The committee believes** that it is the responsibility of the health professions to stimulate adequate training in HIV infection and AIDS. One way to speed this process is to incorporate questions about AIDS and HIV infection into examinations for medical speciality and subspeciality board certification and state professional licensure; another is to offer continuing medical education courses. **The committee recommends** that basic curricula in education programs of all medical and health professions be modified to ensure adequate training in the diagnosis, prevention, and treatment of HIV infection and AIDS, as well as in infection control measures.

Doctors and nurses alike have begun to report increasing psychological and emotional strain from working with AIDS patients. Fears of becoming infected, the higher level of care needed for patients who often suffer severe physical and mental deterioration, and the "emotional brutalization" that comes from providing such care are common. There are few formal support groups for these beleaguered providers, although they must maintain their own health in order to give effective care. **The**

committee recommends that research funding be made available to examine the feasibility and study the effectiveness of programs to alleviate stress in health workers who care for AIDS patients.

Costs of Health Care for Persons with AIDS

Concern has been steadily growing over the economic impact of HIV infection and AIDS on the nation's health care system. However, data to assess the current situation and project the future economic burden are scarce. The direct costs associated with AIDS include hospital and physician services and nursing home and hospice care, as well as biomedical research and public health campaigns. The average lifetime medical expenses (from diagnosis to death) per AIDS patient are estimated to be between $65,000 and $80,000. Indirect costs of the disease include the loss of wages because of illness and the loss of future earnings (which is great because AIDS kills young adults in their most productive years). Most recently, indirect costs have been estimated at $7 billion for the prevalent cases in 1986. Projections of the spread of the disease by 1991 give rise to estimated expenditures totaling $66.5 billion for that year, of which $55.6 billion would be indirect costs.

Health services research, which was strongly recommended in *Confronting AIDS,* has been expanded in the past 2 years and should soon begin to identify the total direct costs of AIDS care, make comparisons of AIDS treatment costs with those of other diseases, compare costs among various stages of HIV-related illness and AIDS, and rank the cost-effectiveness of various organizations of service.

Financing Health Care for Persons with AIDS and Other HIV-Infected Individuals

The problems of financing care for persons with AIDS and other HIV-related conditions reflect the inequities in the entire U.S. health care system in relation to the uninsured and uninsurable, the plight of the poor in getting care, continuing underfunding for disease prevention, insufficient capabilities for care outside of institutions, and inadequate care for the chronically ill. **The committee believes** that all individuals have a right to equitable access to adequate medical care and that society has an ethical obligation to ensure such access.

In the meantime, Medicaid covers health care for much of the welfare population, including 40 percent or more of AIDS patients. Medicare, for the aged and disabled, covers very few AIDS patients because they often do not survive the required waiting period to qualify for benefits. Private health insurance may be covering a dwindling share of AIDS patients because of changes in patient demographics and because insurers are making plans to limit their exposure to financial risk.

Possible Financing Mechanisms

The committee has examined a number of proposals to improve health care coverage for persons with AIDS and other HIV-infected individuals. Some would encourage private insurers through government subsidy; others would modify Medicaid to make it more uniform among the states; still others would set up state insurance risk pools. The committee appreciates the concerns that have been voiced about singling out AIDS patients and others with HIV-related illnesses for special consideration in the financing of health care. However, because the AIDS crisis is disrupting the health care delivery system in many areas of the country, an interim financing solution is needed. **The committee endorses** an AIDS federal grant program as an interim measure to ensure that AIDS patients and those with HIV-related conditions have access to appropriate and cost-effective care.

A federal task force has recommended that state Medicaid and private insurers consider reimbursement, but with cost-sharing provisions to limit the burden on public funds, for costly AIDS therapies once the Food and Drug Administration has approved them for treatment under a special new status called the treatment investigational new drug, or IND. **The committee would extend** the task force recommendation to require such reimbursement. However, in the future, it may be necessary to develop a mechanism to establish priorities for coverage among potential therapies.

Although an AIDS federal grant program directing money to the states and reimbursement for costly experimental therapies would be temporary solutions to the problems of health care financing, a more comprehensive and equitable scheme is needed. **The committee urges** the federal government to take the lead in developing a comprehensive and coherent national plan for delivering and financing care for HIV-infected and AIDS patients. Any financing strategy of this kind should be guided by the following principles: (1) coverage from the time of HIV infection, (2) consideration of relief for hard-hit communities, (3) shared responsibility between public and private sectors for the financing of care, and (4) payment mechanisms that encourage the most cost-effective types of care.

THE BIOLOGY OF HIV AND BIOMEDICAL RESEARCH NEEDS

HIV Biology

Appreciable progress has been made recently in understanding how HIV compromises human defenses and causes AIDS. As our knowledge increases, however, so does its complexity. A second human retrovirus, HIV-2, has been identified and linked to a growing number of cases of immunodeficiency diseases that are clinically indistinguishable from the disease caused by HIV-1. HIV-2 infection is most prevalent in West Africa. Researchers have also discovered that the HIV-1 genome contains a number of novel genes that are without known counterparts in other retroviruses. Further understanding of the functions of these genes and the proteins they code for could speed the development of drugs and vaccines against AIDS. In the meantime, more viruses that strongly resemble HIV are being found in monkeys, cows, and cats, a development that may lead to valuable animal models of AIDS.

The HIV replicative cycle offers a number of opportunities for interruption by antiviral interventions. The recent discovery that the HIV-1 target cells have a particular molecule (called a CD4 receptor) on their surface that binds to an envelope protein of HIV-1 (gp120) has made this stage of HIV replication the object of increased attention. Another area of consideration involves the inhibition of reverse transcriptase, the lack of which would disrupt another essential replicative stage. Researchers also now recognize that the cells that are targets for HIV include the macrophages as well as the particular T cells of the immune response. The macrophages not only migrate freely but, unlike the T cells, are not greatly harmed by virus infection. Macrophage transport of HIV into the brain may be the cause of AIDS dementia.

Studies of HIV have revealed a variety of processes that were not previously known to occur in human cells, another example of the classic dependence of science on serendipity for unanticipated answers. For this reason, increasing the funds devoted to AIDS without a concomitant strengthening of all basic biomedical research is shortsighted. Thus, **the committee recommends** that funding for basic research in all areas of biology should continue to grow rather than be curtailed in favor of AIDS-targeted research.

Drug Development and Testing

Applying recent accomplishments of basic research to drug development requires organizational coordination. A promising new form of such cooperation is the National Cooperative Drug Discovery Groups of the National Institute of Allergy and Infectious Diseases (NIAID). Groups such as these and other investigators are exploring new approaches to drug development, as well as screening existing compounds for possible effectiveness against HIV. One example of a new treatment approach that is currently being tested is the combination of zidovudine (i.e., AZT) with an immune response modifier such as macrophage colony-stimulating factor.

The U.S. drug approval process, which is regulated by the Food and Drug Administration (FDA), is the most rigorous in the world. The approval of a new drug generally involves tests in animals and then a three- or sometimes four-phase series of clinical (human) trials for safety and efficacy. However, in response to the urgency of the AIDS crisis, FDA has moved to speed up some portions of its review and has established a new category of investigational new drugs called the treatment IND, which allows manufacturers to distribute a drug for use before FDA review has been completed.

A prototype of this procedure brought zidovudine (AZT) into relatively wide use quickly; more recently, trimetrexate, a drug used to treat the pneumonia common to AIDS patients, was approved under the new regulations. Yet FDA action for greater alacrity in getting drugs into testing, coupled with the intensity of drug development surrounding AIDS, could tax the agency's present capabilities. **The committee believes** that FDA resources for new drug approval should be commensurate with the task. In addition, although the ingenuity of FDA in designing new regulations to hasten the availability of drugs against HIV is admirable, **the committee recommends** that an outside evaluation of the treatment IND process be conducted after enough time has elapsed to determine its possible unanticipated consequences for any new drugs.

HIV infection and AIDS have generated a pressing need to develop and test experimental drugs and to make effective drugs widely available as soon as possible. The committee recognizes the frustration, fear, and anger of people with HIV infection, who may feel a lack of urgency in the drug development process. Nonetheless, **the committee believes** that once drugs are through phase I testing for toxicity, carefully controlled trials are still the fastest, most efficient way to determine what treatments work.

Although the best-designed clinical trial would enroll the fewest people needed to demonstrate a drug's effectiveness, persons with HIV infection want very much to participate in clinical trials. **The committee believes** that, following scientifically sound guidelines, wider access to clinical trials can be gained by broadening their geographic base, by extending trials to previously untapped populations including women, IV drug abusers, and pediatric patients, and by testing all compounds that might possibly be effective. Those groups conducting trials have the responsibility to communicate with the public about their availability and to encourage wide participation.

NIAID's establishment of AIDS clinical trial units (ACTUs) across the nation offers a mechanism for such communication. The 35 ACTUs are sites at which investigators and patients can be enlisted for large-scale, standardized collaborative clinical trials to determine the worth of a new drug. **The committee believes** that, to the greatest extent possible, trials should take place within well-established sites for drug testing.

Finally, the committee abhors the exploitation of people with HIV infection and AIDS by those promoting and selling "effective" therapies that are in fact unproven.

Vaccine Development and Testing

The prevention of HIV infection by vaccination continues to pose fundamental difficulties. Most of the experimental work employs portions of the viral envelope as the vaccine antigen to eliminate the possibility that the vaccine itself could be infectious. Vaccines of this type have been shown to induce antibody synthesis in mice and chimpanzees, including synthesis of neutralizing antibodies, which block HIV infection in tissue culture. However, the neutralizing antibodies did not block HIV infection in chimpanzees. These experimental results tend to mirror clinical observations, in which no correlation is seen between the level of neutralizing antibodies and the progress of the natural infection in patients.

We are no closer now to having a licensed vaccine against HIV than we were 2 years ago. Nevertheless, experiments point to some procedural measures that should be taken when a potential vaccine is found. The vaccine approval process is similar to that for drugs in that candidate vaccines are tested in three phases of trials, the last being a large-scale, controlled field trial with a sufficiently large number of subjects (at sufficiently high risk of infection) to determine whether the vaccine protects people (at a statistically significant level) against disease. FDA standard practice has generally been that a vaccine must show protective efficacy in an accepted animal model before tests can progress to human volunteers. However, given the potentially disastrous effects of the AIDS epidemic, FDA has approved human trials for two vaccine candidates in the absence of proof of protective efficacy in animals. There has been appreciable controversy about the wisdom of this move. **The committee believes** that human trials of HIV vaccine candidates should proceed only when (1) protection against infection has been demonstrated in chimpanzees (HIV), in macaques (SIV), or in another suitable animal model or (2) the vaccine candidate rests on fundamental new knowledge of the relevant human response that cannot be adequately modeled in animals. **The committee also believes** that planning should begin now for large-scale human efficacy trials of as yet undeveloped vaccines.

Roundtable on Drugs and Vaccines

The Institute of Medicine (IOM) conducted conferences in 1987 on the development of drugs to treat AIDS and the development of vaccines to prevent HIV infection. Each of the two events brought together scientists, clinicians, pharmaceutical industry representatives, and policymakers to consider ways to speed the availability of effective therapy and protection against HIV. The participants found the meetings so productive that they asked the IOM to undertake additional conferences. As a result, IOM has established the Roundtable on the Development of Drugs and Vaccines Against AIDS to spur progress in the discovery, regulation, legislation, and clinical application of measures to stem the epidemic. **The committee endorses** the establishment of the Roundtable on the Development of Drugs and Vaccines Against AIDS and encourages active participation by all sectors.

Animal Models of AIDS

The development of model systems, in which an animal infected with HIV shows the same symptoms and exhibits the same course of disease progression found in human AIDS patients, is essential to the campaign against the disease. The use of simian immunodeficiency virus (SIV) to infect Old World primates such as rhesus macaques results in an animal model that quickly develops an AIDS-like disease with a subsequent high death rate. **The committee believes** that SIV infection in macaques and the resulting disease are the best parallels at this time to human HIV infection and should be vigorously exploited. However, chimpanzees will also continue to figure prominently in AIDS research; for example, they are now the animal of choice when HIV is used to challenge vaccinated animals to determine whether a vaccine provides safe, effective protection. Yet chimpanzees for research purposes (like other primates) are in short supply. Thus, **the committee recommends** that plans for breeding, conserving, and otherwise expanding the present stock of chimpanzees be examined. This expansion may require increased funding.

Considering the amount of experimental work that lies ahead to stem the epidemic, the exclusive use of primates as animal models is infeasible. A small animal model is also desirable; in particular, a mouse model (mice being small, plentiful, and well understood) would be a veritable breakthrough in AIDS research. **The committee believes** that whatever its final form, the development of a small animal model for AIDS is of utmost importance. If efforts to develop such a model are carried out under carefully regulated, safe laboratory conditions, the committee would strongly support further work in this area.

Resources for the Campaign

Existing facilities are inadequate for further advances in research against HIV: very few laboratories are equipped to handle the virus safely. The federal government has provided additional funding of $24 million for the National Institutes of Health (NIH) to channel to extramural sites for facility improvement, and more than $19 million has been appropriated for NIH intramural upgrading. These new allocations, however, are only a modest beginning in the facility improvements needed for AIDS research. **The committee recommends** that the director of NIH, in consultation with research scientists from within and without the institutes, assess the need for and costs of new intramural and extramural facilities for AIDS research. This information should be forwarded to Congress for evaluation and subsequent action.

To support AIDS research by providing reagents to scientists, NIAID has established the AIDS Research and Reference Reagent Program. Scientist participation at this point, however, is only voluntary. **The committee recommends** that NIH stipulate that all investigators receiving NIH funds must make their AIDS-related reagents available to the distribution center, and thereby to all qualified investigators, after publication of their research. In addition, **the committee supports** the development by NIH, perhaps through the reagent program, of an HIV/SIV research "starter kit" that would enable qualified new investigators to begin research more easily.

Confronting AIDS recommended that federal appropriations for research related to this disease reach at least $1 billion a year by 1990. At the present rate of increase, it appears that this goal will be met. The 1988 NIH budget for AIDS research is $467.8 million, and the proposed 1989 budget is $587.6 million. Approximately $300 million more is proposed for AIDS research in 1989 by the Centers for Disease Control, the Alcohol, Drug Abuse, and Mental Health Administration, and FDA. **The committee believes** that when federal research expenditures for AIDS reach $1 billion annually, an assessment of the need for further increases should be made. It is important to ensure that other federal research programs are not penalized by a long-term disproportionate growth of the AIDS budget.

INTERNATIONAL ASPECTS OF AIDS AND HIV INFECTION

Of the 158 countries or territories that report to the World Health Organization (WHO), 133 had at least one case of AIDS as of March 1988. A cumulative total of more than 81,000 cases has been reported from countries on all continents. However, the reporting of cases to WHO is incomplete. U.S. officials estimate that the U.S. reporting system captures only about 80 percent of AIDS cases; much smaller proportions of actual cases are probably being captured in countries with few or any epidemiological data systems. Consequently, WHO estimates that there are at least 150,000 AIDS cases worldwide and between 5 and 10 million (closer to 5 million) HIV-infected persons.

Three patterns of AIDS are differentiated on the world map. In North America, parts of South America, many Western European countries, Australia, and New Zealand, most AIDS cases occur among homosexual or bisexual men and urban IV drug abusers. In most of Africa and parts of the Caribbean, most cases occur among heterosexuals. In Eastern Europe, the eastern Mediterranean, Asia, and most of the Pacific, only small numbers of cases have been reported thus far. The WHO Global Programme on AIDS has been working in the past year to (1) provide support to national AIDS control and prevention programs and (2) conduct global AIDS-related activities (e.g., surveillance and research in the biomedical, social, and epidemiological sciences).

The rationale for United States involvement in international AIDS activities is more broadly based than the protection of American troops and tourists. AIDS can destabilize the work force and the economy in developing countries whose advancement has been aided by U.S. dollars. AIDS can also reverse the advances in infant and child survival in countries in which our help only recently has brought improvement. Finally, some countries offer promising opportunities for collaborative AIDS research because they have different disease patterns and a higher prevalence of HIV-2 infection.

American activities in international work against AIDS are conducted by many federal agencies. Contributions to WHO's Global Programme were $1 million in 1986 and $5 million in 1987; they will be about $15 million in 1988. Philanthropic foundations are also beginning to fund AIDS activities. In addition to these contributions, however, **the committee believes** that the United States has a special responsibility in international health efforts to control AIDS because of our exceptional resources in public health specialists and biomedical scientists, the large number of infected persons in the United States, and our relative affluence.

WHO's program on AIDS is also supported, in a sense, by the other divisions of WHO, which are funded by regular budget assessments of assenting United Nations member countries. At last reckoning, the United States was in arrears on its regular budget assessment. **The committee strongly urges** that the United States pay its assessed contributions to WHO in total as soon as possible.

The committee is encouraged by the United States' response to the needs of the international campaign against AIDS. Yet effective planning for U.S. participation requires that we know the detail and extent of activities in which we are already engaged. The committee responsible for *Confronting AIDS* could find no such information 2 years ago; the present committee has also failed to find these data. **The committee urges** that a data base for international AIDS research activities be established and maintained.

A NATIONAL COMMISSION ON HIV INFECTION AND AIDS

In *Confronting AIDS*, the Institute of Medicine/National Academy of Sciences (IOM/NAS) Committee on a National Strategy for AIDS highlighted deficiencies in the efforts being directed against the AIDS epidemic and in the employment of the nation's resources in that task. The 1986 report also identified as a major concern a lack of cohesiveness and strategic planning throughout the national endeavor and recommended the creation of a national commission on AIDS.

The committee carefully weighed the question of whether or not to reaffirm the IOM/NAS recommendation to establish a national commission on AIDS, and in doing so evaluated the quality of leadership in several components of government and in the private sector. The Presidential Commission on the Human Immunodeficiency Virus Epidemic (which concludes the work authorized by its year-long charter in June 1988) has demonstrated the effectiveness of focused attention in bringing diverse public and private resources to bear on a national problem. Unfortunately, however, the commission is short-lived. The coordination offered by the Federal Coordinating Committee on Information, Education, and Risk Reduction on AIDS, chaired by the assistant secretary for health of the Department of Health and Human Services (HHS), has facilitated communication but has not set policy that spans all departments of the executive branch. Within HHS, coordination has been carried out by the Public Health Service Executive Task Force on AIDS. Two new offices, the National AIDS Program Office (to expand and replace the task force) and, at the NIH level, the Office of AIDS Research, will continue to streamline progress within the Public Health Service, but their responsibility is not the overarching leadership that the committee feels is lacking. Finally, private organizations, state and local governments, foundations, volunteer groups, and professional organizations have all made enormous contributions, but the absence of a coherent national policy condemns many of them to "reinvent the wheel" when it comes to AIDS policies and programs.

Still, there have been areas of progress: biomedical research, some improvements in public education manifested in the recent all-household mailing planned by CDC and the continuing superb leadership of Surgeon General C. Everett Koop, improvements in the FDA drug approval process, and the ongoing CDC surveillance efforts. Nevertheless, the committee has concluded that the federal response has been too uneven. Inadequacies persist in the provision and financing of health care, in setting standards for antibody testing and antidiscrimination, in address-ing IV substance abuse, and in furnishing overarching direction for all components of the government and the private sector. The committee considered a separate AIDS agency to remedy these deficiencies but concluded that such a body, cutting as it would across already established programs, would cause unnecessary disruptions.

The nation has suffered from the absence of strong federal leadership. Although generally reluctant to recommend the establishment of new government entities, in light of past successes with the commission approach (e.g., the Social Security Commission), **the committee reaffirms** the 1986 recommendation that a national commission on AIDS and HIV infection be established. The committee would assume an advisory rather than an operating role and be responsible for:

- adopting as its scope a broad view of the epidemic that spans all components of the public and private sectors;
- monitoring the course of the epidemic;
- evaluating research, health care, and public health needs;
- formulating recommendations for altering the direction or intensity of health care, public health, and research efforts as the problem evolves;
- setting the tone for educational campaigns;
- assuming an advisory and catalytic role in stimulating appropriate action by federal, state, and local government bodies, industry, the academic scientific community, and private foundations and organiza-tions;
- encouraging greater U.S. contributions to international efforts;
- monitoring and advising on related legal and ethical issues;
- reporting to the American public to clarify points of possible confu-sion such as the extent and danger of heterosexual spread or the effectiveness of condoms; and
- providing a forum for all involved and interested parties.

To carry out these responsibilities, the commission must have certain attributes. It should:

- be endorsed at the highest levels of government—both by the President and Congress;
- have sufficient national and international stature and credibility for its advice to influence all participants in the struggle against AIDS; and
- be able to engage all of the diverse public and private resources that can be brought to bear on AIDS and its associated problems.

Considering these responsibilities and attributes, the committee pro-poses the establishment of a national commission on AIDS with a 5-year, renewable term. The commission chair should be a senior, recognized leader, engaged full time in this capacity and reporting directly to the President. In addition to the chair, the commission should consist of eight other members, each of whom is a senior expert of national stature in one of the areas of particular relevance to AIDS. Each commissioner should in turn head a panel of experts to explore such topics as research (biomedical, health care services, and social sciences), the provision and financing of health care, public health and education, epidemiology and modeling, law and ethics, and the United States' international role in combating AIDS. The commission should have ample professional staff and a sufficient budget. In addition, consideration should be given to establishing a $10 million discretionary fund that would be spent through existing agencies to allow quick responses to new, unforeseen opportunities.

The establishment of a national commission signals a major commitment to national leadership for preventing and controlling HIV infection and AIDS. HIV infection is a rapidly moving target; a sustained, well-guided effort is needed if we are to remain attentive to its course and thwart its effects.

1

Introduction

The past four decades have witnessed unprecedented success in controlling infectious diseases, an achievement that has created great confidence in medicine's ability to conquer sickness. Yet in only a few years, the epidemic of human immunodeficiency virus (HIV) and acquired immune deficiency syndrome (AIDS) has shaken this confidence and revived fears at least as old as the medieval plagues.

Indeed, the plagues and more recent pestilences offer parallels to the AIDS epidemic that may provide some useful lessons. Bubonic plague, a bacterial disease spread by rats and fleas, caused a succession of epidemics throughout Europe between the fourteenth and eighteenth centuries. The worst of these, called the Black Death, wiped out at least one-quarter of the population of Europe (Gottfried, 1983; Zuger and Miles, 1987). Accounts of the period describe a society grappling with many of the same questions AIDS has provoked: tensions between individual liberties and the public good, the responsibilities of physicians toward their patients, and the attribution of moral meaning to biological phenomena.

In a period closer to our own, the first decades of the twentieth century offer syphilis as an example of an epidemic disease with features similar to those of AIDS, the control of which raised similar questions. As Brandt (1987) has noted, the parallels in this instance are particularly striking: they relate to science, public health, and social values.

The limitations in our knowledge of AIDS and HIV infection and the epidemic's lack of amenability thus far to a purely technological solution

27

mirror medicine's experience with syphilis. Paul Ehrlich discovered a treatment for syphilis—salvarsan—that he hoped would be the first of an arsenal of "magic bullets," drugs that would seek out and destroy particular diseases. Yet even penicillin, a more effective cure, has not eradicated the disease. When penicillin was introduced in 1943, the incidence of syphilis was 72 cases per 100,000 people; by 1956, it had fallen to about 4 per 100,000. By 1987, however, the incidence had risen to 15 cases per 100,000 and continues to rise (CDC, 1988a).

Public health measures present another area for comparisons between the two epidemics. The public health response to syphilis in the early years of this century included what are by now familiar components: educational programs (those of the Victorian era unabashedly stressed chastity as contrasted with "safer sex") and screening and testing for infection. Public health measures to combat syphilis also comprised a dramatic campaign to close red-light districts. A crackdown in the districts during World War I resulted in the jailing of more than 30,000 prostitutes, but this program of detention and isolation had no impact on rates of venereal disease, which increased dramatically during the war.

Perhaps the strongest parallel between AIDS and syphilis is that they are both sexually transmitted diseases, a characteristic that often brings social values forcefully into play. The reality of sexually transmitted diseases threatened the strong Victorian values of discipline and restraint and the social sanction of sex only within marriage. Among other manifestations of opprobrium, in those times as in our own, there arose a distinction predicated on how the infection was obtained, a distinction between "innocent" victims of disease (children and unknowing family members) and others who, according to prevailing moral values, were less deserving of sympathy and medical support (Brandt, 1987).

The similarities between the AIDS epidemic of the present and epidemics of the recent past illustrate that each major epidemic of a fatal infectious disease is not unique in human history but nevertheless is an unusual event in its own time. Polio and smallpox are more recent examples of feared and calamitous epidemics that were eventually controlled by the advent of a vaccine; in the case of smallpox, a worldwide eradication effort was also necessary. There are important differences between AIDS and past epidemics, however, and between AIDS and other diseases of our time that also exact a heavy human toll. As the committee assessed problems and potential solutions in the areas of public health, health care, research, and national leadership, a recurring question emerged: Should extraordinary measures be taken in response to the AIDS epidemic and all its ramifications, given the magnitude and dimensions of other afflictions such as heart disease and cancer?

The committee believes that AIDS is a special case among current diseases. Its characteristics define a unique pattern; although it shares particular features with other diseases, no one disease, past or present, encompasses all the challenges posed by AIDS.

AIDS is an infectious, fatal disease for which there is now no cure. All infected persons appear to remain infectious, both during the long asymptomatic incubation period of HIV infection and during symptomatic disease. This protracted infectiousness is unusual in the history of infectious diseases. The primary sufferers of AIDS come from what is ordinarily a healthy and productive population group: young adults. The Centers for Disease Control (CDC) calculate premature mortality in the United States according to total years of potential life lost before age 65. Against a backdrop of overall decline in years of potential life lost, AIDS has moved from 13th in 1984 to the 8th leading cause of premature mortality in 1986 (CDC, 1988b). The absolute mortality caused by AIDS to date may be exceeded by other major diseases, but the steep slope of its rise and the youth of its victims are unmatched.

Because AIDS first occurred in the United States among already stigmatized groups—homosexual and bisexual men and intravenous (IV) drug abusers—the social response to it has been complicated by moralistic assignments of blame for vulnerability to the disease, much as in earlier days when plague was seen as divine retribution. The persistent fear of casual transmission, in the face of mounting evidence to the contrary, is reminiscent of theories that syphilis was transmitted by toilet seats, pens, and doorknobs, beliefs that lingered well past the time when scientific evidence had proven them groundless. These social constructions of disease, and the fertile ground they provide for restrictive or discriminatory social responses, also set AIDS apart as a matter for special concern. The way in which traditional public health responses are complicated by these features of AIDS is discussed in Chapter 4.

There are other aspects of the AIDS epidemic that set it apart. A disproportionate burden in the care of AIDS patients falls on certain geographic locations where the prevalence of infection is high. In fact, the AIDS epidemic is really a series of discrete epidemics in particular population subgroups in particular places. Society was unprepared for the numbers of patients generated by infection with HIV. Furthermore, the AIDS caseload began to mushroom at a time when hospital beds were being eliminated. If a business-as-usual approach is taken, one consequence of the epidemic may be the decline of hospitals and health care systems in high-prevalence areas. (This aspect of the epidemic is discussed in Chapter 5.) The fundamental uncertainty about the epidemic's future course (see Chapter 3), in contrast to other conditions such as heart disease or cancer for which the burden of illness is more predictable, lends urgency to the need for attention. In addition, the international spread of the disease brings special responsibilities to the United States (see Chapter 7) because of our exceptional resources in public health and biomedical personnel, the large numbers of infected persons in the United States, and our relative affluence.

A further compelling argument for now focusing special attention on AIDS is that future HIV infections are preventable by modifying the behavior that brings individuals into contact with the virus. IV drug abuse and sexual behavior may be both biologically and socially based and are not always voluntary in the simplest sense. Yet the potential exists for their modification through education, counseling, and treatment. In addition, increasingly detailed epidemiological knowledge about the modes of spread of the disease constitutes a firm foundation of data on which to construct public health programs responsive to the precise contours of the epidemic (Osborn, 1988). We may be in the midst of a disaster, but we also have the means to avert future devastation.

Whenever a system is brought into play to cope with AIDS—be it a social, biomedical research, or medical care system—its deficiencies are exposed. (A few examples are the financing of care, the organization of medical services, foster care, the availability of drug abuse treatment, and the coordination of research efforts.) Once AIDS is considered a special case, however, a broader range of solutions to the problems posed by the AIDS crisis opens up. There are three viable categories of approaches: (1) strengthening programs within the context of existing systems; (2) developing new schemes that resolve general problems brought into focus by AIDS; and (3) formulating AIDS-specific solutions (this kind of specific response is often fragmented from the system as a whole, but its advantage is that it can be quickly deployed to respond to an emergency). With these approaches in mind, the committee has tried to lay out a number of options in making recommendations for further action against the AIDS epidemic.

The committee is aware of the possible dangers in granting any one disease special status—in particular, that attention and resources might be diverted from other important conditions. In shaping its recommendations, the committee took particular care to advise against such diversion. Furthermore, just as the results of our experience with other diseases (e.g., cancer) have equipped us to address the challenge of HIV infection and AIDS, so will solutions to the AIDS crisis produce benefits in diverse and possibly unforeseen areas that may well be applicable to other illnesses. These areas include basic science, drug and vaccine development, the financing of health care, alternative health care settings, knowledge of human behavior, relationships between health care providers and patients, drug abuse prevention and treatment, and compassionate treatment of the sick and disabled. Rather than overshadowing efforts in other fields, considering AIDS a special case may illuminate new directions in the management of other illnesses.

REFERENCES

Brandt, A. M. 1987. No Magic Bullet: A Social History of Venereal Disease in the United States Since 1880. New York: Oxford University Press.

CDC (Centers for Disease Control). 1988a. Continuing increase in infectious syphilis—United States. Morbid. Mortal. Wkly. Rep. 37:35–38.

CDC. 1988b. Quarterly report to the Domestic Policy Council on the prevalence and rate of spread of HIV and AIDS in the United States. Morbid. Mortal. Wkly. Rep. 37:223–226.

Gottfried, R. S. 1983. The Black Death. New York: Free Press.

Osborn, J. 1988. AIDS: Politics and science. N. Engl. J. Med. 318:444–447.

Zuger, A., and S. H. Miles. 1987. Physicians, AIDS, and occupational risk. Historic traditions and ethical obligations. J. Am. Med. Assoc. 258:1924–1928.

2

HIV Infection and Its Epidemiology

In the 20 months since the publication of *Confronting AIDS,* much has been learned about the clinical history of HIV infection and about the dimensions of the epidemic. New information has arisen from continuing clinical observation, surveillance systems, and epidemiological studies. In this chapter, we focus on some important aspects of the disease and the epidemic in areas in which new data have either confirmed or altered initial impressions or in which a deeper understanding of the disease has emerged. These areas include the causative agent of AIDS, the proportion of seropositive persons who will develop AIDS, HIV infection as a continuum of conditions, the modes and efficiencies of HIV transmission, and the prevalence and incidence of HIV infection and the dimensions of the epidemic in the United States (global epidemiology is discussed in Chapter 7).

HIV: THE ETIOLOGIC AGENT OF AIDS

Early in the epidemic, epidemiological analysis of the pattern of the spread of AIDS showed it to be reminiscent of that for hepatitis B virus, an observation that pointed scientists in the right direction in their search for an etiologic agent. In 1983 and 1984 several researchers identified a retrovirus that is now understood to be HIV as the cause of AIDS. **The committee believes that the evidence that HIV causes AIDS is scientifically conclusive.**

That a particular organism causes a disease is demonstrated by a confluence of evidence linking the two: HIV and AIDS have been so linked in time, place, and population group. For example, in San Francisco, the examination of frozen blood from a cohort of homosexual men showed the appearance of antibodies to HIV as early as 1978. At that time, the prevalence of HIV infection was probably less than 5 percent in the population of male homosexuals in San Francisco. The first cases of AIDS in homosexual men in San Francisco were detected in 1981 (CDC, 1981). This association between the cumulative incidence of HIV infection and of AIDS cases is the epidemiological pattern that must exist if HIV and AIDS are causally associated: the virus must be newly introduced into the population, it must become widely prevalent, and its dissemination must precede the incidence of AIDS (Winkelstein, 1988).

The conjunction heralded by the joint appearance of HIV and AIDS has been confirmed by their continued association. HIV seropositivity rates in defined subpopulations of homosexual men in San Francisco and New York City and in IV drug abusers in New York City are associated with later cases of AIDS in the same groups (Curran et al., 1988). In San Francisco, these subpopulations can be further broken down by neighborhood of residence, in which the association between HIV seropositivity and AIDS is also high (Winkelstein et al., 1987b). Conversely, AIDS is unknown in populations that are free of HIV antibodies.

The virus has been isolated from persons with AIDS; as assay techniques have improved, close to 100 percent of affected individuals can be found to harbor the virus (Booth, 1988). The virus is not found in persons who are not at risk for infection. These points are supported by epidemiological data from the ongoing San Francisco Men's Health Study, which began in 1984. Among 374 homosexual men who remained uninfected with HIV during the first 30 months of follow-up, no cases of AIDS occurred. Among 36 homosexual men who became infected with HIV during this period, 3 cases of AIDS (8 percent) occurred. Among 399 study subjects who were infected with HIV when they entered the study, 52 (13 percent) developed AIDS. None of the heterosexual men in the study acquired HIV infection, and none developed AIDS. The probability that this distribution might have occurred by chance is less than one in a million (Winkelstein, 1988).

Perhaps the clearest evidence linking HIV to AIDS is to be found in the tragic results of blood transfusions in the United States and around the world. The transmission of HIV in contaminated blood and blood products has been clearly linked to AIDS (Curran et al., 1984); in the United States, over 1,500 reported cases of AIDS are associated with blood transfusions. Since routine screening of the blood supply for antibodies to HIV began in 1985, HIV transmission by this route has practically disappeared. Nevertheless, 13 recipients from 7 donors who initially tested negative for HIV antibodies are known to have acquired

HIV infection between March 1985 and October 1987 (Ward et al., 1988). The 7 donors, who were tested at the time of donation, probably had negative test results because testing occurred soon after infection and before the development of detectable antibodies. On later retesting, however, all 7 donors were found to have detectable HIV antibodies in their blood. Of the 13 recipients, 1 developed AIDS, and 3 developed HIV-related illnesses. Of the 3 developing illness, 1 was an infant twin who received transfusions shortly after birth; her fraternal twin, who received no transfusions, remained healthy. Thus, 13 people with no other risk factors became infected, and 4 of them developed the illness after receiving transfusions from donors who were initially thought to be free of infection. After careful investigation, the donors were found, in fact, to have HIV infection.

The causal role of HIV in AIDS is also supported by the high risk (30 to 50 percent) of perinatal HIV transmission from an infected mother to her infant (CDC, 1987b) and the subsequent diagnosis of AIDS in the infected infants.

The pathogenesis of HIV infection—how the organism causes disease—is still incompletely understood. Several mechanisms have been proposed for the profound immunodeficiency that results from HIV infection, including the aggregation of uninfected and infected T lymphocytes into multinucleated syncytia that subsequently die, the infection of stem cells, and the inhibition of lymphocyte functions by viral products. A complete understanding of a disease's pathogenesis, however, is not a prerequisite to knowing its etiology.

PROPORTION OF INFECTED INDIVIDUALS WHO WILL DEVELOP AIDS

As epidemiological cohorts of HIV-infected individuals are observed over time, a larger and larger proportion of seropositive persons has been seen to develop AIDS. The available data suggest that the great majority of HIV-infected persons will eventually progress to AIDS in the absence of effective therapy to slow or halt the infection's progression.

The cohort of individuals that has been studied longest in relation to AIDS is a group of gay men in San Francisco who were enrolled in a study of hepatitis B virus vaccine in the late 1970s. As part of the study, blood samples were collected, from which serum was saved and frozen. Because this group of men was later found to be at high risk for AIDS, samples of the frozen serum were analyzed for HIV infection, and infected individuals have been followed for clinical and laboratory evidence of AIDS. Almost no cases of AIDS occurred during the first 2 years after infection was discovered. After 8½ years, more than 40 percent of the infected cohort has developed AIDS; a similar proportion has developed symptoms of HIV infection and is expected to progress to AIDS. Statistical modeling of the incidence of AIDS in this cohort predicts the possibility that 100 percent will develop AIDS within 13 years after initial infection (G. W. Rutherford, San Francisco Department of Public Health, personal communication, 1988).

The analysis of another cohort of 288 seropositive homosexual men in San Francisco who were seropositive when the study began shows that 22 percent have developed AIDS after 3 years of observation. Another 19 percent have clinical symptoms of infection, and an additional 24 percent demonstrate laboratory evidence of immunologic compromise. Projections for this cohort are that 50 percent of the men will develop AIDS within 6 years of observation (or probably 9 years of infection) and that many more will develop the disease in subsequent years (Moss et al., 1988).

Data from individuals infected with HIV through blood transfusions and data from persons with hemophilia suggest that the rate of progression from HIV infection to AIDS increases with age. The exception to this pattern is newborns, who have the highest progression rate of all age groups (Eyster et al., 1987; Medley et al., 1987). The progression rate in adults with hemophilia appears to be similar to that in male homosexuals (Goedert and Blattner, in press).

THE SPECTRUM OF HIV INFECTION

In grappling with a new disease, especially one that quickly assumes epidemic proportions, terminology and definitions become vital for clinical management of patients, data gathering and research, and decisions about coverage and reimbursement. In 1982 CDC developed a definition of AIDS for surveillance purposes that relied on the presence of opportunistic infections and malignancies; in August 1987 the definition was revised to incorporate two other syndromes indicative of AIDS: dementia and wasting syndrome (see Appendix B). Yet fairly early in the epidemic, it became apparent that many infected individuals who suffered from clinical symptoms and laboratory abnormalities signaling the presence of HIV infection did not meet the CDC criteria for the disease. For example, persistent generalized lymphadenopathy (PGL) was thought to be associated with an increased risk of developing AIDS, especially when combined with oral candidiasis and certain laboratory abnormalities. Another group of patients displayed other chronic symptoms of AIDS—fever, weight loss, night sweats, chronic diarrhea, and fatigue—and a high proportion of this group also exhibited laboratory abnormalities. Even so, these patients did not fit what had become the standard definition of the disease, although some of them seemed to develop AIDS at a rapid pace. They were described as having AIDS-related complex (ARC), and the ARC clinical syndrome was eventually incorporated in a CDC definition (although it was never used as a basis for case reporting). Clinicians noted, however, that even this definition failed to include some patients who appeared to be at high risk for progressing to AIDS. A third, more broadly defined syndrome was termed the AIDS-related condition.

Today, with a better understanding of the natural history of HIV infection and with more precise laboratory assessments of disease progression, **the committee believes that the term ARC is no longer useful, either from a clinical or a public health perspective, and that HIV infection itself should be considered a disease.** It is more accurate to describe HIV infection as a continuum of conditions, ranging from the acute, transient, mononucleosis-like syndrome associated with seroconversion, to asymptomatic HIV infection, to symptomatic HIV infection, and, finally, to AIDS, a spectrum that encompasses a great variety of clinical symptomatology. The terms ARC and PGL do not have the precise prognostic implications they were once thought to have. For instance, it is now known that the presence of persistent, generalized lymphadenopathy in and of itself does not imply a worse prognosis than HIV seropositivity. For clinical (treatment or research) purposes, a patient can be more accurately described by a combination of a description of symptoms and laboratory evidence of immune dysfunction rather than by terms such as ARC or PGL.

Experience with cohorts of infected individuals indicates that a majority of HIV-infected individuals shows some evidence of progressive immunodeficiency and is likely to develop AIDS in the absence of effective therapy. AIDS, a dramatic and devastating syndrome, caught the attention of physicians and public health officials earlier than the milder manifestations of HIV infection, but it is now clear that AIDS is end-stage HIV infection. Like many other progressive disease processes, both infectious and noninfectious, HIV has an asymptomatic period that varies in length.

Viewing HIV infection as a disease is important because it may eventually be amenable to treatment. The drug zidovudine (i.e., AZT) has been shown to prolong the life of AIDS patients; it and other drugs are currently being tested to determine whether they also halt or slow disease progression in infected asymptomatic individuals. If an effective therapy is found, HIV infection will need to be treated early, just as diseases such as gonorrhea are often diagnosed and treated in asymptomatic infected patients. Even though no treatment is available, diagnosing HIV infection is still important now so that opportunistic infections and malignancies

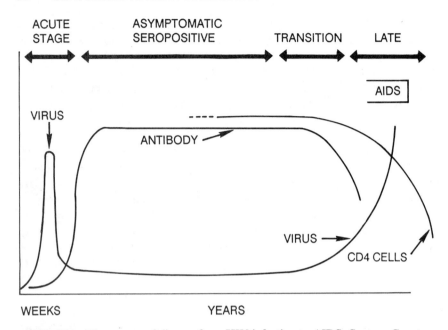

FIGURE 1   The course of disease from HIV infection to AIDS. Source: Courtesy of David Baltimore, Whitehead Institute for Biomedical Research, Cambridge, Massachusetts.

can be recognized as early as possible. Many treatments for these complications are more effective and less toxic when initiated early.

Considering HIV infection a disease is important to other aspects of the AIDS crisis. From a public health perspective, the population of most interest is the group infected with the virus, because these persons are capable of infecting others. In addition, as discussed in Chapter 5, medical care coverage should be based on symptoms associated with HIV infection rather than on arbitrary definitions of when "disease" begins. A terminology that reflects the progression of the disease from the initial, acute stage of infection to asymptomatic HIV infection and finally to symptomatic HIV infection and AIDS (Figure 1) would be useful for clinical treatment and for society's management of the disease. CDC has developed a classification system (see Appendix B) that might form the basis for such a terminology.

MODES AND EFFICIENCIES OF HIV TRANSMISSION

Epidemiological data continue to support the observation that HIV transmission is limited to sexual contact, the sharing of contaminated needles and syringes, exposure to infected blood or blood products, transplantation of infected organs or tissue, and transmission from mother to child either across the placenta or during delivery. A recent follow-up investigation of more than 1,100 AIDS cases that were initially reported to CDC as having no identified risk factors has shown that transmission in these individuals was also limited to the recognized routes (Castro et al., 1988). Finally, additional data from studies of health care workers (CDC, 1988d), nonsexual household contacts (Friedland and Klein, 1987), and insect bites (CDC, 1986) all support the conclusion that HIV is not transmitted by casual contact or insect bites. A change in HIV transmission modes would be biologically unprecedented in a virus. There is no evidence that HIV is capable of such a change.

Heterosexual Transmission

It has been clearly documented that HIV infection can be transmitted from men to women and from women to men through vaginal and anal intercourse (Fischl et al., 1987; Goedert et al., 1987; Padian et al., 1987a; Peterman et al., 1988). So far, however, the heterosexual spread of the virus in the United States has been confined mainly to persons whose sexual partners acquired HIV by other means—for example, by sharing contaminated needles and syringes or from blood transfusions.

Evidence to date shows that the spread of infection among heterosexuals has been rather slow in instances in which neither partner can be classified in a known risk category (CDC, 1988b). In nine seroprevalence surveys of heterosexual men and women attending sexually transmitted disease (STD) clinics in six cities, the prevalence of HIV infection ranged from 0 to 2.6 percent (CDC, 1987b). STD clinics treat individuals in the community who, because of their sexual behavior, are most likely to be infected with HIV. In studies conducted in clinics in which data were collected during personal interviews and not through self-administered questionnaires, and in which seropositive individuals were reinterviewed to obtain better information about their risk status, the prevalence of HIV infection ranged from 0 to 1.2 percent among persons with no known risk factors. The results obtained from large-scale studies of over 36 million blood donations and 1.5 million military personnel (in which there are indications of the self-exclusion of persons at high risk) show that the overall prevalence of HIV has been less than 1 percent in these populations for the period 1985 to 1987. This low prevalence among heterosexuals (compared to the 20 to 50 percent prevalence among male homosexuals) appears to indicate that the virus is not spreading rapidly in populations that are considered to be primarily low-risk groups.

To become complacent in the face of this apparent trend would be a mistake, however. Heterosexual transmission of the virus is an established fact; although the numbers are small, cases acquired through heterosexual transmission are the fastest growing group of AIDS cases in the United States. Indeed, in parts of Africa, heterosexual transmission of HIV is great enough to sustain AIDS in an epidemic status (see Chapter 7). It is useful to review the African experience with AIDS and attempt to pinpoint conditions that may augur changes in the patterns of disease spread in the United States.

It is believed that, in Africa, HIV infection appeared in great numbers first in the heterosexual community and that prostitution has played a major role in its spread. Prostitution is not uncommon in some urban areas in central and east Africa, and the prevalence of HIV infection is quite high (25 to 88 percent) among the prostitutes tested in some of those areas (Kreiss et al., 1986; Piot et al., 1988). Case-control studies have also shown that sexual activity with female prostitutes is more common among men with AIDS than among controls; African patients with AIDS also report contact with more heterosexual partners than do controls (Quinn et al., 1986). On the other hand, homosexuality and IV drug abuse do not play a major role in HIV transmission in Africa (Piot et al., 1988). In addition, STDs, in particular, genital ulcers, are fairly prevalent in some sexually active populations in Africa and are associated with an increased risk of infection, perhaps by providing a more direct portal of entry into the bloodstream. The contamination of the African blood supply and frequent exposure to unsterilized needles and syringes in both medical settings and ritual practices may also be important factors in the spread of AIDS among the African heterosexual population. Furthermore, African heterosexual adults show chronically activated immune systems more frequently than American heterosexual men, which may be a factor that increases their susceptibility to HIV infection (Quinn et al., 1987).

The pattern of disease spread in the United States has been much different. Here, the epidemic began in a few cities and within a closed community—male homosexuals—in which high-risk behaviors were practiced (multiple partners and receptive anal intercourse). These behaviors enhanced the rapid spread of HIV infection within that community, which also had high STD rates, another factor that may have increased the risk for HIV infection. The observation that the spread of HIV infection into the heterosexual community appears to be much slower suggests that one or more of the following may be true: (1) there has been relatively little sexual contact between this pool of infected men and heterosexuals; (2) heterosexuals probably change partners less frequently than homosexual men; and (3) vaginal intercourse may not spread the virus as easily as anal intercourse. Consequently, HIV infection in the heterosexual population in the United States has been somewhat contained.

Similarly to the appearance of disease among homosexual men, HIV infection also became pronounced in communities of IV drug abusers who practiced high-risk behaviors—in this instance, frequent drug injections and the sharing of contaminated drug injection equipment. These behaviors are the functional equivalents of frequent receptive anal intercourse and multiple sexual partners among homosexual men. Here also, the spread of infection was rapid but contained (Robertson et al., 1986; Des Jarlais et al., 1988). The potential for the spread of infection beyond the IV drug-abusing population is discussed below.

Will HIV infection reach epidemic proportions in the "general" heterosexual population in the United States, and are the conditions necessary for such an epidemic already in place? Sustaining the spread of the disease requires a "chain of transmission" from individuals practicing high-risk behaviors to their partners and from them to individuals with no known risks. This chain of transmission would have to include sufficient numbers of infected women interacting with men who would not otherwise be at high risk. Such a reservoir of infected women might be created in several ways: one mechanism is bisexuality; another probably more significant avenue is IV drug abuse (Guinan and Hardy, 1987; Moss et al., 1987). Of all IV drug abusers, 90 percent are heterosexuals, and 30 percent are women. Moreover, between 30 and 50 percent of female IV drug abusers have engaged in prostitution. Thus, there exists the possibility that a pool of infected prostitutes might be created (whose source of infection is the sharing of contaminated needles and syringes). HIV infection could then enter the heterosexual community from male customers of female prostitutes.

To date, most of the cases of AIDS among heterosexuals have resulted from IV drug abuse, and the number of infected addicts is growing. Moreover, seroprevalence among heterosexuals with no known risk factors is higher in areas of the country in which seroprevalence among IV drug abusers is high. This correspondence means that IV drug abusers play a pivotal role in the spread of HIV to adults through heterosexual transmission (and to infants through perinatal transmission).

For 1987, a 30 percent increase in syphilis was reported in the United States (CDC, 1988c), primarily among heterosexuals. Higher rates were reported for blacks and Hispanics than for whites. In addition, the areas reporting the largest absolute increases in syphilis cases (i.e., Florida, New York City, and California) were also areas that have high rates of HIV infection. The increases in syphilis cases suggest that behavior that increases the probability of HIV infection among heterosexuals is not being effectively curtailed.

In sum, the evidence to date is that heterosexual HIV transmission occurs from men to women and from women to men through vaginal and anal intercourse. The virus is capable of spreading among heterosexuals, but so far the prevalence of infection in the heterosexual population with no known risks for infection is low. Yet the extent of future heterosexual spread is uncertain. A "window of opportunity" apparently exists for preventing the further spread of infection to the heterosexual population.

Efficiencies of Transmission

The modes of HIV transmission are well documented. What is not as clear is how easily or how "efficiently" HIV is transmitted by a particular route if an individual is exposed. Specially designed epidemiological studies provide information that helps to estimate the probability of HIV transmission by the various known routes.

Blood Transfusions. The efficiency of this transmission route can be estimated using studies of the recipients of blood from donors who were subsequently found to have AIDS or HIV antibodies. Between 66 and 100 percent of blood transfusion recipients became infected if donors either tested positive for antibodies to HIV or later became antibody positive or developed AIDS (Ward et al., 1987). Furthermore, recipients were more likely to become infected if the transfusion occurred close to the time the donor developed symptoms. All recipients of blood transfusions became infected if the donors developed AIDS within 23 months of the donation (Ward et al., 1987). Thus, the large dose of the virus a transfusion represents, coupled with this particular route, appears to be quite efficient as a transmission path.

Perinatal Transmission. Risk of transmission can also be estimated from studies that evaluate the risk that an HIV-infected pregnant woman will deliver an infected infant. The results from such studies suggest that the probability of HIV transmission from mother to infant ranges from 30 to 50 percent (CDC, 1987b). Some studies suggest that the risk of transmission is higher for infants born to mothers who have symptoms of HIV infection during pregnancy or who show evidence of immunosuppression (Mok et al., 1987; Nzilambi et al., 1987; Piot et al., 1988).

IV Drug Abuse. Information on HIV transmission through the sharing of contaminated needles and syringes is hard to gather because of the illicit nature of IV drug abuse. However, several studies have shown that once HIV is introduced into a community, its spread is rapid among IV drug abusers and a majority of them soon becomes infected (Novick et al., 1986; Robertson et al., 1986; Des Jarlais et al., 1988). In New York City, where there are large numbers of infected IV drug abusers, the patterns of needle-sharing behavior include the practice of renting used needles and other drug paraphernalia in "shooting galleries" in which IV drug abusers gather (Friedland and Klein, 1987). Studies of IV drug abusers have shown an association between HIV seropositivity and both the frequency of drug injections and the sharing of drug injection equipment (Chaisson et al., 1987b; Marmor et al., 1987).

Homosexual Transmission. The risk of HIV transmission from receptive anal intercourse between homosexual men has been estimated, although partner tracing among homosexuals can be difficult in situations in which there have been multiple sexual partners (Grant et al., 1987). Cohort and case-control studies of homosexual men (Darrow et al., 1987; Kingsley et al., 1987; Moss et al., 1987; Winkelstein et al., 1987) show that the risk of HIV infection is greatest for persons who engage in receptive anal intercourse. The risk of infection is less for partners who engage in insertive anal intercourse, and the risk appears even lower for oral receptive intercourse.

Heterosexual Transmission. Estimates of the risk of heterosexual transmission have been derived from studies of the sex partners of infected persons. In this study design, an index case (the infected person) is identified, and the antibody status of his or her sexual partner is determined at entry and observed over time. In several studies of female partners of IV drug abusers, the risk of infection was reported to be about 50 percent (Curran et al., 1988). Studies of the male sex partners of female IV drug abusers found similarly large risks of infection, although the numbers of male partners tested were small. In these studies, HIV transmission by the sharing of contaminated needles and syringes cannot be ruled out.

The risk of transmission is lower for female partners of hemophiliacs and bisexual men and for partners of transfusion-infected persons than it is for male or female partners of IV drug abusers (Padian, 1987; Padian et al., 1987a; Curran et al., 1988; De Gruttola and Mayer, 1988; Johnson, 1988). In studies of the wives or female partners of hemophiliacs, the risk of infection was about 10 percent. Studies of female partners of bisexual men reported a risk of transmission of around 25 percent. Risks of similar magnitude have been found in studies of the spouses of transfusion-infected persons. In a recent study, of the 55 wives who had sexual contact with their infected partners, 10 (18 percent) became seropositive (Peterman et al., 1988). In this study, the risk of infection was not related to the number of sexual contacts a woman had with her infected spouse; in fact, seropositive wives reported fewer sexual contacts and were somewhat older than seronegative wives. This result suggests that, in addition to behavioral factors, biological factors probably play a role in determining how easily HIV is transmitted. There may be differences in transmissibility as a result of changes in the infectiousness of the infected individual over time. Thus, heterosexual contact during periods of high infectiousness may be more likely to transmit the virus than contact during periods of low infectiousness. A similar finding has been reported from a cohort study of partners of infected hemophiliacs. In this study, the best predictor of HIV trans-mission was the absolute number of T-helper lymphocytes in the hemophiliacs, suggesting that, as their immune systems became more suppressed, they were more likely to infect their sex partners, regard-less of the frequency of sexual contact or the duration of their infection (Goedert et al., 1987).

Another finding from the investigation of spouses of transfusion-infected persons was a higher rate of transmission from men to women than from women to men. Whereas 10 of 55 wives (18 percent) became seropositive through sexual contact with their infected husbands, only 2 of 25 husbands (8 percent) became seropositive through sexual contact with their infected wives. Although this difference was not statistically significant, the finding that HIV transmission may be more efficient from men to women than from women to men has been reported in other studies (Padian, 1987; De Gruttola and Mayer, 1988).

Needle-Stick Transmission. Studies among health care workers of accidental needle-stick injuries or cuts with sharp objects provide infor-mation on the risk of HIV infection by this route. As of December 31, 1987, a collaborative surveillance study conducted by CDC had followed 489 health care workers who sustained needle-stick exposures to infected blood and for whom both acute- and convalescent-phase serum samples were obtained. Three of the 489 health care workers (0.6 percent) had seroconverted within 6 months of exposure. Two other prospective studies of health care workers in the United States are also assessing the risk of HIV transmission from accidental needle-stick exposure. As of April 15, 1988, a similarly designed study at the University of California at San Francisco had reported that 1 of 180 health care workers (0.5 percent) seroconverted after at least 6 months of follow-up (J. L. Gerberding and H. F. Chambers, personal communication [updating Gerberding et al., 1987], 1988). As of April 30, 1988, the National Institutes of Health had obtained both acute and convalescent serum samples at least 6 months after exposure for 108 health-care workers with needle-stick injuries; none had seroconverted (D. K. Henderson, per-sonal communication [updating Henderson et al., 1986], 1988). The results from these studies, as well as from studies conducted in England and Canada, suggest that the risk of transmission from needle-stick exposure is less than 1 percent and probably closer to 0.5 percent. In most instances, these risks are associated with *one episode* of exposure, in contrast to the studies of sexual partners, which involve multiple expo-sures over time.

Relative Efficiencies of HIV Transmission

Several investigators have estimated the probability of HIV transmission for different modes of transmission (e.g., per episode of heterosexual intercourse or per screened blood transfusion), but these estimates are uncertain because the calculations are based on very limited information (Grant et al., 1987; Padian et al., 1987b; Hearst and Hully, 1988; Ward et al., 1988). Neither is it possible to rank routes of transmission from the greatest to the least efficient with complete certainty. Factors other than the route appear to determine whether transmission of the virus occurs; these factors include the dose (inoculum size) of virus transferred, the frequency of exposure, differences in host susceptibility, variation in infectiousness of an infected person over time, possible differences in virulence among HIV isolates, and the presence of other sexually transmitted diseases or other cofactors. In addition, study designs differ, which makes it difficult to compare results.

However, some preliminary conclusions can be drawn. The recipients of infected blood transfusions are at very high risk of infection, as are children born to infected mothers. Studies of infected IV drug abusers also report high rates of infection for this group, suggesting that the sharing of contaminated needles and syringes combined with frequent injections carries a high risk of infection. The sexual partners of IV drug abusers have a greater risk of becoming infected than the sexual partners of individuals who were infected by other routes, suggesting that the mode of transmission may be either heterosexual transmission or the unacknowledged sharing of contaminated needles and syringes. Studies of the sex partners of individuals who were infected by routes other than IV drug abuse show much lower risks of infection, as do studies of the risk of infection from accidental needle-stick exposure. It is important to note that, although the risk of infection from one episode of heterosexual sex and one needle-stick injury may be roughly equivalent, studies of sexual transmission involve repeated exposures over the course of years, whereas needle-stick injury studies usually involve one or a few episodes. Although it seems intuitively correct that risk increases with increased exposure, other factors (for instance, the apparent inability of a particular infected person to transmit the virus) may intervene.

In sexual transmission, the risk of infection is greater for the receptive partner in anal intercourse than for the insertive partner. Vaginal intercourse is probably less efficient than receptive anal intercourse as a transmission route; preliminary evidence also suggests that, in vaginal intercourse, infectivity from men to women is somewhat greater than from women to men.

PREVALENCE AND INCIDENCE OF HIV INFECTION
IN THE UNITED STATES

The importance of accurate descriptions of the prevalence and incidence of HIV infection, both at present and for the future, cannot be overstated. Defined cases of AIDS are only the clinical end stage of the devastating effects produced by HIV infection. The description of HIV infection by demographic characteristics and other distinguishing features helps determine which groups to target for intervention strategies to prevent the further spread of infection.

HIV Prevalence in Groups at Recognized Risk

In November 1987, CDC summarized current knowledge of the prevalence and incidence of HIV infection for various segments of the United States population according to age, sex, race or ethnic group, and geographic area (CDC, 1987b). The report reviewed data obtained from several sources (including federal agencies, health departments, and medical centers) on the prevalence of HIV infection as measured by the presence of HIV antibodies in the blood (i.e., seroprevalence).

The observed prevalence of HIV infection is highest in those risk groups that account for the majority of AIDS cases reported to CDC. Still, caution is needed in interpreting prevalence data. For example, the prevalence of HIV infection may be seen to vary in STD clinics in different geographic areas because the background prevalence in any two communities may be different. Other problems in comparing data arise from differences in questionnaire design, the inclusion or exclusion of symptomatic individuals in reports of seroprevalence, and differences in the demographic characteristics of the individuals being tested. Further, reported prevalence may be higher or lower than the true prevalence for a given group depending on who "walked in the door" (i.e., most of these surveys are based on self-selected samples).

Estimates of the prevalence of HIV infection in homosexual and bisexual men based on data from 23 cities range from 10 to 70 percent, with most estimates falling between 20 and 50 percent (CDC, 1987b). Prevalence is highest in cohorts of homosexual men in San Francisco. Yet the data probably overestimate the true prevalence of HIV infection in this group because most of the respondents to these surveys were persons who were either seeking medical attention for STDs or who were concerned that their past or present sexual behavior had placed them at risk (Curran et al., 1988).

The populations of IV drug abusers appear to be less mobile than the population of homosexual men, as larger differences in HIV prevalence are reported by geographic area. Surveys consistently show very high prevalence (50 to 60 percent) in major East Coast cities with geographic or close cultural connections to New York City and northern New Jersey; prevalence is much lower (less than 5 percent) in other areas of the country (CDC, 1987b). Most of the surveys measuring prevalence in IV drug abusers are conducted at facilities for chronic heroin abuse treatment. It is thought that only 10 to 20 percent of the estimated 1.2 million drug abusers in the United States are currently in treatment and that those not in treatment may be habitual users whose risk for HIV infection is even greater (CDC, 1987b).

The prevalence of HIV infection for persons with hemophilia ranges from 15 percent to more than 90 percent, depending on the type and severity of hemophilia and, in turn, the amount of clotting factor received (CDC, 1987b). Persons with severe hemophilia A have the highest prevalence (approximately 70 percent), whereas persons with hemophilia B or mild hemophilia A have a somewhat lower prevalence (approximately 35 percent). Within these clinical categories, however, prevalence is uniform throughout the country, reflecting the distribution of clotting factor concentrate received before 1985. Only hemophiliacs who seek treatment are tested; consequently, the prevalence reported here may be an overestimate of the true prevalence for hemophiliacs as a group (CDC, 1987b).

The prevalence of HIV in female prostitutes in the United States varies from 0 percent to more than 50 percent. Seropositivity is higher in black and Hispanic prostitutes than in white prostitutes. The differences in prevalence appear to be related to the extent of IV drug abuse in the groups tested and the background HIV prevalence in IV drug abusers in the area (CDC, 1987b).

In studies of seroprevalence conducted among persons who are heterosexual sex partners of HIV-infected persons but who have no other identifiable risk factors for HIV infection, prevalence ranged from less than 10 percent to 60 percent (CDC, 1987b). As noted earlier in this chapter, surveys in STD clinics of heterosexual men and women who do not belong to any risk group and who do not have partners in any risk group report prevalences ranging from 0 percent to 2.6 percent, depending on the population studied and the method of data collection. Seroprevalence is higher among heterosexuals in areas in which seroprevalence in IV drug abusers is high. However, such studies may overrepresent the true prevalence of HIV among heterosexuals because people surveyed in STD clinics may be more sexually active than the "general" heterosexual population.

HIV Prevalence Among Selected Segments of the General Population

The prevalence of HIV infection in the population at large has been estimated primarily from studies of various special populations: blood donors, civilian applicants to the military, Job Corps entrants, sentinel hospital patients, and newborn infants (whose antibody status at birth reflects the presence or absence of antibodies in their mothers) (CDC, 1987b). More than 36 million blood or plasma donations in the United States have been tested for HIV antibodies since 1985. HIV prevalence among first-time donors for the period 1985 to 1987 was 0.04 percent. Prevalence was much higher for men than for women and higher for blacks and Hispanics than for whites. Since October 1985, blood samples from over 1.5 million applicants for military service have also been tested for HIV antibodies. The prevalence of HIV infection increases with age for applicants between the late teens and late twenties. Prevalence by birth year cohorts also increased from the first screening period (1985–1986) to the second (1986–1987). As with blood donors, seropositivity was higher for men than for women and higher for blacks and Hispanics than for whites. The overall prevalence (for October 1985 to September 1987), adjusted for the age, sex, and racial and ethnic composition of the U.S. adult population aged 17 to 59 years, was 0.14 percent. Since March 1987, HIV antibody screening has been conducted for new members of the Job Corps who participate in residential training programs. This program recruits rural and inner-city disadvantaged youths aged 16 to 21. Provisional data from the first 25,000 entrants showed a seroprevalence of 0.33 percent. The prevalence of infection in the nation as a whole is probably higher than what has been observed in blood donors, applicants to the military, and Job Corps entrants, as persons at highest risk for infection are probably underrepresented.

To avoid the self-selection bias associated with volunteer programs, anonymous HIV antibody testing has also recently begun on selected hospital patients (excluding AIDS cases and other conditions related to HIV infection) at sentinel hospitals. Based on the first 8,668 test results, the age- and sex-adjusted prevalence of infection was 0.32 percent. This sample represents hospitalized patients who are at low risk for infection. In addition, the hospitals selected to participate in the program may service specialized segments of the community; therefore, the data collected are not representative of all hospitalized patients.

Several states have begun programs to assess the prevalence of HIV infection in women of childbearing age by testing for HIV antibodies in their newborns. Maternal antibodies against HIV cross the placenta and are therefore present in the baby's blood. A baby with antibodies to HIV may or may not itself be infected; however, the presence of antibodies in the baby's blood always indicates that the mother is infected. Neonatal blood specimens are routinely collected in hospitals to test for metabolic disorders; the test for HIV antibodies has been added to this program. A recent study has reported that 1 of every 476 women (0.2 percent) giving birth in Massachusetts was antibody positive during the period December 1986 to June 1987. The prevalence of HIV infection differed according to the type and location of the maternity hospitals. Prevalence was highest in inner-city hospitals (0.8 percent), lower in mixed urban and suburban hospitals (0.25 percent), and lowest in suburban and rural hospitals (0.09 percent) (Hoff et al., 1988). In New York, the prevalence of HIV infection among women delivering babies in hospitals in the five New York City boroughs between November 1987 and February 1988 was 1.45 percent; the prevalence of HIV infection among women delivering babies in hospitals outside the metropolitan area was 0.18 percent (Novick et al., 1988).

Incidence of New Infections

Data on the incidence (the number of new infections over time) of HIV infection are more difficult to obtain than prevalence data, but they are crucial for longer term projections of the course of the epidemic. Evidence from eight cohort studies of gay men suggest a lower HIV incidence rate in that population for 1985–1987 than in the earlier part of the decade (CDC, 1987b). This observed decline in the incidence of infection may be attributed to several factors, but it is consistent with reports of a decline in other sexually transmitted diseases in this group (CDC, 1988c) as well as changes in sexual behavior (Winkelstein et al., 1987a). Serologic screening of blood and plasma donors and heat treatment of factor concentrate, as well as efforts to exclude donors at high risk, have also reduced the rate of new infection among transfusion recipients and hemophiliacs since 1985. In contrast, HIV incidence appears to be increasing in IV drug abusers in New York City and San Francisco (Chaisson et al., 1987a; Des Jarlais et al., 1987; Schoenbaum et al., 1987). These data suggest that the epidemic of HIV infection in the United States may be viewed as a series of overlapping smaller epidemics, each with its own dynamics and time course (Curran et al., 1988).

National Estimates of HIV Infection

In 1986, CDC estimated the size of various segments of the population that were known to be infected (i.e., male homosexuals, IV drug abusers, hemophiliacs, heterosexuals with no known risks), as well as the prevalence of HIV infection for each of these groups. It then calculated from these estimates that 1 to 1.5 million people in the United States were currently infected with HIV. In November 1987, CDC reviewed these estimates and modified them slightly based on new information about the size of the various populations and new seroprevalence data for these groups. In retrospect, the 1986 estimates made by CDC appear to have been too high. CDC now estimates that between 945,000 and 1.4 million Americans currently are infected with HIV. The major limitation of both the original and the revised estimates is the unknown size of the homosexual population that engages in at-risk behaviors (CDC, 1987b). CDC will continue to update national estimates of the prevalence of HIV infection as more information is gathered. Other groups and investigators have also estimated the prevalence of HIV infection in the United States; these estimates have been both higher and lower than those made by CDC, ranging from 400,000 to 2.2 million for the end of 1987 (De Gruttola and Lagakos, 1987; Harris, 1987). Such estimates provide an overall picture of the magnitude of the epidemic; however, seroprevalence and incidence data on specific groups at risk are more important because they offer the necessary information to target prevention strategies and evaluate their effectiveness in curbing the epidemic.

The Program of HIV Surveys and Studies

CDC has responded to the urgent need to monitor the spread of HIV infection by instituting a series of seroprevalence studies and surveillance systems (Dondero et al., 1988). In approximately 30 metropolitan areas in the United States, blood samples will be routinely collected from persons treated at STD clinics, drug abuse treatment centers, family planning and women's health clinics, and tuberculosis clinics, as well as from selected hospital admissions and newborns. These studies will provide local officials with information on HIV prevalence so that interventions can be designed to control HIV infection in specific settings. The surveys of newborns will provide some of the most valuable information because sample selection is unbiased; the entire population of childbearing mothers is included. As noted earlier, testing for HIV antibodies, which will occur in approximately 30 states, will be added to already existing programs that routinely test newborns for metabolic disorders. These surveys will, therefore, be population based and, by providing information on the antibody status of newborns, will reflect the prevalence of infection in mothers delivering in these hospitals.

In addition to these activities, studies of HIV infection will continue in civilian applicants to the military services, active duty military personnel, blood donors, and Job Corps entrants. Surveys of HIV prevalence will also be conducted in other populations of special interest such as patients from emergency rooms, patients using other hospital services, students on college campuses, and prisoners. The National Center for Health Statistics (NCHS) will also conduct a study to determine the feasibility of a nationwide household seroprevalence survey. In addition, NCHS also plans to include anonymous HIV antibody testing of an estimated 17,000 blood specimens collected from adults over a 6-year period as part of the National Health and Nutrition Examination Survey.

It is important to note that some of these surveys will be "blinded" (i.e., HIV antibody testing will be done on blood specimens collected for other purposes with personal information on the individual permanently removed) to avoid the uninterpretable impact of self-selection bias. Other surveys, however, will be nonblinded. In these settings, volunteer participants will be interviewed to evaluate risk factors for HIV transmission.

AIDS CASES IN THE UNITED STATES

In October 1986, when *Confronting AIDS* was published, approximately 24,500 cases of AIDS had been reported to CDC. As of May 1988, 62,200 cases of AIDS had been reported since June 1981, and 35,051 of these had ended in death (CDC, 1988a). An additional 10 to 20 percent of cases are believed to have been missed by the surveillance system. The number of cases reported each year continues to increase, although the rate of increase is less steep than it was earlier in the decade. Cases have been reported from all 50 states and the District of Columbia.

Since the publication of *Confronting AIDS,* the distribution of cases by risk group as well as by sex, race, age, and geographic area has not changed substantially: 63 percent of cases are homosexual or bisexual men not known to have abused IV drugs, 19 percent are heterosexual IV drug abusers, 7 percent are both male homosexuals and IV drug abusers, 1 percent are patients with hemophilia and related disorders, 4 percent are persons who acquired the disease through heterosexual contact, 3 percent are recipients of blood transfusions, and 3 percent are cases in which risk information is undetermined because it is incomplete (patients have died, refused to be interviewed, or have been lost to follow-up) or the patients are still under investigation. This 3 percent also includes men reporting contact with a prostitute and patients with no identifiable risk factor. Of the 981 cases of AIDS among children that had been reported to CDC by May 1988, 77 percent are offspring of a parent with AIDS or at high risk for AIDS. Of the remaining pediatric cases, 6 percent are children with hemophilia, 14 percent are transfusion recipients, and 4 percent are children for whom risk information cannot be determined.

Over the past 2 years, the largest increases in new cases have been observed in two groups: heterosexual partners of HIV-infected individuals and children whose mothers abuse IV drugs or are sexual partners of men at high risk. There is an overrepresentation of blacks and Hispanics in both of these groups. The only group showing a steady decline in AIDS incidence over the past 2 years has been children with transfusion-associated AIDS. This decline is attributed to the screening of blood and blood products that began in early 1985 and to the rather short incubation period of 12 months or less observed for children with transfusion-associated AIDS. It is now thought that more than 80 percent of HIV infection in children can be directly linked to IV drug abuse in the mother or father.

THE DEMOGRAPHIC IMPACT OF AIDS

AIDS has already begun to alter the demographic characteristics of New York City and San Francisco. A disease that was virtually unknown to Americans 8 years ago, AIDS is now the leading cause of death in New York City among men aged 25 to 44 and women aged 25 to 34. In 1986, mortality from AIDS was the eighth leading cause of years of potential life lost before the age of 65 in the United States (CDC, 1988b). Recent data from New York City indicate that 1 of every 66 infants born between November 1987 and February 1988 tested positive for HIV antibodies, reflecting the prevalence of HIV infection in women of childbearing age in that city (Novick et al., 1988). In San Francisco, approximately 50 percent of the male homosexual population is infected with the virus, suggesting the possible future devastation of a large component of the city's population. In 1986, New York City and San Francisco accounted for approximately 40 percent of all AIDS cases; by 1991 these two cities will account for less than 20 percent of cases nationwide (Morgan and Curran, 1986), suggesting that other metropolitan areas will soon face major economic and demographic losses.

AIDS cases occur in higher proportions in black and Hispanic populations than in white populations (on the West Coast, the proportion is 3 times higher in black and Hispanic than in white populations and 12 times higher on the East Coast), mainly as a result of higher HIV prevalence in black and Hispanic IV drug abusers and their sex partners and offspring. Recent data also suggest that the virus is spreading more rapidly among blacks and Hispanics at risk than among other population groups, especially in Northeastern cities, suggesting that the future composition of AIDS cases will consist primarily of poor, urban minorities.

FUTURE RESEARCH NEEDS

Epidemiological studies are the main source of information on the prevalence and incidence of HIV infection and AIDS, the modes and efficiencies of HIV transmission, the proportion of infected individuals who progress to AIDS, serologic markers of disease progression, and the distribution of behaviors associated with increased exposure to HIV. Epidemiological studies have also provided some of the strongest evidence for the association between HIV infection and AIDS. Whether or not these studies are prevalence or incidence surveys, cohort or case-control in design, they provide essential data to understand and control the epidemic.

Although much has been learned about the epidemiology of HIV infection, more research is needed to address its many unanswered questions. **The committee therefore strongly urges continued epidemiological research in support of appropriate prevention and control measures.** CDC must be provided with the necessary funding to ensure that personnel, space, and technical resources are adequate to the task of continuing epidemiological research.

REFERENCES

Booth, W. 1988. A rebel without a cause of AIDS. Science 239:1485–1488.

Castro, K. G., A. R. Lifson, C. R. White, T. J. Bush, M. E. Chamberland, A. M. Lekatsas, and H. W. Jaffe. 1988. Investigations of AIDS patients with no previously identified risk factors. J. Am. Med. Assoc. 259:1338–1342.

CDC (Centers for Disease Control). 1981. Kaposi's sarcoma and *Pneumocystis* pneumonia among homosexual men—New York City and California. Morbid. Mortal. Wkly. Rep. 30:305–308.

CDC. 1986. Acquired immunodeficiency syndrome (AIDS) in western Palm Beach County, Florida. Morbid. Mortal. Wkly. Rep. 35:609–612.

CDC. 1987a. Antibody to human immunodeficiency virus in female prostitutes. Morbid. Mortal. Wkly. Rep. 36:157–161.

CDC. 1987b. Human immunodeficiency virus infection in the United States: A review of current knowledge. Morbid. Mortal. Wkly. Rep. 36(suppl. 6):1–48.

CDC. 1987c. Revision of the CDC surveillance case definition for acquired immunodeficiency syndrome. Morbid. Mortal. Wkly. Rep. 36(suppl. 1):3S-15S.

CDC. 1988a. AIDS weekly surveillance report—United States, May 16. Atlanta, Ga.: CDC.

CDC. 1988b. Changes in premature mortality—United States, 1979–1986. Morbid. Mortal. Wkly. Rep. 37:47–48.

CDC. 1988c. Continuing increase in infectious syphilis—United States. Morbid. Mortal. Wkly. Rep. 37:35–38.

CDC. 1988d. Update: Acquired immunodeficiency syndrome and human immunodeficiency virus infection among health-care workers. Morbid. Mortal. Wkly. Rep. 37:229–239.

Chaisson, R. E., D. Osmond, A. R. Moss, H. W. Feldman, and P. Bernacki. 1987a. HIV, bleach, and needle sharing. Lancet 1:1430.

Chaisson, R. E., A. R. Moss, R. Onishi, D. Osmond, and J. R. Carlson. 1987b. Human immunodeficiency virus infection in heterosexual intravenous drug users in San Francisco. Am. J. Public Health 77:169–172.

Curran, J. W., D. N. Lawrence, H. Jaffe, J. E. Kaplan, L. D. Zyla, M. Chamberland, R. Weinstein, K.-J. Lui, L. B. Schonberger, T. J. Spira, W. J. Alexander, G. Swinger, A. Ammann, S. Solomon, D. Auerbach, D. Mildvan, R. Stoneburner, J. M. Jason, H. W. Haverkos, and B. L. Evatt. 1984. Acquired immunodeficiency syndrome (AIDS) associated with transfusions. N. Engl. J. Med. 310:69–75.

Curran, J. W., H. W. Jaffe, A. M. Hardy, W. M. Morgan, R. M. Selik, and T. J. Dondero. 1988. Epidemiology of HIV infection and AIDS in the United States. Science 239:610–616.

Darrow, W. W., D. F. Echenberg, H. W. Jaffe, P. M. O'Malley, R. H. Byers, J. P. Getchell, and J. W. Curran. 1987. Risk factors for human immunodeficiency virus (HIV) infections in homosexual men. Am. J. Public Health 77:479–483.

De Gruttola, V., and S. W. Lagakos. 1987. The value of doubling time in assessing the course of the AIDS epidemic. Paper prepared for the Institute of Medicine Workshop on Modeling the Spread of Infection with Human Immunodeficiency Virus and the Demographic Impact of Acquired Immune Deficiency Syndrome, Washington, D.C., October 15–17.

De Gruttola, V., and K. H. Mayer. 1988. Assessing and modeling heterosexual spread of the human immunodeficiency virus in the United States. Rev. Infect. Dis. 10:138–150.

Des Jarlais, D. C., S. R. Friedman, M. Marmor, H. Cohen, D. Mildvan, S. Yancovitz, U. Mathur, W. El-Sadr, T. J. Spira, J. Garber, S. T. Beatrice, A. S. Abdul-Quader, and J. L. Sotheran. 1987. Development of AIDS, HIV seroconversion, and potential cofactors for T4 cell loss in a cohort of intravenous drug users. AIDS 1:105–111.

Des Jarlais, D. C., S. R. Friedman, and R. L. Stoneburner. 1988. HIV infection and intravenous drug use: Critical issues in transmission dynamics, infection outcomes, and prevention. Rev. Infect. Dis. 10:151–158.

Dondero, T. J., M. Pappaioanou, and J. W. Curran. 1988. Monitoring the levels and trends of HIV infection: The Public Health Service's HIV Surveillance Program. Public Health Rep. 103:213–220.

Eyster, M. E., M. H. Gail, J. O. Ballard, H. Al-Mondhiry, and J. J. Goedert. 1987. Natural history of human immunodeficiency virus infections in hemophiliacs: Effects of T-cell subsets, platelet counts, and age. Ann. Intern. Med. 107:1–6.

Fischl, M. A., G. M. Dickinson, G. B. Scott, N. Klimas, M. A. Fletcher, and W. Parks. 1987. Evaluation of heterosexual partners, children, and household contacts of adults with AIDS. J. Am. Med. Assoc. 257:640–644.

Friedland, G. H., and R. S. Klein. 1987. Transmission of the human immunodeficiency virus. N. Engl. J. Med. 317:1125–1135.

Gerberding, J. L., C. E. Bryant-LeBlanc, K. Nelson, A. R. Moss, D. Osmond, H. F. Chambers, J. R. Carlson, W. L. Drew, J. A. Levy, and M. A. Sande. 1987. Risk of transmitting the human immunodeficiency virus, cytomegalovirus, and hepatitis B virus to health care workers exposed to patients with AIDS and AIDS-related conditions. J. Infect. Dis. 156:1–8.

Goedert, J. J., and W. A. Blattner. In press. The epidemiology and natural history of human immunodeficiency virus. In AIDS: Etiology, Diagnosis, Treatment and Prevention, 2nd ed., V. T. DeVita, S. Hellman, and S. A. Rosenberg, eds. Philadelphia: Lippincott.

Goedert, J. J., M. E. Eyster, R. J. Biggar, and W. A. Blattner. 1987. Heterosexual transmission of human immunodeficiency virus: Association with severe depletion of T-helper lymphocytes in men with hemophilia. AIDS Res. Hum. Retrovir. 3:355–361.

Grant, R. M., J. A. Wiley, and W. Winkelstein. 1987. Infectivity of the human immunodeficiency virus: Estimates from a prospective study of homosexual men. J. Infect. Dis. 156:189–193.

Guinan, M. E., and A. Hardy. 1987. Epidemiology of AIDS in women in the United States: 1981 through 1986. J. Am. Med. Assoc. 257:2039–2042.

Harris, J. E. 1987. The AIDS epidemic: Looking into the 1990s. Technol. Rev. 90:59–64.

Hearst, N., and S. B. Hulley. 1988. Preventing the heterosexual spread of AIDS. Are we giving our patients the best advice? J. Am. Med. Assoc. 259:2428–2432.

Henderson, D. K., A. J. Saah, B. J. Zak, R. A. Kaslow, H. C. Lane, T. Folks, W. C. Blackwelder, J. Schmitt, D. J. LaCamera, H. Masur, and A. S. Fauci. 1986. Risk of nosocomial infection with human T-cell lymphotropic virus type III/lymphadenopathy-associated virus in a large cohort of intensively exposed health care workers. Ann. Intern. Med. 104:644–647.

Hoff, R., V. P. Berardi, B. J. Weiblen, L. Mahoney-Trout, M. L. Mitchell, and G. F. Grady. 1988. Seroprevalence of human immunodeficiency virus among childbearing women. Estimation by testing samples of blood from newborns. N. Engl. J. Med. 318:525–530.

Johnson, A. M. 1988. Heterosexual transmission of human immunodeficiency virus. Br. Med. J. 296:1017–1020.

Kingsley, L. A., R. Kaslow, C. R. Rinaldo, Jr., K. Detre, N. Odaka, M. VanRaden, R. Detels, B. F. Polk, J. Chmiel, S. F. Kelsey, D. Ostrow, and B. Visscher. 1987. Risk factors for seroconversion to human immunodeficiency virus among male homosexuals. Lancet 1:345–349.

Kreiss, J. K., D. Koech, F. A. Plummer, K. K. Homles, M. Lightfoote, P. Piot, A. R. Ronald, J. O. Ndinya-Achola, L. J. D'Costa, P. Roberts, E. N. Ngugi, and T. C. Quinn. 1986. AIDS virus infection in Nairobi prostitutes. Spread of the epidemic to east Africa. N. Engl. J. Med. 314:414–418.

Marmor, M., D. C. Des Jarlais, H. Cohen, S. R. Friedman, S. T. Beatrice, N. Dubin, W. El-Sadr, D. Mildvan, S. Yancovitz, U. Mathur, and R. Holzman. 1987. Risk factors for infection with human immunodeficiency virus among intravenous drug abusers in New York City. AIDS 1:39–44.

Medley, G. F., R. M. Anderson, D. R. Cox, and L. Billard. 1987. Incubation period of AIDS in patients infected via blood transfusion. Nature 328:719–721.

Mok, J. Q., C. Giaquinto, A. De Rossi, I. Grosch-Worner, A. E. Ades, and C. S. Peckham. 1987. Infants born to mothers seropositive for human immunodeficiency virus. Preliminary findings from a multicentre European study. Lancet 1:1164–1168.

Morgan, W. M., and J. W. Curran. 1986. Acquired immunodeficiency syndrome: Current and future trends. Public Health Rep. 101:459–465.

Moss, A. R. 1987. AIDS and intravenous drug use: The real heterosexual epidemic. Br. Med. J. 294:389–390.

Moss, A. R., D. Osmond, P. Bacchetti, J.-C. Chermann, F. Barre-Sinoussi, and J. Carlson. 1987. Risk factors for AIDS and HIV seropositivity in homosexual men. Am. J. Epidemiol. 125:1035–1047.

Moss, A. R., P. Bacchetti, D. Osmond, W. Krampf, R. E. Chaisson, D. Stites, J. Wilber, J.-P. Allain, and J. Carlson. 1988. Seropositivity for HIV and the development of AIDS or AIDS related condition: Three-year follow-up of the San Francisco General Hospital cohort. Br. Med. J. 296:745–750.

Novick, D. M., M. J. Kreek, D. C. Des Jarlais, T. J. Spira, E. T. Khuri, J. Ragunath, V. S. Kalyanaraman, A. M. Gelb, and A. Miescher. 1986. Abstract of clinical research findings: Therapeutic and historical aspects. Pp. 318–320 in Proceedings of the 47th Annual Scientific Meeting, Committee on Problems of Drug Dependence (1985), L. Harris, ed. Rockville, Md.: National Institute on Drug Abuse.

Novick, L. F., D. Berns, R. Stricof, and R. Stevens. 1988. New York State Department of Health newborn seroprevalence study. Interim report draft. Albany. March 15.

Nzilambi, N., R. W. Ryder, F. Behets, H. Francis, E. Bayende, A. Nelson, J. M. Mann, et al. 1987. Perinatal HIV transmission in two African hospitals. P. 158 in Abstracts of the Third International Conference on AIDS, Washington, D.C., June 1–5.

Padian, N. S. 1987. Heterosexual transmission of acquired immunodeficiency syndrome: International perspectives and national projections. Rev. Infect. Dis. 9:947–960.

Padian, N., L. Marquis, D. P. Francis, R. E. Anderson, G. W. Rutherford, P. M. O'Malley, and W. Winkelstein, Jr. 1987a. Male-to-female transmission of human immunodeficiency virus. J. Am. Med. Assoc. 258:788–790.

Padian, N., J. Wiley, and W. Winkelstein. 1987b. Male-to-female transmission of human immunodeficiency virus (HIV): Current results, infectivity rates, and San Francisco population seroprevalence estimates. P. 171 in Abstracts of the Third International Conference on AIDS, Washington, D.C., June 1–5.

Peterman, T. A., R. L. Stoneburner, J. R. Allen, H. W. Jaffe, and J. W. Curran. 1988. Risk of human immunodeficiency virus transmission from heterosexual adults with transfusion-associated infections. J. Am. Med. Assoc. 259:55–58.

Piot, P., F. A. Plummer, F. S. Mhalu, J.-L. Lamboray, J. Chin, and J. M. Mann. 1988. AIDS: An international perspective. Science 239:573–579.

Quinn, T. C., J. M. Mann, J. W. Curran, and P. Piot. 1986. AIDS in Africa: An epidemiologic paradigm. Science 234:955–963.

Quinn, T. C., P. Piot, J. B. McCormick, F. M. Feinsod, H. Taelman, B. Kapita, W. Stevens, and A. S. Fauci. 1987. Serologic and immunologic studies in patients with AIDS in North America and Africa. The potential role of infectious agents as cofactors in human immunodeficiency virus infection. J. Am. Med. Assoc. 257:2617–2621.

Robertson, J. R., A. B. V. Bucknall, P. D. Welsby, J. J. K. Roberts, J. M. Inglis, J. F. Peutherer, and R. P. Brettle. 1986. Epidemic of AIDS related virus (HTLV-III/LAV) infection among intravenous drug abusers. Br. Med. J. 292:527–529.

Schoenbaum, E. E., P. A. Selwyn, D. Hartel, R. S. Klein, K. Davenny, and G. H. Friedland. 1987. HIV seroconversion in intravenous drug abusers: Rate and risk factors. P. 117 in Abstracts of the Third International Conference on AIDS, Washington, D.C., June 1–5.

Ward, J. W., D. A. Deppe, S. Samson, H. Perkins, P. Holland, L. Fernando, P. M. Feorino, P. Thompson, S. Kleinman, and J. R. Allen. 1987. Risk of human immunodeficiency virus infection from blood donors who later developed the acquired immunodeficiency syndrome. Ann. Intern. Med. 106:61–62.

Ward, J. W., S. D. Holmberg, J. R. Allen, D. L. Cohn, S. E. Critchley, S. H. Kleinman, B. A. Lenes, O. Ravenholt, J. R. Davis, M. G. Quinn, and H. W. Jaffe. 1988. Transmission of human immunodeficiency virus (HIV) by blood transfusions screened as negative for HIV antibody. N. Engl. J. Med. 318:473–478.

Winkelstein, W., Jr. 1988. Epidemiological observations on the causal nature of the association between infection by the human immunodeficiency virus and the acquired immunodeficiency syndrome. Paper presented at the Scientific Forum on the Etiology of AIDS, American Foundation for AIDS Research, Washington, D.C., April 9.

Winkelstein, W., Jr., M. Samuel, N. S. Padian, J. A. Wiley, W. Lang, R. E. Anderson, and J. A. Levy. 1987a. The San Francisco Men's Health Study. III. Reduction in human immunodeficiency virus transmission among homosexual/bisexual men, 1982–86. Am. J. Public Health 76:685–689.

Winkelstein, W., Jr., D. M. Lyman, N. Padian, R. Grant, M. Samuel, J. A. Wiley, R. E. Anderson, W. Lang, J. Riggs, and J. A. Levy. 1987b. Sexual practices and risk of infection by the human immunodeficiency virus. The San Francisco Men's Health Study. J. Am. Med. Assoc. 257:321–325.

3

Understanding the Course of the Epidemic

To alter the course of the HIV epidemic, planners must estimate, as early and as precisely as possible, how it will progress. Such predictions, like any forecasts, are necessarily based on available information, however incomplete it may be. The techniques used in efforts to bridge the gaps in information are forms of mathematical modeling. This chapter describes the uses of models and potential means of sharpening the projections they provide.

In 1986 the U.S. Public Health Service (PHS) projected numbers of AIDS cases and deaths through 1991. So far the reported number of cases has closely followed these projections. PHS estimated that by the end of 1991 there will have been a cumulative total of 270,000 AIDS cases in the United States and 179,000 deaths. These projections were derived from a model based on a statistical trend analysis of AIDS cases reported to CDC through May 1986, corrected for reporting delays (Morgan and Curran, 1986). Such models depend on the assumption that observed trends of the disease (e.g., the distribution of cases by age, sex, geographic location, and risk group) will not change with time. Another method to forecast short-term projections of the number of AIDS cases uses information about the period between HIV infection and AIDS, and AIDS incidence data (Brookmeyer and Gail, 1986). For the short term, the projections produced by this method are similar to those made by CDC.

Near the time that this update is published, a second PHS conference will be held to revise short- and long-term projections of HIV seroprevalence and AIDS cases and deaths.

57

THE USES OF MODELS

Mathematical models are used to project the prevalence and incidence of HIV infection and AIDS in specific regions or populations, define the conditions necessary for a given subpopulation to sustain an epidemic, assess the possible consequences of educational interventions aimed at modifying sexual behavior and drug abuse, help plan for health care services, clarify what data are required to predict future trends, and interpret existing data (May and Anderson, 1987; Hyman and Stanley, in press). A range of models, from simple to complex, can be constructed. The challenge, however, is to build models that are simple enough to be useful but complex enough to reflect the realities of the disease.

Since 1986 there has been some progress in refining the different types of models that have been used and in defining the types of questions to which they are applicable (Jager and Ruitenberg, 1987; IOM, 1988). Forecasts of the future course of the epidemic depend heavily on underlying assumptions about the transmission dynamics of HIV infection. Modeling these dynamics is extremely difficult because of the large number of biological and behavioral variables required to describe the spread of HIV infection. For example, assumptions must be made about the length of time from a person's initial infection to the manifestation of disease and the relative infectiousness of a person during this time, assumptions that are less important in diseases such as gonorrhea and syphilis, which have shorter incubation periods. In addition, modeling is complicated by the knowledge that the epidemic's characteristics have changed and will continue to change over time with modifications in personal and cultural behaviors and progress in prolonging life and reducing infectivity with antiviral therapy (Hyman and Stanley, in press).

One important attribute of models is that they help clarify the assumptions that underlie different projections and the extent to which the assumptions are sensitive to different parameters (May and Anderson, 1987; De Gruttola and Mayer, 1988). Modeling the AIDS epidemic is a dynamic process; as additional data on biological and behavioral factors are collected, these assumptions can be refined and the projections improved.

Models can produce widely differing projections of the future number of AIDS cases while accurately describing the present picture of the epidemic (De Gruttola and Mayer, 1988). Yet currently available knowledge does not enable researchers to determine which projections are correct. The limitations of the data that are used in models greatly influence their capacity to predict the future accurately.

DATA NEEDS

Current projections about AIDS rely heavily on a limited number of data sets, some of which may be unreliable. (For example, data collected in the 1940s is routinely used to estimate the size of the homosexual population.) The following kinds of information have been identified by modelers as essential for improving the reliability of projections.

• Better information is needed about HIV seroprevalence in particular risk groups. Information on the seroprevalence of HIV in defined groups coupled with a knowledge of disease progression will allow more reliable projections of the future number of AIDS cases than will reliance on the reported numbers of cases.

• Facts are needed about sexual behavior: the number of sexual partners people have, the partner selection process, the duration of partnership, the frequency and nature of sexual contacts, and the numbers of people involved in high-risk sexual behavior. Available data on sexual behavior in certain segments of the population may be sufficiently flawed that accurate qualitative data may serve modelers better than quantitative data obtained from selected nonrepresentative samples (IOM, 1988).

• More data are required on the size of the IV drug-abusing population, patterns of sharing needles and syringes among drug abusers, and the interactions between drug abuse and sexual behavior.

• Projections made by models are highly sensitive to certain assumptions about HIV transmission and disease progression. For example, information is needed about the effect of such cofactors as other infections, the variability of infectiousness in an infected individual over the course of infection, the factors that precipitate the transition from asymptomatic to symptomatic states, and the percentage of people who will progress from HIV infection to AIDS.

The paucity of information on the behavioral factors influencing the spread of HIV infection has led the Commission on Behavioral and Social Sciences and Education (CBASSE) of the National Research Council to establish the Committee on AIDS Research and the Behavioral, Social, and Statistical Sciences. The committee has been charged to identify ways in which social science expertise can help curb the epidemic. Its work will include an assessment of the adequacy of available data on the scope of the epidemic, the distribution within the population of behavior that sustains it, and an examination of educational efforts to prevent the spread of HIV infection in various subpopulations. The committee's first report is scheduled for release in the fall of 1988.

Accurate forecasting of the AIDS epidemic depends in large measure on better knowledge of human sexual and IV drug-abusing behavior.

Research in the social sciences, particularly in understanding such behavior, has been inadequate in the past. The committee expects that the CBASSE study will report in detail on the data needs in these areas, propose improved data collection methods, and clarify what is known about the number of people who engage in behavior that spreads HIV infection. The committee adds its endorsement to the importance of the social and behavioral studies needed to understand the epidemic.

The committee strongly supports continued research efforts to develop better ways to refine predictions about the future course of the AIDS epidemic and to evaluate potential intervention strategies. To this end, IOM/ NAS plans to conduct a series of workshops on modeling over the next 2 years. Modelers, data collectors, and policymakers should meet regularly to ensure that modelers are asking questions for which data can be collected and that data collection is proceeding along lines that will yield information useful to modelers. The questions asked must also be relevant for policymakers.

It is important to keep modeling efforts in perspective. Their importance lies in the way projections can help mold prevention strategies and plan care for the sick. Although exact numbers may be important for such purposes as determining the number of hospital beds needed for AIDS patients, trends may be equally useful for targeting interventions. It is likely that the number of AIDS cases will continue to grow for many years, probably into the next century—a prediction based on estimates of the number of individuals currently infected, the projected increase in the distribution of the incubation period, and the proportion of infected individuals who will eventually develop AIDS. Strategies aimed at changing behavior to prevent transmission of the virus thus remain the first priority in the effort to control HIV infection.

REFERENCES

Brookmeyer, R., and M. H. Gail. 1986. Minimum size of the acquired immunodeficiency syndrome (AIDS) epidemic in the United States. Lancet 2:1320–1322.

De Gruttola, V., and K. H. Mayer. 1988. Assessing and modeling heterosexual spread of the human immunodeficiency virus in the United States. Rev. Infect. Dis. 10:138–150.

Hyman, J. M., and E. A. Stanley. In press. Using mathematical models to understand the AIDS epidemic. Mathematical Biosciences.

IOM (Institute of Medicine). 1988. Report of the Workshop on Modeling the Spread of Infection with Human Immunodeficiency Virus and the Demographic Impact of Acquired Immune Deficiency Syndrome, Washington, D.C., October 15–17, 1987.

Jager, H. J. C., and E. J. Ruitenberg. 1987. The statistical analysis and mathematical modelling of AIDS. AIDS 1:129–130.

May, R. M., and R. M. Anderson. 1987. Transmission dynamics of HIV infection. Nature 326:137–142.

Morgan, W. M., and J. W. Curran. 1986. Acquired immunodeficiency syndrome: Current and future trends. Public Health Rep. 101:459–465

4

Altering the Course of the Epidemic

AIDS and the HIV epidemic present a fundamental challenge to
"guardians" of the public health. This chapter discusses the range of
possible public health interventions, the resources and talents that will be
necessary to implement them, and the hallmarks of programs that are
both responsive to the crisis and consonant with a respect for human
dignity and individual freedom. It also highlights the needs of IV drug
abusers and several problem areas that will require more attention, such
as the impact of AIDS on minorities.

FEATURES OF PUBLIC HEALTH PROGRAMS

Certain properties of the HIV epidemic distinguish it from other dread
diseases and prompt special concerns in fashioning a public health
response. The incubation period of AIDS may be a number of years;
asymptomatic carriers of the virus appear to be infectious for the
remainder of their lives. Public health programs are based on the
presumption that this is so. AIDS is also a disease of behaviors—
generally private, consensual behaviors such as sexual intercourse and IV
drug abuse. Finally, the groups at greatest risk of infection were already
subject to social stigma and prejudice; that vulnerability entails unique
considerations for public health officials (Walters, 1988).

In considering how to fashion interventions to confront the HIV
epidemic, it is useful to review the conceptual framework for the
operation of public health programs. They are frequently classified by the

level of prevention they are intended to provide: primary, secondary, or tertiary; that is, by efforts to prevent the problem altogether, to detect the problem early and provide definitive treatment, or to avert or mitigate the long-term consequences of the problem. Programs organized to combat the HIV epidemic can be considered in that manner, although some program activities may have an effect on more than one type of prevention.

Primary prevention, which is aimed at preventing new cases of infection, focuses on three groups. First, there are those who have not begun to engage in high-risk behaviors, principally young persons who are not sexually active or who do not abuse drugs. Activities may be directed at preparing these individuals to avoid risk behavior entirely or to learn safer practices prior to initiation. Second, there are those who engage in high-risk behavior but who have not yet been infected. These individuals may be approached to stop the risk behavior or to learn safer practices. Finally, those persons who are currently infected can be supported in practices that minimize the opportunities for transmitting the virus to uninfected persons.

Secondary and tertiary levels of prevention are harder to define in the absence of definitive treatment for HIV infection. Current research indicates that there is a role for early case finding, not only for the contribution early identification can make to primary prevention but also to allow for medical supervision of the asymptomatic individual and for medical care of the symptomatic person. As additional treatment methods are developed, it may be possible to define a tertiary prevention level.

The committee believes that the HIV epidemic should prompt a reexamination of the fiscal and institutional barriers that impede effective public health efforts in all program areas related to the control of HIV infection. Public health efforts to combat the spread of HIV infection are not limited to programs with "AIDS" in their titles. Sexually transmitted disease clinics (Aral et al., 1986; Solomon and DeJong, 1986), drug abuse treatment centers (Carlson and McClellan, 1987), private physicians' offices (Koop, 1987b), hospitals, and other health care clinics are all appropriate places for HIV education, counseling, and testing. In fact, many of the programs designed to combat gonorrhea, syphilis, chlamydia, chancroid, and other sexually transmitted diseases will themselves have a direct bearing on the AIDS epidemic, as will efforts to combat drug abuse. The continued reprogramming of funds from these activities to AIDS programs may have a deleterious net impact on the public health.

ANTIDISCRIMINATION PROTECTIONS

Evidence accumulated since the publication of *Confronting AIDS* gives us further confidence in our conclusions about the modes of HIV transmission (see Chapter 2). There are no grounds for discriminating against persons with AIDS or HIV infection because of fears that they pose a health risk in the workplace or in housing. The fear of AIDS can be a healthy and useful reaction when it helps people avoid behaviors that put them at risk of contracting HIV infection. Unreasonable fears can have a debilitating effect on both the individual and the body politic (Eisenberg, 1986).

The committee believes that the fear of discrimination is a major constraint to the wide acceptance of many potentially effective public health measures. Public health programs will be most effective if they are accompanied by clear and strict sanctions to prevent unwarranted discrimination against those who are infected with HIV or who are at risk of infection.

In many instances, discrimination has thwarted access to health care (hospitals, nursing homes, dental care, and private physicians' services), employment, housing, education, health insurance, and even funeral services (Rapoport and Parry, 1987; Dickens, 1988).

A few systematic studies have attempted to determine the range and scope of AIDS-related discrimination and legal protections (National Gay Rights Advocates, 1986; ASTHO, 1987). Although it is impossible to tell whether AIDS-related discrimination has paralleled the rise in AIDS cases, dramatic anecdotal accounts reflect problems that increasingly confront those with AIDS or with lesser manifestations of HIV infection, those who are without symptoms but are seropositive, or those who are merely members of risk groups. For example, an apparent rise in violence against gays has been attributed to fears of AIDS (NGLTF, 1988).

Many court cases have been filed involving victims of AIDS-related discrimination in a variety of settings (Boorstin, 1987), and complaints have been docketed with state and local human rights commissions. Courts have ordered schools to admit HIV-infected students and have allowed teachers with AIDS to remain on duty in the classroom. It is likely that many other episodes of discrimination are being resolved privately, or they may simply not be pursued by AIDS patients who are too debilitated to press their claims (Ansberry, 1987).

Protection from irrational discrimination is a hallowed function of U.S. law (Parmet, 1987). In particular, Section 504 of the Federal Rehabilitation Act of 1973 specifically proscribes discrimination against "otherwise qualified" disabled or handicapped individuals in programs receiving federal funds. Although persons with AIDS may readily establish their disabled status, the legal posture of those who are seropositive but asymptomatic may be unclear. These individuals may not be considered handicapped under common law or statutory definitions although they may still face discrimination and threats to their livelihood, health, or residence.

A case decided by the U.S. Supreme Court since the publication of *Confronting AIDS* involving a teacher with tuberculosis would seem clearly to extend the protections of Section 504 to HIV-infected individuals who display symptoms. Yet in a footnote, the Court explicitly reserved judgment about the status of asymptomatic carriers of infectious diseases (*School Board of Nassau County, Florida* v. *Arline*, 107 U.S. 1129, 1987). However, the Ninth Circuit Court of Appeals has recently held that Section 504 specifically covers AIDS in finding that a public school teacher with AIDS could not be dismissed because of his illness (*Chalk* v. *U.S. District Court for the Central District of California*, No. 87-6418, 840 F.2 701, February 26, 1988).

The committee supports the enactment of a federal statute specifically designed to prevent discrimination on the basis of HIV infection or AIDS. The committee also supports the consideration by states and localities of statutes and ordinances designed to prevent discrimination in employment, education, housing, health insurance, or the receipt of health care services. However, the committee does not support measures that would abrogate insurers' rights to distinguish among applicants for life insurance. States should consider whether their handicapped antidiscrimination, civil rights, education, and insurance laws sufficiently address HIV infection and AIDS. Executive orders and administrative regulations are other possible avenues of reform. It may also be appropriate to review the time it takes to consider claims—if discrimination charges take years to resolve, many AIDS patients may die before their rights can be upheld.

EDUCATION

Educational efforts to foster and sustain behavioral change remain the only presently available means to stem the spread of HIV infection.

This statement is no less true today than it was in 1986 when *Confronting AIDS* was published. At that time, IOM/NAS lamented the failure of the United States to mount an aggressive, effective AIDS education campaign, calling such efforts woefully inadequate. The past 2 years, on the other hand, have seen many state and local efforts to educate the general public and those in high-risk groups, as well as a nationwide education campaign funded by the federal government and directed by CDC. These significant efforts are laudable. Nevertheless, formidable obstacles to effective AIDS education remain. Merely communicating information about the risks of infection will not suffice; individuals must also have the motivation and means to translate an awareness of risk into changes in fundamental areas of human behavior.

The committee believes that the urgency of the HIV epidemic warrants a multiplicity of educational efforts, including the use of paid advertising on television or in other media. Currently, a number of federal entities, including the armed forces, the postal service, Amtrak, and the mint use paid advertising—over $300 million worth each year. Administrative restrictions from the Department of Health and Human Services (HHS) preclude CDC from doing the same. The committee is aware of concerns about paying for advertising: that paid advertising for AIDS could have a detrimental effect on the amount of time or space donated for public service announcements in general. Nevertheless, it is doubtful that public service announcements are adequate to the task of increasing public awareness of the risks of HIV infection and encouraging behavioral change. **The gravity of the HIV epidemic is such that CDC, like other government entities, should be allowed to purchase advertising time and space and should be supplied with the funds to do so. Any administrative regulations that preclude such actions should be withdrawn immediately.**

Content of the Message

The implementation of AIDS education programs has continued to founder over questions involving their content. Although a great deal is known about the modes of transmission of the virus, much of this information is difficult to convey. Only the scientist or physician trained in epidemiology may be able to appreciate the fact that HIV is at once fragile and deadly—unable to live outside of the body for very long and yet lethal once it is introduced by sexual intercourse or through the bloodstream. Yet it is essential that educational programs convey to the public this scientifically accurate message. Moreover, these efforts should be aimed beyond those in what traditionally have become identified as high-risk groups. The further spread of HIV is sufficiently daunting to warrant educational efforts to promote personal caution and prudent behaviors on the part of all sexually active persons.

The linking of HIV transmission to sexual behavior and IV drug abuse raises concerns about the propriety of the educational message, concerns that have not abated since the publication of *Confronting AIDS*. Those who view homosexual relations, heterosexual relations outside of marriage, or IV drug abuse as immoral may believe that frank, straightforward educational or public health programs encourage such activities. These concerns continue to stymie educational efforts (Booth, 1987b).

The committee believes that government at all levels, as well as private sources, should continue to fund effective, factual educational programs designed to foster behavioral change. This may mean supporting AIDS education efforts that contain explicit, practical, and perhaps graphic advice targeted at specific audiences about safer sexual practices and how to avoid the dangers of shared needles and syringes.

Confronting AIDS expressed skepticism about the approach taken by CDC in establishing local boards to review the degree of explicitness of AIDS educational materials (the so-called "dirty words" issue) because of concern that such a process might keep explicit information from those for whom it would be most beneficial. Efforts to stifle candid materials that discuss safer sexual practices and that are targeted at appropriate audiences may take a toll in human lives. In 1987 an amendment to the HHS appropriations bill (P.L. 100-202, Title 5, Sec. 514, 1988) passed the House and Senate with overwhelming majorities. It precludes the use of CDC funds for educational materials "that promote or encourage, directly, homosexual sexual activities" (Booth, 1987a). Explicit information on the risks associated with gay sex and the way those risks can be minimized does not "promote or encourage" homosexual activities. Its sole function is to help homosexuals avoid an illness that endangers their lives and those of their sexual partners and costs the nation billions of dollars.

School-Based Education

The committee believes that school-based educational programs are an essential part of efforts to increase awareness of the risk of HIV and to combat the spread of infection. Ideally, such education would begin at a young age, with a level of detail and explicitness appropriate for the age group. Education about sexuality and drug abuse, including specific information about HIV, should be part of a systematic and comprehensive program of health education.

Many states have initiated some kind of AIDS education program. At the time of publication of *Confronting AIDS,* nine states had statutes that specifically allowed or mandated public school classroom teaching about sexually transmitted diseases. Since then, at least nine more states have passed similar statutes, some of which specifically address AIDS (Associated Press, 1988).

A number of states have also acted in the absence of specific legislation. By early 1987 half of the nation's largest school districts had instituted some kind of HIV education program. Unfortunately, in many states, HIV education proposals have hit formidable roadblocks. The locus of responsibility for shaping the content of AIDS curricula remains a highly charged issue, reflecting historical tensions between state and local control of education. State mandates also vary widely as to the degree of parental control that may be permitted. Some states have provisions that allow parents or guardians to inspect curricular material in advance or to exempt their children from the courses (Koop, 1987a).

Colleges are another key site for AIDS prevention and education efforts. Because of the lengthy incubation period of the virus and the timing of the onset of sexual (and drug abuse) activity, there may be few cases of fulminant AIDS among college students. Nevertheless, many may be infected (Hein, 1987). Recent reviews of college-level activities have identified the college campus as a particular gap in AIDS education efforts (Biemiller, 1987; Caruso and Haig, 1987).

Within the college setting, there are many opportunities for reaching students with AIDS prevention messages (Fraser, 1987). Dormitory advisors, health centers, and peer groups are beginning to offer HIV counseling on some campuses. More campuses are beginning to offer serologic testing or, if not, to advertise off-campus services. At some colleges, condoms are available through clinics, bookstores, or dormitories. A few schools are also carefully evaluating the effectiveness of various program mixes.

Effect of Educational Programs

Awareness of AIDS is widespread. The deaths from AIDS of a number of celebrities have rendered the disease less of an abstraction. During the 12-month period ending October 1987, the number of Americans who reported that they knew someone with AIDS grew from 4 to 6 percent (*New York Times*, 1988). The ways in which HIV is spread are also widely known. According to the National Health Interview Survey of August 1987, 92 percent of the public know that AIDS can be contracted by having sex with someone who is infected; more than 80 percent believe that condoms are a somewhat or very effective means of avoiding infection. Unfortunately, serious misunderstandings persist: 25 percent of the general public believe incorrectly that HIV can be acquired by donating blood; 38 percent believe incorrectly that mosquitoes are a likely mode of transmission; and 21 percent believe incorrectly that there is a risk of infection from merely working near someone with AIDS (Dawson et al., 1987).

The committee believes that more studies are needed to determine the effects of various types of educational campaigns on specific populations. For example, there have been few systematic assessments of the impact of AIDS education programs or media efforts on the behavior of heterosexuals (as opposed to the impact on their beliefs or understanding). The National Research Council's CBASSE study on AIDS research and the behavioral, social, and statistical sciences (see Chapter 3) will explore the effectiveness of educational interventions in depth. The committee's report, to be released in the fall of 1988, will present general principles of health behavior and recommendations about AIDS intervention strategies.

Especially critical are educational efforts aimed at persons at risk within minority populations. The prevalence of AIDS in the black and

Hispanic communities is substantially higher than the prevalence among whites. Culturally specific programs to address the needs of minority communities, especially in the inner cities, are of paramount importance. In August 1987 CDC sponsored a conference on minorities and AIDS, the outgrowth of which has been a number of new efforts in this regard. A second such conference is planned for the summer of 1988.

Gay and Bisexual Men

Community-based programs in the two cities hardest hit by the epidemic, New York and San Francisco, are the oldest examples of aggressive HIV educational efforts. These programs began at the grass roots level with privately raised funds and volunteer support from many in the gay community. Today, they feature a multipronged attack funded by a variety of government and private sources and include media campaigns, peer counseling, literature distribution, and support groups. In addition, local efforts in cities such as New York, Boston, San Francisco, and Los Angeles have been expanded to the state level. It has been shown that substantial changes in behavior can be effected among gay and bisexual men in areas with firmly established gay social and political structures (Winkelstein et al., 1987).

Unfortunately, even the dramatic changes that have occurred in San Francisco and New York are faint reassurance when half or more of the male homosexual population may already be infected (Fineberg, 1988). The high rates of seropositivity among gay men in these cities and the widespread appreciation of the risk posed by AIDS are not sufficient reasons to abandon educational efforts for homosexual men or curtail local, state, or federal government funding support, despite the claims of some critics (Kilpatrick, 1987). The mere understanding that one may be at risk will not necessarily translate into sustained behavioral change in the absence of concerted educational and counseling efforts.

The challenge also remains to educate and inculcate behavioral change among gay men outside of urban areas with active gay social communities and among men who may not see themselves as belonging to the gay community but who nevertheless engage in homosexual behavior that puts them at risk. **The committee also believes it is essential to develop effective methods for reaching youth who are just becoming homosexually active.**

AIDS and Condoms

Condoms are a generally effective means of preventing the spread of HIV infection and a number of other sexually transmitted diseases.

Studies of the effectiveness of condoms as a barrier against HIV and other viral agents have resulted in recommendations for the use of latex (as opposed to natural membrane) condoms, supplemented by creams or jelly containing nonoxynol 9, a proven virucidal agent (Rietmeijer et al., 1988). Condoms are regulated as medical devices under the Federal Food, Drug, and Cosmetics Act, and the Food and Drug Administration (FDA) has recently moved to ensure the adequacy of condom manufacture. FDA batch testing and manufacturer quality control programs have resulted on occasion in product recalls.

Ensuring that condoms meet quality specifications is only an initial step, however. The occasional failure of condoms is more likely to be attributable to "user failure" than to "product failure" (CDC, 1988a). Greater familiarity with condom use should be fostered to promote a willingness to incorporate them routinely into heterosexual and homosexual intercourse. Health care professionals need to advise their patients in detail about how to use condoms. CDC has issued a detailed review of the role of condoms in the prevention of sexually transmitted diseases including detailed guidelines for their use (CDC, 1988a).

One obstacle to effective AIDS education has been the long-standing refusal of the media to accept commercial condom advertising in the belief it would offend a substantial portion of their audience. In 1987 some companies relented, including the *New York Times, Newsweek,* and *Time, Inc.* (Aiken, 1987). These changes in policy were accompanied by the proviso that the advertising message stress the role of condoms in disease prevention rather than in contraception. Although a few local television affiliates have broken ranks and agreed to accept condom advertising, the networks have continued to balk. Many have pointed out the irony of the numerous steamy sexual encounters that take place on daytime TV soap operas and during prime time with seldom even a mention of the need to exercise precautions.

The committee believes that there must be continued attention to the development of policies to foster the use of condoms. Allowing condoms to be advertised through the major media, increasing the number and types of outlets for their sale and distribution, and taking steps to ensure their quality are among the measures the committee has considered. In addition, continued education is needed to ensure their effective use.

HIV ANTIBODY SCREENING AND TESTING

The proper role of tests for HIV infection has continued to be one of the most controversial AIDS-related public policy issues. Arguments for and against testing (of individuals) and screening (of populations) depend largely on the circumstances in which the tests are to be applied. In order to assess the utility of testing or screening in any particular setting, it is essential that the purpose of such activities be clearly spelled out. A few possible rationales related to public health and medical care include the following:

• HIV antibody (and, possibly in the future, antigen) screening is essential to ensure the *safety of donated blood, tissues, and organs.*

• Antibody screening is critical in *surveillance and planning* to obtain geographic and demographic data about the spread of disease. These data are needed to plan targeted public health efforts and earmark patient care services.

• Increased antibody testing is also an adjunct to *patient care.* The advent of zidovudine (i.e., AZT) trials in asymptomatic individuals is one additional reason asymptomatic persons at risk might wish to know their status. In patients with new symptoms that suggest HIV infection, HIV antibody testing should be part of a diagnostic workup.

• Testing and counseling may also help foster *individual behavioral change.* Testing may be especially useful to women of childbearing years confronted with reproductive decisions.

• HIV testing may be useful in identifying index cases, which will allow the *identification of contacts* and others who may have been exposed, such as female partners of bisexual men or recipients of contaminated blood products. Testing will ascertain whether exposed persons have become infected.

• Screening has also been proposed as an adjunct to *infection control* procedures in hospitals to help ensure that appropriate precautions are exercised when invasive procedures are performed on seropositive patients.

These varied rationales offer a backdrop against which to examine the array of proposals for more widespread testing. Yet a number of other factors must also be taken into account: the social and psychological ramifications of the test, the expense of testing and the labor-intensive nature of counseling, the accuracy of the test in terms of the number of false-positive and false-negative results (in both the ideal and the "real world" laboratory settings), and the degree to which test information can be protected from unauthorized access (Barry et al., 1987). Attributes of the population to be screened are also critical factors. The degree to which a population is at risk and the reservoir of infection within the population to be screened are further considerations. Institutionalized populations pose special concerns (Gostin and Curran, 1987).

Technical Considerations

Tests to measure the development of antibodies against HIV have been commercially available since the spring of 1985. Eight different tests have been licensed for antibody detection, including seven enzyme-linked immunoassay (ELISA) tests and one Western blot test kit. As of 1987 these tests had been approved by FDA for clinical diagnostic use in addition to their original purpose of screening the blood supply. Since their introduction, a number of manufacturing modifications have been approved to bolster the sensitivity (the test's performance among infected individuals), specificity (the test's performance among uninfected individuals), and reproducibility of test results.

The accuracy of currently marketed HIV antibody tests compares quite favorably with other medical diagnostic tests and has been borne out by experience in the nation's two largest screening programs: blood banks and the military.

The more widespread testing programs that have been proposed under a variety of public and private auspices have prompted concerns about the ability to replicate the military's record of testing accuracy (Burke, 1987). The risk of false-positive results (which is greater in the screening of low-prevalence populations) and the danger of imposing an unnecessary burden of fear and stigma on uninfected individuals have been sources of misgivings about expanding screening programs (Okie, 1987). The issue of the number of false test results that might have to be endured to achieve the intended public health result of screening programs presents ethical and political as well as technical questions (Meyer and Pauker, 1987).

The committee believes the federal government should give more attention to establishing standards for laboratory proficiency in HIV antibody testing, setting criteria for interpreting assays, and instituting quality assurance procedures. When appropriate, FDA should continue to move rapidly to license new diagnostic tests. Additional resources should be provided to allow state and local governments to expand their testing capabilities, shorten waiting periods, and improve the quality of test results.

Informed Consent and Confidentiality

In addition to ensuring that tests for infection with HIV are accurate, properly confirmed, and conducted by experienced, proficient laboratories, other essential requisites of testing and screening (in addition to counseling) include securing the consent of the individual to be tested and maintaining the confidentiality of the results.

Courts have forcefully articulated the right of a legally competent person to direct his or her own medical care. Yet state statutes and case law do not necessarily require informed consent for HIV antibody testing in all cases. It is common practice for physicians to order batteries of laboratory tests for their patients without detailed explanations of each test or more specific consents other than that inferred from the patient's presenting for treatment. (In fact, the possible overuse of medical tests has come under increasing fire.) A few states have clarified the law by requiring specific consent for HIV antibody testing. Still, in the past year, there have been a number of accounts of patients who were tested without their knowledge or consent (Henry et al., 1988a,b).

In addition to underscoring the need for counseling to precede and follow the administration of an HIV antibody test, *Confronting AIDS* recommended that in no case should a test be made without the subject's prior knowledge (or that of a duly appointed proxy when the test subject's competence is questioned). The informed consent process should entail a discussion of the clinical and behavioral implications of the test results, including the accuracy of the test and its potential for encouraging behavioral change. Also critical are discussions of potential psychological and social ramifications. The person to be tested should be aware of the third parties to whom the test results must (or may) be divulged. In hospitals, for example, an array of individuals have legitimate access to patient charts. Testing and screening should take place only in the context of pretest and posttest counseling. As discussed elsewhere in this chapter, to encourage the use of the test to promote behavioral change and as a diagnostic tool in the clinical setting, it is essential that confidentiality and antidiscrimination sanctions be in place and be understood and enforced.

To secure the cooperation of those at risk of HIV infection in coming forth voluntarily to be tested, test results must be kept confidential (Sherer, 1988). People will be more likely to undergo testing voluntarily if they believe that inappropriate disclosures of HIV testing information, which could result in the loss of jobs, housing, or insurance coverage, will not occur. **The committee believes that laws and regulations with strict sanctions to prohibit willful or negligent unauthorized disclosure of HIV antibody test results are an essential component of the public health effort.** Such laws must address both public health and medical records and be coupled with sound recordkeeping practices. Exceptions to confidentiality provisions must have a solid basis in public health law or policy and must be clearly justified.

Laws regulating the confidentiality of health records tend to be complicated, overlapping, and even conflicting (IHPP, 1987). Complexities arise in distinguishing between hospital records and those maintained by private physicians or between records kept in private versus public institutions. Some states protect medical records from court review because of the testimonial privilege deriving from the doctor–patient relationship (although frequently this extends only to psychiatrists). Questions may arise in transferring records from one state to another.

AIDS has been a catalyst in some states for a new look at the entire range of protection afforded various types of medical records. Other states have considered the confidentiality of HIV antibody test results specifically. Of the dozen or so states that have instituted HIV antibody reporting requirements, only Colorado, Idaho, and Wisconsin have simultaneously strengthened confidentiality provisions (although other states may rely on existing public health statutes).

California and Massachusetts are examples of states that have enacted statutes that severely restrict the scope of disclosure of HIV antibody test results and severely punish negligent or willful breaches of confidentiality. Some state laws are so restrictive that they have been criticized for impeding patient care by precluding the sharing of information about patients' HIV antibody status among health care providers.

The range of exceptions that have been suggested to the general rule of confidentiality and the context in which breaches have occurred suggest how complex these rules may be in their application. Lawsuits have been filed against blood banks to reveal the identities of donors who may be implicated in transfusion-related HIV transmission, and courts have decided for and against disclosure. Employees in health care institutions and emergency medical personnel have asserted a right to know the serologic status of their patients, especially following accidental exposure to blood or bodily fluids through needle sticks or similar accidents. A number of states have enacted statutes requiring that emergency medical personnel be informed of a patient's HIV infection status if it becomes known subsequent to their contact with the patient; in some states, morticians must likewise be informed if they are handling the body of someone who has died from AIDS.

Concerns about confidentiality have extended even beyond the death of persons with AIDS. One court, in upholding the right of a newspaper to print that a local resident had died of AIDS, noted that the public's right to be informed of the reality of AIDS in its own local community was not merely "gratification of idle curiosity." Physicians have cautioned, however, that the continued confidentiality of such information helps to ensure that doctors accurately and completely report causes of death (Lambert, 1988).

Of course, statutes and regulations by themselves will not absolutely guarantee confidentiality, however severe the sanctions provided for breaching it. HIV-infected individuals may themselves share knowledge of their status with friends, neighbors, or coworkers, who may in turn disseminate the information further. Statutes enacted to provide privacy protections may subsequently be repealed or limited by case law interpretations; medical records are frequently subject to subpoena in the absence of specific protections. The sanctions established by statutes may also be of little use when it is impossible to trace the source of the unwarranted disclosure of information. **The committee believes that, in addition to reviewing statutory protections of medical confidentiality, it will also be necessary at the local level for hospitals and other medical care institutions to review their recordkeeping policies and apprise their staff of their responsibilities to protect patient privacy.**

Voluntary Testing

The committee believes that tests for HIV infection will play an increasingly useful role on a range of fronts in the battle against its spread. **The committee recommends expanded voluntary testing combined with counseling of all those whose behavior may have put them at risk for exposure to HIV.** Those whose test results are positive have a moral obligation to take the necessary steps to inform and protect their sexual or needle-sharing partners.

Antibody status is a powerful piece of information—individuals may differ considerably in their psychological and behavioral responses to such knowledge (Martin, 1986). Screening and testing programs must be linked to programs with adequate staff and funding to offer pretest and posttest counseling for both seropositive and seronegative individuals (CDC, 1987b).

Opponents of testing for homosexual men and others at high risk have argued that such persons should simply act "as if" they were infected because the admonitions would be the same for those who tested positive or negative. Both need to heed advice about safer sex and the sharing of needles and syringes—if negative, to preserve one's negative status, or if positive, to protect one's partners from infection. In the absence of a cure or vaccine, testing opponents believe that the potentially adverse social consequences of such tests, in terms of the risk of losing employment, housing, friends, or insurance coverage, are simply too great (Helquist, 1987).

The belief that a knowledge of antibody test results encourages healthier behaviors animates much of public health policy related to AIDS. It is therefore critical to understand whether this is actually and not merely intuitively correct. The differences in behavioral responses on learning of a positive or negative test result, as well as the determinants of individual variations, should be the subjects of continued study. (Apart from the possible behavioral impact of knowledge of antibody test results, it is important that people know their antibody status so they can receive appropriate health care and therapy should it become available.)

Virtually all of the studies to date have been conducted with self-identified gay men in large cities. More research is needed on homosexual men outside of the few urban areas that have been the epicenters of HIV infection. Another important research direction is an assessment of the impact of HIV on gay youths who are just entering sexual maturity. Relatively few cases of AIDS have appeared among adolescents; nevertheless, 20 percent of all AIDS cases occur among those aged 20 to 29, suggesting that many young people are being infected during their teenage years.

The committee believes further studies to assess the behavioral impact of testing are essential. For example, there are virtually no data on the effects of knowledge of antibody test results on family planning decisions (Grimes, 1987; Cotton, 1988). There are also no published studies demonstrating that women or heterosexual men are more likely to practice safer sex when they know their antibody test result, whether positive or negative.

Mandatory Screening

The committee has weighed the potential public health benefits of various mandatory screening programs against their problems and has concluded that, at this time, in only a few instances can mandatory testing be endorsed.

Mandatory screening programs, especially those aimed at low-risk groups, are likely to be ineffective, counterproductive, and distracting. Mandatory screening of low-risk groups may divert resources from more worthwhile educational and voluntary programs, identify too few individuals at risk, and produce many false-positive test results; it may also have untoward social consequences that would outweigh any possible benefits. **The committee believes that, at this time, the only mandatory screening appropriate for public health purposes involves blood, tissue, and organ donation.**

Nevertheless, screening programs that cast the net more widely among low-risk groups have garnered political as well as popular support, regardless of whether they are likely to reduce the spread of HIV (Hentoff, 1987). To examine the merits of some of the plethora of mandatory testing and screening program proposals, what follows are highlights of experiences with programs and data that have come to light since the publication of *Confronting AIDS*.

Blood, Tissue, and Organs

The screening of blood and blood products for HIV is a universal standard of practice in this country. The advent of serological screening in addition to self-deferral of persons at risk has made the nation's blood supply much safer. Yet there remains a small but identifiable risk of HIV infection for recipients of screened blood because of the possibility that recently infected donors are still antibody negative and consequently escape detection by available tests. There is also a possibility of human error in the blood labeling or inventory process. Given current understanding of the prevalence of HIV infection and the sensitivity of the screening tests now in use, it is estimated that 1 out of every 40,000 to 50,000 HIV-infected blood donations escapes detection (Ward et al., 1988). New, more sensitive technologies to detect antigen may make the blood supply even safer in the future.

The appreciable, albeit small, continuing risk of HIV transmission through blood underscores the need for those who have engaged in high-risk behaviors to refrain from donating blood for transfusion. Blood banks should continue to implement procedures whereby prospective donors may "self-defer" without being stigmatized, providing a form the donor can check off privately to earmark donated blood for research (rather than transfusion purposes). Increased support for alternative test sites and other centers for voluntary, anonymous testing will reduce waiting times for test results and mitigate any desire to donate blood merely to determine HIV status. The risk of the transmission of HIV is one of the reasons for the judicious use of blood and blood components and careful evaluation of the clinical indications for transfusion.

The transplantation of infected tissues and organs has also been cause for concern. FDA and CDC, in concert with the American Fertility Society, the American Association of Blood Banks, and the American College of Obstetrics and Gynecology, have recently issued more detailed recommendations on HIV antibody screening for semen banking and organ and tissue transplantation (CDC, 1988b).

Hospital-Based Screening

The committee encourages hospitals and other health care facilities to implement the "universal precautions" recommended by CDC and the American Hospital Association. These precautions involve a number of infection control measures to ward against exposure to any blood or body fluids (CDC, 1987c). The committee believes that, for the purpose of infection control, universal blood and body fluid precautions are preferable to any type of widespread hospital-based screening program. Implementing such a program might have the paradoxical effect of causing health care workers to ease infection control procedures for patients who are actually infected but who test negative during the "window" of time between infection by the virus and the development of measurable antibodies.

Nevertheless, the committee believes that, although mandatory screening of all hospital patients is inappropriate, the current situation warrants more widespread use of HIV antibody tests in the hospital setting on a voluntary, informed basis. For many individuals, being admitted to a hospital is a rare encounter with the health care system. Physicians and other caregivers, when appropriate, should use this opportunity to ascertain the patient's level of risk of HIV infection by taking a detailed sexual and drug abuse history. The assessment of risk should also be influenced by the prevalence of infection in the geographic area. If testing is medically indicated, it should proceed with the patient's understanding and cooperation.

Premarital Screening

The considerable political and popular appeal of premarital screening proposals is reflected in the number of bills on the subject introduced in 1987—nearly 80 in 35 states (Gostin, 1987b). Premarital screening proposals have been advanced in the belief that AIDS should be treated in a manner similar to and no less seriously than syphilis. Historically, states have screened couples for evidence of syphilis and other sexually transmitted diseases before issuing marriage licenses (Brandt, 1987). Yet more than 20 states have repealed their premarital blood test regulations since 1980, leaving fewer than half the states with such requirements (Hunter, 1987). Today, such tests are viewed as an inefficient and costly means of discovering too few prospective spouses with sexually transmitted diseases (Cleary et al., 1987).

The trend away from premarital screening also reflects the fact that marriage is not the precursor to sexual activity, or even to childbearing, that it once was. The average age of initiation of sexual activity reported in a 1983 study was 15.7 years for men and 16.2 years for women; the average age for marriage was 26.7 and 23.1 years, respectively (Hunter, 1987). Nor would premarital screening necessarily be prenatal screening. In New York City, where about 40 percent of the pediatric AIDS cases have occurred, 83 percent involve the children of unwed parents.

Despite the idea's initial appeal, only a few states have acted on premarital screening proposals. These include Louisiana, Illinois, and Texas (where screening is mandated only if the seropositivity rate among the general population reaches a certain point). Utah, with a statute that has been criticized as possibly unconstitutional, bans the marriage of antibody-positive individuals (Gostin and Ziegler, 1987).

The Illinois statute, which is part of a comprehensive package of AIDS bills, mandates premarital testing. Press accounts of the initial experience with the Illinois program told of an unexpected number of couples seeking testing at public clinics, thus increasing the burden on already overtaxed facilities and counseling staff. The law appears to have discouraged marriage within the state by encouraging couples to apply for marriage licenses in nearby states without testing requirements. An AIDS program director in a newspaper interview described the program as "providing intensive, one-on-one counseling to the people who need it least" (Wilkerson, 1988). Legislators have already moved to repeal the statute.

The committee reaffirms the position adopted originally in *Confronting AIDS* **that testing marriage license applicants is inadvisable.** It does, however, support the approach that requires potential applicants for marriage licenses to be informed of the risks of HIV transmission.

Female Prostitutes

Prostitution, defined as the exchange of sexual services for drugs or money, is of special concern in the HIV epidemic. By engaging in multiple sexual encounters, prostitutes heighten their risk of HIV infection. Prostitutes are a potential nexus for the heterosexual spread of AIDS because their clients may become infected and in turn infect their partners. They also risk transmission of HIV to any offspring. Studies of HIV antibodies in prostitutes have reported seroprevalence ranging from 0 to more than 50 percent (CDC, 1987a). Seroprevalence has varied dramatically from city to city, generally paralleling the cumulative incidence of HIV infection among women in the area and tending to be more than twice as high for black and Hispanic prostitutes as for white and other prostitutes. The prevalence of HIV infection is highest in the northern New Jersey and Miami areas and lowest in Nevada, where the Nevada Board of Health requires prostitutes in county-licensed brothels to test negative for HIV antibodies as a condition of employment.

Although female prostitutes historically have experienced higher levels of sexually transmitted diseases than the public at large, with HIV the primary risk factor seems to be IV drug abuse. Prostitutes are more likely than the public at large to engage in IV drug abuse; they are also at heightened risk when their male partners are themselves drug abusers.

As with other groups at particular risk of HIV infection, there has been evidence among prostitutes of considerable awareness of the threat of HIV and some behavioral change, mainly the increased use of condoms. There is also some evidence that while prostitutes have been more likely to require that their clients use condoms, they have been less likely to require their husbands or boyfriends to do the same (CDC, 1987a).

Concern about the spread of HIV infection by prostitutes has prompted three states—Nevada, Illinois, and Florida—to enact statutes mandating that prostitutes submit to HIV antibody testing. The Newark, New Jersey, city council passed an ordinance over the mayor's veto that requires antibody testing for anyone convicted of prostitution-related offenses—that is, prostitutes *and* their clients.

The committee believes that mandatory testing of prostitutes at the time of arrest or as a condition of release is not warranted at this time. Policies that tie the determination of HIV antibody status to criminal action are likely to be counterproductive because they may discourage voluntary efforts to seek testing, counseling, and related medical services. Encouraging behavioral change among prostitutes demands especially vigorous counseling and voluntary testing programs. Testing should be offered in conjunction with counseling about condom use, opportunities for drug abuse treatment and vocational rehabilitation, and medical care referral. The California Prostitutes Education Project is an example of programs that offer innovative approaches to educating both male and female prostitutes. Other examples include social service projects (e.g., Covenant House in New York City) that offer a safe haven and counseling for homeless adolescents, including prostitutes (CDC, 1987a).

The committee supports further seroprevalence studies to assess risk in this group and for the larger heterosexual community. The committee did not address the related question of mandatory testing of prisoners; however, it believes the issue deserves further study.

Home-Based Testing

Many of the concerns about testing and screening are captured in the growing debate over the use of home test kits. There are two possible types of such tests. One type, requiring considerable technological advances, would allow non-health care professionals to collect their own blood, perform a test, and interpret the results in the privacy of their own home. A second, simpler method involves a kit merely to draw blood, which is then sent to a private commercial laboratory for analysis. Results would then be delivered over the phone by a "trained counselor" (Miller, 1987). Both of these types of kits would require premarket approval from FDA (*Medical World News,* 1987; Parkman, 1988). Both have the virtue of preserving anonymity. FDA approval of the second type of kit has been sought and denied at this time. The agency requested further study to determine whether the methodology could be safely and properly applied.

The committee believes that home test kits and their associated questions warrant careful review. The principal virtue of HIV antibody tests, apart from screening blood and organ donations, is as an adjunct to a program of education and counseling. Serious questions of accuracy, confidentiality, and counseling remain to be settled before home test kits should be approved. Nevertheless, there may be some individuals who are wary of encounters with the health care system or are fearful of being seen at an alternative testing site or clinic known to offer HIV antibody testing. For such persons, home-based testing may become a viable alternative.

OTHER PUBLIC HEALTH MEASURES

Duty to Warn

One area in which the law has traditionally recognized an exception to the general duties of confidentiality is certain situations in which third parties may be at risk. Case law on the books in many states spells out the duties of physicians to warn specific individuals of foreseeable dangers, including the risk of contracting an infection. Many but not all courts have required that there be specifically identifiable and not merely "statistically probable" victims. Generally, the health care professional must know of some imminent danger to a third party and have some means of preventing the harm. Directly warning the third party at risk may not be required. Merely counseling or dissuading the patient from the avowed course of action might be enough. Informing police or public health authorities might also be reasonable alternatives.

Arguments against applying the duty to warn to persons with AIDS or to asymptomatic seropositive individuals hold that the failure to respect professional confidentiality obligations would deter patients from seeking care and would drive the disease underground. Because of the lack of transmissibility through casual contact, an HIV-infected individual does not imperil his or her neighbors, coworkers, or even those who share the same household. Rather, it is specific drug abuse and sexual practices (unprotected vaginal or anal intercourse) that endanger third parties.

The American Medical Association has offered guidelines regarding physicians' duty to warn in instances in which there is no statute that either mandates or prohibits the reporting of seropositive individuals to public health authorities and in which a physician knows that a seropositive individual is endangering a third party. In such cases the physician should: (1) attempt to persuade the infected patient to cease endangering the third party; (2) if persuasion fails, notify authorities; and (3) if the authorities take no action, notify the endangered third party (AMA, 1987). Further extensions of responsibility are unclear, however. Should the physician warn the spouse or lover of a patient? What about previous sexual partners? What kind of assurances should the physician require that sexual partners have been warned and that the patient is heeding advice about safe sex and not sharing needles?

According to some legal commentators, physicians and public health officials, especially in states with strict HIV confidentiality protections, face potential liability either way they decide (Gostin and Curran, 1987). The Scylla and Charybdis of conflicting professional obligations are not merely hypothetical. A New York City psychiatrist reports having been sued from both directions, by a patient for disclosures made to the patient's wife and by the lover of a gay patient for not disclosing antibody status (*U.S. Medicine*, 1987).

The AIDS Federal Policy Bill of 1987 was drafted to provide for the confidentiality of HIV antibody test results and to prohibit discrimination against persons with AIDS or those at risk. Provisions of the bill allow physicians to use their discretion in warning third parties at risk. Although the bill does not impose a duty on physicians one way or the other, it does protect them from liability in the event of breached confidentiality in such circumstances.

Contact Notification

Contact notification can occur in two contexts. Aside from a physician's statutory or professional obligations to warn third parties who have had intimate contact with HIV-infected persons, at the risk of breaching patient confidentiality, such warnings may also take place with the voluntary cooperation of the infected individual and within the private doctor–patient relationship. Health care professionals should encourage seropositive patients to notify their sexual or needle-sharing partners. Physicians may offer to assume that responsibility themselves or merely offer to provide further advice. Those who are notified will have the opportunity to seek serologic testing or further diagnostic information.

Contact notification may also involve local public health officials who investigate and notify the sexual or needle-sharing partners of HIV-infected individuals ("index cases," in the public health lexicon). In many states, these programs are specifically authorized by venereal disease statutes (although AIDS is usually not classified as a venereal disease). Statutes give the public health official the power or duty to inquire about the person's previous and current sexual partners. These more aggressive programs still depend on the voluntary cooperation of those who will be asked to share the identity of their partners because the laws establishing such programs do not give specific authority to compel infected individuals to disclose partners' names—through contempt citations, for example (Curran et al., 1987). The record of public health officials in preserving the confidentiality of information uncovered in the implementation of contact notification programs is remarkably good (Fox, 1986).

The feasibility of contact tracing among high-risk groups in areas with a high prevalence of HIV infection—for example, among gay men in urban settings such as San Francisco and New York City—has been viewed skeptically. Those in high-risk groups may know already what behaviors put them at risk; they would not, however, know whether or not they had become infected.

The committee believes that voluntary contact notification programs can be useful in preventing the spread of HIV infection. Trained counselors in local public health departments have experience in notifying contacts of patients with other venereal diseases; the ethos of client confidentiality is highly valued. Contact notification programs provide for the notification of sexual or drug abuse partners of infected individuals who are afraid, embarrassed, or unwilling to notify partners themselves. The health department can notify the contact without revealing the identity of the index case. These programs may be of greatest value when directed at those who otherwise might be unaware they had risked infection. For example, San Francisco has pursued a limited program to notify female contacts of bisexual men (Echenberg, 1987).

Reporting of HIV-Seropositive Cases

Approximately a dozen states now require the reporting of seropositivity. Several rationales have been offered for this requirement. First, the reporting of all seropositive test results broadens the state's information base about the prevalence of infection in the state. Second, reporting seropositive index cases facilitates the contact notification process. Third, reporting HIV infection is consistent with the view that the disease is really a continuum from HIV infection to AIDS. Finally, treating HIV infection and AIDS like other reportable diseases helps to dissipate some of the stigma associated with HIV infection and thus "normalize" the disease.

Although the committee recognizes these arguments, **it believes that mandatory reporting of seropositive test results with identifiers should not be required at this time.** Contact notification does not necessarily demand the reporting of seropositive cases with identifiers. Furthermore, for determining seroprevalence rates, well-designed population surveillance studies are more useful than ad hoc collections of cases in which the size of the underlying populations is unknown. The committee believes that the effect of mandatory reporting may be to discourage individuals from seeking voluntary testing, a cost that does not justify its potential benefits. Neither are the arguments about treating HIV infection like other diseases sufficiently compelling to risk deterring individuals from being tested.

Personal Control Measures

Since the publication of *Confronting AIDS*, there has been increasing attention given to measures aimed at controlling the behavior implicated in the spread of HIV infection, whether through isolation or quarantine, criminal penalties, or civil liability for the intentional transmission of the virus. Scores of criminal cases have been filed involving intentional or reckless attempts to transmit HIV through sexual conduct, giving blood, spitting, or biting. Since the HIV epidemic first appeared, a few states, including Colorado, Connecticut, Indiana, and Florida, have even enacted statutes providing for the isolation of infectious disease carriers.

The problems with many of these measures are manifest: it is difficult to determine intent and to predict with certainty who among the infected are dangerous to others; enforcing prudent behavior is difficult when private sexual activity is involved; the incubation period of the virus makes the determination of causation problematic; and only the poorest and most disenfranchised individuals are likely to come within the bounds of personal control measures (Field and Sullivan, 1987; Gostin, 1987a). Despite these difficulties, if it can be demonstrated that a person knowingly or recklessly transmits HIV to unwitting partners, there is no reason why such an individual should be beyond the reach of the law. There have been a number of celebrated cases of "recalcitrant" individuals who refused to conform in their behavior to the advice of health officials. (For example, "Patient Zero" was the centerpiece of a popular chronicle of the AIDS epidemic [Shilts, 1987].)

The use of criminal law sanctions or legal provisions for isolation will not address the core problems of the spread of HIV infection; nevertheless, the inability or unwillingness of authorities to deal with such hard cases may undermine confidence in those who are entrusted with the protection of the public health. It is unclear how the numerous laws already on the books would apply to HIV and AIDS, given some of the properties (especially the incubation period of the virus) that distinguish AIDS from other sexually transmitted diseases. Indeed, such laws may be ineffective, protecting neither the public health nor civil liberties. **The committee believes that there may be rare instances in which the state should act to restrict the personal liberties of some infected individuals, and states should review their statutes to ensure that such authority exists.** Legal measures to restrict personal liberty should be used only when the following conditions have been met: (1) the individual is infected; (2) the individual is putting others at risk; (3) voluntary efforts to prevent the individual from jeopardizing others have failed; and (4) the restrictive measure is the least restrictive alternative available. Furthermore, restrictive measures should also entail the provision of intensive counseling, job training, and other supportive actions designed to induce behavior change. The time involved should be short and clearly limited.

AIDS AND IV DRUG ABUSE

Confronting AIDS highlighted the needs of IV drug abusers and noted that this group had not received as much media attention as other risk groups. This situation is changing with recognition of the looming danger that IV drug abuse poses for the user, his or her needle-sharing or sexual partner, and his or her offspring (Des Jarlais et al., 1988). IV drug abusers are the second largest group of AIDS sufferers; they are the persons most likely to transmit HIV to heterosexual partners. There are an estimated 1.2 million drug abusers in the United States who inject drugs, including heroin and, increasingly, cocaine. Approximately 30 percent of these drug abusers are women.

Three-quarters of the IV drug-related AIDS cases come from the New York City metropolitan area, where seroprevalence among IV drug abusers is estimated to be anywhere from 50 to 60 percent (Des Jarlais and Friedman, 1987; Lange et al., 1988). Retrospective reviews of the medical records of drug-related deaths in New York City have uncovered many more deaths (for example, from bacterial endocarditis and tuberculosis) than were originally believed to be related to HIV. The link of IV drug abuse to AIDS is of particular concern to inner-city minority communities, particularly blacks and Hispanics (Ginzburg, 1987).

The committee believes that the gross inadequacy of federal efforts to reduce HIV transmission among IV drug abusers, when considered in relation to the scope and implications of such transmission, is now the most serious deficiency in current efforts to control HIV infection in the United States. Correcting this deficiency will require special efforts directed particularly but not exclusively at black and Hispanic populations at risk in New York City and New Jersey (Brown et al., 1987; Rogers and Williams, 1987).

The committee supports a number of strategies in the short and long terms to prevent drug abuse and to avoid the risk of HIV infection when such prevention is not possible. **The committee urges a greater commitment on the part of federal, state, and local governments to the rapid, large-scale expansion of drug abuse treatment slots, both in residential drug-free treatment centers and in methadone maintenance facilities, to offer immediate access to all addicts who request treatment.** Without substantially increased funding, however, treatment on demand is a laudable yet distant goal. In January 1988 there were 29,400 methadone maintenance treatment slots for an estimated 200,000 IV drug abusers in New York City. More than 60 percent of those slots were taken by long-term clients who had been on methadone for 2 or more years (Thomas, 1988). Official waiting lists contain at least a thousand names; thousands of others are assuredly deterred by the prospect of a wait of a month or more.

Creating and funding more treatment slots will entail training and hiring more counselors and physicians as well as securing more office space, but these are not the only impediments to more ready access to methadone maintenance. Much of the historical development of methadone clinics has involved philosophical debates over the medical versus moral models of treatment and the competing merits of methadone versus drug-free programs (Newman, 1987). The HIV epidemic has quieted some of this debate, and there has been more willingness to loosen some of the restrictions that accompany the dispensing of methadone. In October 1987 the National Institute on Drug Abuse and FDA proposed lifting the requirement that methadone clinics hire a counselor for every 50 patients. In December 1987 the American Medical Association also recommended loosening enrollment restrictions (Thomas, 1988). Others have urged that physicians in private practice be allowed to prescribe methadone.

Intervention Innovations

The committee supports the increased use of former IV drug abusers as community health workers to provide "one-on-one" risk reduction counseling and materials to drug abusers who are not in treatment, including instruction in the use of bleach to sterilize injection equipment. This program points up one important requirement of effective intervention programs—they must reach beyond treatment centers, as no more than 20 percent of IV drug abusers attend treatment programs in any given year.

In San Francisco, former drug abusers and experienced drug counselors distributed thousands of 1-ounce vials of bleach, accompanied by instructions for addicts on how to clean "works" (drug injection equipment). A study by an independent research group surveyed 387 addicts at four sites in the San Francisco area. Before the program, only 3 percent reported using bleach to clean needles and syringes, although 34 percent used "possibly safe" methods such as boiling syringes or rinsing them with alcohol or hydrogen peroxide. One year later, the results of a survey of 440 addicts showed that 68 percent used bleach to clean their equipment, while another 8 percent used "possibly safe" techniques (Watters, 1988). According to one of the architects of the program, "[t]he outreach workers, and not the bleach bottles are the linchpins of our program; their street wise skills are essential to empower the IVDUs [intravenous drug users] to take health maintenance into their own hands, and to reinforce adherence to risk-avoidance measures" (letter to R.

Widdus from J. A. Newmeyer, Haight-Ashbury Free Medical Clinic, San Francisco, October 13, 1987).

New Jersey has designed a coupon program using vouchers that entitle prompt entry into drug treatment slots. This policy may allow more precise targeting of the IV drug abuser at greatest risk of infection or in greatest need of intervention while also matching the appropriate treatment modality with the particular characteristics of the user. Reports indicate that 84 percent of the distributed coupons were redeemed in the first 3 months of the program (Jackson and Rotkiewicz, 1987).

Distribution of Sterile Needles and Syringes

Confronting AIDS concluded that, because not all IV drug abusers will be able to abandon drug abuse or switch to safer, noninjectable drugs, "[i]t is time to begin experimenting with public policies to encourage the use of sterile needles and syringes by removing legal and administrative barriers to their possession and use." Some tentative results from needle exchange programs in other countries support this recommendation, and **the committee continues to believe that evaluation of the effectiveness of providing sterile needles and injection equipment to drug abusers in certain circumstances is an essential part of planning a prevention strategy.**

At least four countries—the Netherlands, the United Kingdom, Australia, and Switzerland—have begun to experiment with free, government-supported needle exchange programs, and all report encouraging results (Lofton, 1988). At a meeting sponsored by the World Health Organization, the Netherlands reported that needle sharing declined from 75 percent to 25 percent from 1985 to 1987. WHO officials caution, however, that programs may not be transplanted readily from one country to another, and they urge nations to begin with small pilot programs.

In this country, reluctance to begin to experiment with such programs for fear of encouraging drug abuse has begun to give way to concerns about the risk of AIDS. In New York, where a state statute bans the sale of sterile needles and syringes without a prescription, a proposal to institute such an experiment was made as early as August 1985 by the New York City health commissioner. (Although New York is one of 12 states with statutes banning the sale of sterile needles, the state health commissioner is empowered to waive parts of the law for experimental purposes.) Yet city and state government officials had difficulty agreeing on details of the scope of the programs or the experimental design.

In early 1988 a number of events conspired to prompt a change in policy. Concern about the spread of HIV infection in New York City was underscored by a study showing that 1 of every 61 babies born there tested positive for HIV antibodies (Novick et al., 1988). In another development, ADAPT, a well-respected local drug treatment group, threatened to break the law openly and distribute sterile needles and syringes. With these added pressures, New York State and City agreed to an experimental program to issue sterile needles and equipment to addicts on methadone maintenance program waiting lists in targeted neighborhoods in which drug abuse was rampant (Raymond, 1988b). These needle and syringe exchange programs may be viewed as a way to attract addicts into treatment during which they can be counseled not only about the danger of contaminated needles and syringes but also about unprotected sex.

There are a number of other short- and long-term approaches to the problems of IV drug abuse that deserve attention, both on their own merits and because the stakes are now higher as a result of the HIV epidemic. In particular, the widespread variations in seroprevalence among even needle-sharing drug abusers highlight the opportunity for interrupting the spread of infection in this group (see Chapter 2). As one tack, **the committee supports the immediate extension of serologic testing and counseling for HIV infection to all appropriate settings in which IV drug abusers are seen.** Programs should also be developed to promote self-help support groups of former and current drug abusers as a means of providing education about AIDS and drug abuse among at-risk groups. Some treatment centers have designed programs of this type to counsel the families of abusers as well and to assist in obtaining housing, child care, and legal assistance (Raymond, 1988a).

Some long-term strategies that deserve increased attention include intensified efforts to prevent IV drug abuse by educating teens and preteens in high-risk populations. Research and evaluation are critical to ascertain which interventions work best.

RESOURCES

Unlike biomedical research, which is traditionally and overwhelmingly a federal responsibility, funds for AIDS prevention and education rightfully come from a variety of sources, including federal, state, and local governments. It is thus somewhat more difficult to determine whether one of the goals of *Confronting AIDS*—providing by 1990 $1 billion a year in "newly available funds" for public health and education—is being reached. The goals for public health and education were set with the recognition that, instead of being the sole funding source, the federal government is "the only possible majority funding source."

Various private sources have also been marshalled, and charitable contributions in the form of foundation support and individual funding of local AIDS service-providing groups remain a critical part of the effort.

Contributions from private individuals are not only monetary; they also take the form of thousands of hours of volunteer time.

The current administration request for $1.3 billion for AIDS in fiscal year 1989 represents a substantial (37 percent) increase over the actual funding of the preceding fiscal year. Of the total Public Health Service AIDS budget, $400 million is earmarked for prevention efforts under the category of public health control measures. This total includes a small portion for the prevention of transfusion-acquired AIDS and the development and evaluation of blood tests ($26 million). The lion's share ($374 million) is reserved for information and education programs directed at the following audiences: the public at large ($50 million); school- and college-aged youths ($36 million); high-risk or infected individuals ($241 million, including $162 million for testing, counseling, and referrals); and health care workers ($44 million). In addition, communities will receive $93 million for the development of expanded programs to treat drug abusers and another $41 million to develop drug abuse prevention strategies.

The committee is encouraged by the growth in federal funding and by the heightened commitment of state and local governments, foundations (Wells, 1987; Seltzer, 1988), and the private sector (Allstate, 1988). Yet the shortfall is still considerable. The committee believes that several critical areas of AIDS prevention and education still need an infusion of personnel and funds.

Perhaps the single greatest concern is the lack of availability of treatment facilities for IV drug abusers and the lack of support for programs to eliminate or reduce drug abuse or to mitigate the danger of shared injection equipment. **The committee believes that a substantial sum of money will have to be spent for these purposes, well beyond the $1 billion originally proposed for AIDS public health and education measures.** IOM/NAS is currently conducting a congressionally mandated study to assess the adequacy of third-party coverage for substance abuse treatment. The study's assessment of the cost of such treatment will supplement the information already compiled by the Presidential Commission on the Human Immunodeficiency Virus Epidemic. That information was used by the commission as the basis of their recommendation that $1.5 billion annually will be necessary for drug abuse treatment and education. The waiting lists for entry into treatment programs are a clear indication that the caliber of the ammunition in the war on drugs needs to be increased.

A number of other specific programs are deserving of particular mention—for example, the support of counseling linked to antibody testing. There is a growing realization of the need for such counseling—that is, beyond the short-term counseling of antibody-positive individuals.

In a health care system skewed toward the reimbursement of procedures rather than counseling, this need is particularly acute, especially if HIV antibody testing is going to be increasingly relied on as a public health measure. The long-term impact of such knowledge is critical. Counselor training and the development of counseling programs must accompany the expansion of testing efforts. The recent demand for testing in sexually transmitted disease clinics and family planning and maternal and child health clinics is currently outstripping the availability of trained counselors. Because they are labor intensive, expanded counseling programs will require a major infusion of funds.

Minority groups are not being adequately reached by current educational and outreach efforts. The rates of syphilis cases are an example. Syphilis has declined significantly among gay and bisexual white men; at the same time, there have been small increases in the number of cases among black and Hispanic gay and bisexual men—and substantial increases among heterosexual black and Hispanic men and women. Educational efforts to foster changes in sexual behavior are critical for minority communities. Sexually transmitted disease programs, family planning clinics, and maternal and child health centers that cater to minority clients are all critical vehicles for this effort and are in dire need of greater federal support.

REFERENCES

Aiken, J. H. 1987. Education as prevention. Pp. 90–105 in AIDS and the Law, S. Harris, H. Dalton, and the Yale AIDS Law Project, eds. New Haven, Conn.: Yale University.

Allstate Forum on Public Issues. 1988. AIDS: Corporate America Responds. Chicago: Allstate.

AMA (American Medical Association). 1987. Report of the Council on Ethical and Judicial Affairs: Ethical Issues Involved in the Growing AIDS Crisis. Chicago: American Medical Association.

Ansberry, C. 1987. AIDS, stirring panic and prejudice, tests the nation's character. Wall Street Journal, October 9, p. A1.

Aral, S. O., W. D. Mosher, M. C. Horn, and W. Cates. 1986. Screening for sexually transmitted disease by family planning providers: Is it adequate and appropriate? Fam. Planning Perspect. 18:255–258.

Associated Press. 1988. School boards favor AIDS mandate. New York Times, February 27, p. A10.

ASTHO (Association of State and Territorial Health Officials). 1987. Guide to Public Health Practice: AIDS Confidentiality and Anti-Discrimination Principles. Washington, D.C.: Public Health Foundation.

Barry, M. J., P. D. Cleary, and H. V. Fineberg. 1987. Screening for HIV infection: Risks, benefits, and the burden of proof. Law Med. Health Care 14:259–267.

Biemiller, L. 1987. Health experts assail colleges for wasting opportunity to lead AIDS-education drive among students. Chronicle of Higher Education, September 23, p. A37.

Boorstin, R. O. 1987. Criminal and civil litigation on spread of AIDS appears. New York Times, June 19, p. A1.

Booth, W. 1987a. Another muzzle for AIDS education? Science 238:1036.

Booth, W. 1987b. The odyssey of a brochure on AIDS. Science 237:1410.

Brandt, A. M . 1987. AIDS: From social history to social policy. Law Med. Health Care 15:231–242.

Brown, L. S., D. L. Murphy, and B. J. Primm. 1987. Needle sharing and AIDS in minorities. J. Am. Med. Assoc. 258:1474–1475.

Burke, D. S. 1987. HIV screening by the U. S. Army: Two years of experience in quality control. Testimony before the House Committee on Small Businesses, Subcommittee on Regulation and Business Opportunities, Washington, D.C., October 19.

Carlson, G. A., and T. A. McClellan. 1987. The voluntary acceptance of HIV-antibody screening by intravenous drug users. Public Health Rep. 102:391–394.

Caruso, B. A., and J. R. Haig. 1987. AIDS on campus: A survey of college health service priorities and policies. J. Am. Coll. Health Assoc. 36:32–34.

CDC (Centers for Disease Control). 1987a. Antibody to human immunodeficiency virus in female prostitutes. Morbid. Mortal. Wkly. Rep. 36:157–160.

CDC. 1987b. Public Health Service guidelines for counseling and antibody testing to prevent HIV infection and AIDS. Morbid. Mortal. Wkly. Rep. 36:509–515.

CDC. 1987c. Recommendations for prevention of HIV transmission in health-care settings. Morbid. Mortal. Wkly. Rep. 36:1–18.

CDC. 1988a. Condoms for the prevention of sexually transmitted diseases. Morbid. Mortal. Wkly. Rep. 37:33–39.

CDC. 1988b. Semen banking, organ and tissue transplantation, and HIV antibody testing. Morbid. Mortal. Wkly. Rep. 37:57–63.

Cleary, P. D., M. J. Barry, K. H. Mayer, A. M. Brandt, L. Gostin, and H. V. Fineberg. 1987. Compulsory premarital screening for the human immunodeficiency virus: Technical and public health considerations. J. Am. Med. Assoc. 258:1757–1762.

Cotton, D. 1988. Pediatric AIDS: Compelling areas of need in research, treatment, and prevention. Correspondent paper. AIDS Activities Oversight Committee, Washington, D.C.

Curran, W. J., M. E. Clark, and L. Gostin. 1987. AIDS: Legal and policy implications of the application of traditional control measures. Law Med. Health Care 15:27–35.

Dawson, D. A., M. Cynamon, and J. E. Fitti. 1987. AIDS knowledge and attitudes. Provisional data from the National Health Interview Survey, August 1987. Natl. Cent. Health Stat. Advance Data 146:1–11.

Des Jarlais, D. C., and S. R. Friedman. 1987. Editorial review. HIV infection among intravenous drug users: Epidemiology and risk reduction. AIDS 1:67–76.

Des Jarlais, D. C., S. R. Friedman, and R. L. Stoneburner. 1988. HIV infection and intravenous drug use: Critical issues in transmission dynamics, infectious outcomes, and prevention. Rev. Infect. Dis. 10:151–158.

Dickens, B. M. 1988. Legal rights and duties in the AIDS epidemic. Science 239:580–586.

Echenberg, D. F. 1987. Education and contact notification for AIDS prevention. N.Y. State J. Med. 87:296–297.

Eisenberg, L. 1986. The genesis of fear: AIDS and the public's response to science. Law Med. Health Care 14:243–249.

Field, M. A., and K. M. Sullivan. 1987. AIDS and the criminal law. Law Med. Health Care 15:46–60.

Fineberg, H. V. 1988. Education to prevent AIDS: Prospects and obstacles. Science 239:592–596.

Fox, D. M. 1986. From TB to AIDS: Value conflicts in reporting disease. Hastings Cent. Rep. 16:11–15.

Fraser, D. W. 1987. AIDS education in colleges: Recent issues. Correspondent paper. AIDS Activities Oversight Committee, Washington, D.C.

Ginzburg, H. M. 1987. Intravenous drug abusers and HIV infections: A consequence of their actions. Law Med. Health Care 15:268–272.

Gostin, L. 1987a. AIDS: Law, ethics, and public policy. Correspondent paper. AIDS Activities Oversight Committee, Washington, D.C.

Gostin, L. 1987b. Viewpoint. The nucleus of a public health strategy to combat AIDS. Law Med. Health Care 15:226–230.

Gostin, L., and W. J. Curran. 1987. AIDS screening, confidentiality, and the duty to warn. Am. J. Public Health 77:361–365.

Gostin, L., and A. Ziegler. 1987. A review of AIDS-related legislative and regulatory policy in the United States. Law Med. Health Care 15:5–16.

Grimes, D. A. 1987. The CDC and abortion in HIV-positive women (letter). J. Am. Med. Assoc. 258:1176.

Hein, K. 1987. AIDS in adolescents: A rationale for concern. N.Y. State J. Med. 87:290–295.

Helquist, M. 1987. Your HIV status: Should you take the test? The Advocate, July 7, p. 45.

Henry, K., M. Maki, and K. Crossley. 1988a. Analysis of the use of HIV antibody testing in a Minnesota hospital. J. Am. Med. Assoc. 259:229–232.

Henry, K., K. Willenbring, and K. Crossley. 1988b. Human immunodeficiency virus antibody testing: A description of practices and policies at U.S. infectious disease teaching hospitals and Minnesota hospitals. J. Am. Med. Assoc. 259:1819–1822.

Hentoff, N. 1987. The assault on routine AIDS testing. Washington Post, June 28, p. C7.

Hunter, N. D. 1987. AIDS Prevention and Civil Liberties: The False Promise of Proposals for Mandatory Testing. New York: American Civil Liberties Union Foundation.

IHPP (Intergovernmental Health Policy Project). 1987. AIDS: A Public Health Challenge, M. Rowe and C. Ryan, eds., 3 vols. Washington, D.C.: George Washington University.

Jackson, J., and L. Rotkiewicz. 1987. A coupon program: AIDS education and drug treatment. P. 156 in Abstracts of the Third International Conference on AIDS, Washington, D.C., June 1–5.

Kilpatrick, J. J. 1987. Why should we pay to teach gays safe sex? Detroit Free Press, November 17, p. A11.

Koop, C. E. 1987a. AIDS instruction and local control. Wall Street Journal, May 19, p. A28.

Koop, C. E. 1987b. Physician leadership in preventing AIDS. J. Am. Med. Assoc. 258:2111.

Lambert, B. 1988. Confidentiality for AIDS patients is at issue in disputes around the U.S. New York Times, March 4, p. A13.

Lange, W. R., F. R. Snyder, D. Lozovsky, V. Kaistha, M. A. Kaczaniuk, J. H. Jaffe, and the ARC Epidemiology Collaborating Group. 1988. Geographic distribution of human immunodeficiency virus markers in parenteral drug abusers. Am. J. Public Health 78:443–446.

Lofton, D. 1988. Nations report on needle distribution: WHO report backed by some experience. American Medical News, March 4, p. 6.

Martin, J. L. 1986. AIDS risk reduction recommendations and sexual behavior patterns among gay men: A multifactorial categorical approach to assessing change. Health Educ. Q. 13:347–358.

Medical World News. 1987. AIDS home test kit poised to hit market, but FDA's balking. November 9, p. 40.

Meyer, K. B., and S. G. Pauker. 1987. Screening for HIV: Can we afford the false positive rate? N. Engl. J. Med. 317:238–241.

Miller, L. B. 1987. Plans for mail-in kit for testing for AIDS are drawing criticism. New York Times, August 9, p. A1.

New York Times. 1988. SRI-Gallup poll conducted October 1987. January 8, p. B6.

NGLTF (National Gay and Lesbian Task Force). 1988. Anti-Gay Violence: Victimization and Defamation in 1987. Washington, D.C.: National Gay and Lesbian Task Force.

National Gay Rights Advocates. 1986. AIDS and Discrimination: A Survey of the 50 States and the District of Columbia. San Francisco: National Gay Rights Advocates.

Newman, R. 1987. Methadone treatment: Defining and evaluating success. N. Engl. J. Med. 317:447–450.

Novick, L. F., D. Berns, R. Stricof, and R. Stevens. 1988. New York State Department of Health newborn seroprevalence study. Interim report draft, March 15. Albany.

Okie, S. 1987. AIDS "false positives": A volatile social issue. Low-risk groups may have a high error rate. Washington Post, July 23, p. A3.

Parkman, P. D. 1988. Serologic and virologic testing. Correspondent paper. AIDS Activities Oversight Committee, Washington, D.C.

Parmet, W. E. 1987. AIDS and the limits of discrimination law. Law Med. Health Care 15:61–72.

Rapoport, D., and J. Parry, eds. 1987. Legal, Medical, and Governmental Perspectives on AIDS as a Disability. Washington, D.C.: American Bar Association.

Raymond, C. A. 1988a. Combating a deadly combination: Intravenous drug use, acquired immune deficiency syndrome. J. Am. Med. Assoc. 259:329–330.

Raymond, C. A. 1988b. First needle-exchange program approved; other cities await results. J. Am. Med. Assoc. 259:1289–1290.

Rietmeijer, C. A. M., J. W. Krebs, P. M. Feorino, and F. N. Judson. 1988. Condoms as physical barriers against human immunodeficiency virus. J. Am. Med. Assoc. 259:1851–1853.

Rogers, M. F., and W. W. Williams. 1987. AIDS in blacks and Hispanics: Implications for prevention. Issues Sci. Technol. 3:89–94.

Seltzer, M. 1988. Meeting the Challenge: Foundation Responses to Acquired Immune Deficiency Syndrome. New York: Ford Foundation.

Sherer, R. 1988. Physician use of the HIV antibody test. The need for consent, counseling, confidentiality and caution. J. Am. Med. Assoc. 259:264–265.

Shilts, R. 1987. And The Band Played On: Politics, People and the AIDS Epidemic. New York: St. Martins.

Solomon, M. Z., and W. DeJong. 1986. Recent sexually transmitted disease prevention efforts and their implications for AIDS health education. Health Educ. Q. 13:301–316.

Thomas, P. 1988. AIDS prevention for addicts: Methadone favored. Medical World News, January 11, p. 78.

U.S. Medicine. 1987. CNS decrement in AIDS uncertain. U.S. Med. 23:3.

Walters, L. 1988. Ethical issues in the prevention and treatment of HIV infection and AIDS. Science 239:597–603.

Ward, J. W., S. D. Holmberg, J. R. Allen, D. L. Cohn, S. E. Critchley, S. H. Kleinman, B. A. Leves, O. Ravenholt, J. R. Davis, M. G. Quinn, and H. W. Jaffe. 1988. Transmission of human immunodeficiency virus by blood transfusions screened as negative for HIV antibody. N. Engl. J. Med. 318:473–477.

Watters, J. K. 1987. Preventing human immunodeficiency virus contagion among intravenous drug users: The impact of street-based education on risk-behavior. P. 60 in Abstracts of the Third International Conference on AIDS, Washington, D.C., June 1–5.

Wells, J. A. 1987. Foundation funding for AIDS programs. Health Affairs 6:113–123.

Wilkerson, I. 1988. Prenuptial AIDS screening a strain in Illinois. New York Times, January 26, p. A1.

Winkelstein, W., D. M. Lyman, N. Padian, R. Grant, M. Samuel, J. A. Wiley, R. E. Anderson, W. Lang, J. Riggs, and J. A. Levy. 1987. Sexual practices and risk of infection by the human immunodeficiency virus: The San Francisco men's health study. J. Am. Med. Assoc. 257:321–325.

5

Care of Persons Infected with HIV

AIDS and HIV infection have had a profoundly jarring effect on American health care. The relatively sudden appearance of large numbers of patients with a disease notable for its medical complexities and thorny social and ethical issues has highlighted inadequacies in current medical practice and the health care system. In the face of an epidemic, administrators, researchers, practitioners, and policymakers alike are being forced to reconsider how medical care is provided in this country—both in clinical and fiscal terms—and to seek solutions to the social and ethical quandaries that have surfaced during the process.

Confronting AIDS outlined a model of patient care comprising appropriate inpatient services for those most acutely ill and comprehensive outpatient care operating at the interface of hospitals and community-based agencies. Guiding the construction of the model was the principle that, to the greatest extent possible, care should be delivered in the community, rather than in hospitals or clinics, to make it more humane and more cost-effective. Nothing we have learned since 1986 about caring for persons with AIDS suggests the need to change this basic approach. Indeed, what has become clearer is its soundness and the areas in which we are currently succeeding or failing in its implementation.

AIDS-dedicated inpatient units and outpatient clinics appear to be the optimal configuration for providing comprehensive AIDS care. The most effective staffing for such facilities is a multidisciplinary caregiving team that includes skilled generalists trained in AIDS treatment and specialists in such relevant areas as oncology and infectious diseases, as well as

93

physicians trained to conduct clinical trials of drugs and vaccines. The team would also include nurses and allied health personnel specifically trained in AIDS-related care, as well as trained counselors to assist patients (and health care workers) with the social, economic, ethical, and psychological concomitants of AIDS.

Discharge planning involves the necessary arrangements for community or home services that should be made prior to hospital discharge and is a bridge between care in the hospital unit and care in the community. Yet effective discharge planning is often a problem for AIDS patients: gaps in health care financing, combined with a lack of federal, state, and community resources to provide the appropriate array of services, frequently result in disruption in the continuity of care and an increasing burden for public agencies.

Since the publication of *Confronting AIDS,* there has been progress in improving care for patients with HIV infection and AIDS. However, many of the recommendations from that volume remain unaddressed. This chapter highlights some of those continuing concerns: appropriate health care settings for particular patient groups, the responsibilities and needs of health care providers, and the costs of and financing mechanisms for HIV-related care.

CARE NEEDS OF SPECIAL PATIENT GROUPS

The lack of some services, especially those involving residential placement and long-term care, becomes even more critical in the case of particular AIDS patient groups. The committee focused on the needs of three such populations: IV drug abusers, pediatric patients, and patients with dementia or other neuropsychological deficits.

IV Drug Abusers

In certain urban areas, growing numbers of IV drug abusers with AIDS have significantly strained health care resources and focused attention on gaps in the spectrum of care available to AIDS patients. Because IV drug abusers are usually impoverished and have few social supports, they rely almost entirely on the public medical system for care. In many cases, this system may not be sufficient to provide the level of treatment required by patients whose care is often complicated by severe presenting diagnoses, a debilitated state, and drug abuse. Some IV drug abusers with AIDS are also difficult to manage medically because of poor compliance with treatment recommendations. Even when community agencies have the resources to provide the necessary care, they may not be eager to extend services to such patients or their families.

Once they leave the hospital, some drug-abusing patients may require long-term or nursing home care, which can be difficult to secure. In general, nursing homes are reluctant to accept any AIDS patients; they are even more reluctant to care for AIDS patients who also abuse drugs. IV drug abusers may also be homeless, which complicates hospital discharge planning and contributes to extended hospitalizations. New Jersey has implemented a posthospital residential program to provide follow-up care, drug treatment services, home care support, and housing to drug-abusing, homeless, and indigent AIDS and HIV-infected patients (IHPP, 1987). **The committee believes more long-term residential facilities or group homes are needed for AIDS patients who are IV drug abusers.** Those patients with ongoing substance abuse, mental illness, or both, in addition to AIDS, have a special need for these facilities.

Infants and Children

Pediatric AIDS is a growing problem, especially in New York City, northern New Jersey, and southern Florida. Approximately 1,000 cases have been reported nationally in children under 13; nearly 50 percent of these cases have been reported in the past 12 months. More than three-quarters of the total cases occurred among black and Hispanic children (CDC, 1988a). CDC estimates that there will be approximately 3,000 cases of AIDS in children by the end of 1991.

Pediatric AIDS further disrupts families that may be already weakened as a result of parental drug abuse or HIV infection (Boland, 1987). Approximately 75 percent of children who develop AIDS are infected perinatally; about 80 percent of perinatally infected children come from families in which one or both parents are IV drug abusers (Curran et al., 1988). The mothers of these children are usually infected or ill with AIDS themselves; progressive physical illness may limit their ability to care for their children adequately. In addition, children with AIDS are usually poor and bereft of social or community support systems; they remain hospitalized for prolonged periods. When pediatric AIDS patients are discharged, there is frequently a lack of medical follow-up (D. Axelrod, State of New York Department of Health, personal communication, 1988).

All of these circumstances complicate the task of providing adequate care to pediatric patients and their families. Ideally, what is needed is a range of coordinated medical and social services including multidisciplinary inpatient care, outpatient treatment, and community-based support options that include but are not limited to day care, home care, and respite care. Such services allow children to remain with their families— the most desirable course—and may help to preserve the family unit

(PHS, 1987). For children who are homeless or abandoned, foster care may be appropriate, although it is difficult to secure because of unfounded fears of disease transmission through casual household contact (Cotton, 1988). **The committee urges that foster care, community-based residential care, and hospice care programs be developed or expanded to meet the needs of pediatric AIDS patients and their families so that hospitals are no longer the "home of last resort."** To overcome the problem of scarce foster care services, innovative community-based homes may be essential. Currently, adult residential or long-term care facilities are not equipped to care for pediatric patients, and pediatric facilities cannot accommodate the mothers of sick children. Communities should seek to develop "family" homes that would allow children and their mothers (who may require medical and drug abuse treatment services) to remain together.

Patients with Dementia or Other Neuropsychological Deficits

Patients with dementia or other neurological disorders require a level of care that is not appropriately provided in an acute care setting. These patients frequently need custodial care more than treatment, and chronic care or extended care facilities are generally the setting of choice. Yet this intermediate level of care is extremely limited or even nonexistent in many cities. As noted earlier, nursing homes and other long-term care facilities are reluctant to admit AIDS patients, often because of unfounded fears of contagion or difficulties in handling patients with infectious diseases (PHS, 1988). Limited reimbursement for nursing home and skilled nursing facility costs also contributes to the other problems encountered in placing patients with dementia in an appropriate care setting. The break-even costs for long-term care of patients with HIV-related disorders are estimated to be close to $200 to $300 per day; yet most reimbursements for nursing home or skilled nursing facility care are only about $50 per day (Benjamin, 1988).

The committee recommends that skilled nursing facilities or nursing homes providing inpatient long-term or hospice care be made available to AIDS patients who require these services—for example, through the construction of AIDS-dedicated facilities or by offering incentive payments to facilities that are willing to accept AIDS patients.

HEALTH CARE PROVIDERS

Although health care providers continue to enter the field of AIDS patient care, they are not being recruited at a rate commensurate with the epidemic's growth. What is still a relatively small group of providers may soon exceed its physical and emotional capacities to provide care to additional patients. Physicians and other health care workers have an ethical obligation to care for HIV-infected patients; yet this responsibility must be complemented by adequate psychological support, training, and guidance about the occupational risk of HIV infection for health care providers. The following sections examine these issues and propose guidelines for action.

Ethical Aspects of Providing Care

AIDS has forced health care providers to reexamine some of the fundamental tenets of their professions, prompting them to question their obligation to care for patients who may expose them to some risk of infection. This same question has arisen in previous epidemics, but history reveals no consistent response (Zuger and Miles, 1987). The HIV epidemic, however, differs considerably from earlier epidemics. Despite its dire nature, the risk of contagion is not as great, the modes of HIV transmission are known, and the risk to health care workers can be minimized through the prudent use of infection control procedures (Gerberding and the University of California at San Francisco Task Force on AIDS, 1986).

Occupational Risks

Although the probability that a health care provider will acquire HIV infection on the job is low, it is not zero. There have been 15 well-documented and well-publicized cases in which seroconversion followed a health care worker's exposure to the blood or body fluids of an infected patient and in which nonoccupational risk factors were ruled out to a great extent (CDC, 1988b). Included among these cases are those of three health care workers for whom the exact route of transmission is not known; all three had direct, non-needle-stick exposures to blood from infected patients, and all had skin lesions or mucous membrane exposure that may have provided the route of transmission (CDC, 1987b). As discussed in Chapter 2, studies of health care workers following needle-stick exposure or mucous membrane splashes have quantified the risks involved (Henderson et al., 1986; McCray and the Cooperative Needle-stick Surveillance Group, 1986; McEvoy et al., 1987). For example, the occupational risk of acquiring HIV infection is considerably less than that of acquiring hepatitis B virus, a blood-borne virus transmitted in a similar fashion (Gerberding et al., 1987). In 1986 an estimated 18,000 health care workers contracted hepatitis B. It is estimated that there is a 6 to 30 percent risk of infection following needle-stick exposure to hepatitis B virus; in contrast, the risk of acquiring HIV infection from a needle stick is estimated to be less than 1 percent (Grady et al., 1978; Seeff et al., 1978; Vlahov and Polk, 1987; CDC, 1988b).*

Documentation of the risk of occupational HIV exposure has been accompanied by reports of high rates of seropositivity among specific types of patients in certain areas. One such report revealed that, in a series of patients admitted to the emergency room of an urban teaching hospital, 16 percent of the trauma patients aged 24 to 39 were HIV positive (Baker et al., 1987). Health care workers who provide emergency medical care—trauma physicians, nurses, and paramedics—have expressed concern because they often render assistance without knowing the patient or the patient's medical history. Moreover, the exigencies of trauma care may make it difficult to comply with the usual infection control procedures.

Surgeons are particularly concerned about their risk of infection: they are often splattered with blood during the course of an operation or may find their gloves accidentally pierced by sharp instruments or fragments of bone. Some surgeons have refused to care for patients without the reassurance of a seronegative test status; a few prominent surgeons have publicly announced that they will not treat AIDS patients (Gruson, 1987). Among health care workers in general, there appears to be increased concern about the risk of treating HIV-infected patients; there is also a growing willingness to question their ethical obligation to treat such patients. Link and coworkers (1988) surveyed 258 doctors in New York City and found that 25 percent believed it would be ethical to refuse treatment to an AIDS patient. Should such refusals to treat become more routine, the effect on patients and on the health care delivery system could be profound.

Professional Obligations

Professional associations have recently begun to address the HIV threat to their members. Historical precedent and the codes of ethical conduct promulgated by professional associations do not provide specific guidelines for the HIV epidemic. The idea that Americans have the right of equitable access to a basic level of health care has had much popular

---

*Guidelines from CDC (containing detailed and extensive infection control precautions) suggest a protocol to follow in the event of a needle stick or similar exposure to a patient who has AIDS or is seropositive or to a patient whose serologic status is unknown (CDC, 1987a). In addition, HHS and the Occupational Safety and Health Administration of the Department of Labor have issued detailed joint guidelines that specify particular infection control precautions (DOL/DHHS, 1987).

and political support (President's Commission for the Study of Ethical Problems in Medicine and Biomedical and Behavioral Research, 1983). Yet the rights of patients to receive health care do not necessarily translate into the duties of health care providers in treating individual patients, as opposed to the obligation of the medical professions and society as a whole to provide care for infectious persons. In modern ethical discourse, the freedom and discretion of physicians are protected, as well as the rights of patients. It is not clear that physicians have an obligation to expose themselves even to small risks. (Physicians who are employees of hospital emergency rooms or of municipal or other public hospitals are an exception.) Although doctor–patient models based either on rights or a contract would allow physicians considerable latitude in choosing to whom they offer their services, these models have been roundly criticized for reducing medicine to a business. Some critics have called for a medical ethic based on virtue, a model of the doctor–patient relationship that would obligate a physician to assume a degree of personal risk (Pellegrino, 1987).

The debate over professional obligations resulted in the adoption of a policy statement in 1987 by the American Medical Association that a physician "may not ethically refuse to treat a patient whose condition is within the physician's current realm of competence" merely because the patient has AIDS or is seropositive (AMA, 1987, p. 4). The American Nurses' Association has also clarified its position regarding nurses' responsibility to care for HIV-infected individuals: "Nursing is resolute in its perspective that care should be delivered without prejudice, and it makes no allowance for use of the patient's personal attributes or socioeconomic status or the nature of the health problems as grounds for discrimination" (American Nurses' Association, Committee on Ethics, 1986, p. 1). The committee endorses the policies of the American Medical Association and the American Nurses' Association.

The committee believes that the health professions have a compact with society to treat patients with all forms of illness, including HIV infection and AIDS. To deny or compromise treatment to any patient on the grounds that a medical risk is posed to the provider is to break the fundamental trust between patient and caregiver.

In determining hospital policies on infection control, professional codes of ethical duties to patients, and guidelines for dealing with professionals who refuse to treat certain patients, a major question is whether the degree of fear is consonant with the actual risks involved (Eisenberg, 1986). Yet in the case of AIDS, the experts have been unable to agree on the appropriate level of concern and the degree of danger. Moreover, actual risks are not distributed uniformly across all health professions, nor are perceptions of risk or duty consistent among health care workers.

The concepts underpinning the responsibility to care for AIDS patients may have a variety of sociological determinants, including professional values and training. Individual psychological factors and workers' high expectations of occupational safety in the hospital and laboratory environment (in contrast to much of the history of medical care) may also come into play to determine a person's tolerance of risk.

The committee recommends that assessments of the risk of occupational transmission of HIV continue and that new data be published as widely as possible. Techniques to further reduce the risk of occupational HIV transmission should also be explored. Decision making about infection control policies should include representatives of those groups of health care workers who are at greatest risk for infection.

To assume that health care professionals need only a statistical appreciation of risk to assume the mantle of professional virtue in caring for AIDS patients is to deny their humanity. Concerns about AIDS involve symbolic as well as actual dangers. Issues other than nosocomial (hospital-based) transmission may contribute to the reluctance of hospital staff to treat or interact with AIDS patients. More needs to be known about the most effective ways of educating and counseling reluctant or apprehensive personnel. In such efforts, institutional policies frame the issues and have a considerable impact on the attitudes of caregivers.

Health Care Worker Screening

There have been no reported cases of the infection of a patient by a seropositive caregiver in the course of treatment. Nonetheless, a theoretical risk of iatrogenic infection exists and must be considered in addressing the issue of health care worker screening.

Should health care workers who are seropositive continue in their duties, or should they be discharged from their positions or otherwise limited in their practice? Few health care institutions have formal policies in this regard; the relatively few employees who have come to administrators' or the public's attention have been dealt with on a case-by-case basis, sometimes to the accompaniment of considerable publicity. In one instance, a Cook County, Illinois, physician battled his hospital administration to be allowed to continue to practice medicine following his AIDS diagnosis; in another, a Mesquite, Texas, pediatrician was forced to close his private practice after a local newspaper disclosed his seropositive status, even though medical experts affirmed that he represented no danger to his patients.

Serologic testing of health care workers to prevent HIV transmission raises concerns similar to those surrounding the prospect of routine screening of other populations (see Chapter 4). Such measures only discourage some infected health care providers from ascertaining their antibody status and thus prevent them from seeking the assessment, care, and counseling they may need (Adler, 1987). The American College of Physicians and the Infectious Diseases Society of America currently do not recommend routine testing of health care professionals because, according to CDC, there have been no reports of HIV transmission from infected health care workers performing invasive procedures, and such transmission would be expected to occur only rarely, if at all. Adherence to universal blood and body fluid precautions by seropositive health care providers should serve to further minimize any risk of HIV transmission to patients (CDC, 1987b; American College of Physicians and the Infectious Diseases Society of America, 1988).

Should serologic testing programs for health care workers be developed in the future, such programs ought to apply the same principles used to develop screening for other populations (see Chapter 4). That is, informed consent must be secured, confidentiality safeguards must be established, and testing must be accompanied by appropriate counseling for seropositive persons (CDC, 1987a).

The reciprocal concerns of both patients and health care workers about serologic status and HIV transmission in the hospital add further fuel to what has become a continuing debate. **The committee recommends that the Institute of Medicine convene a conference on the ramifications of routine testing for HIV antibodies in health care workers.** The outcome of such a conference may help in the development of testing policies for hospitals and professional associations.

Health Care Provider Training

A major difficulty in organizing the resources of the health care system for AIDS treatment is the multifarious nature of the disease. In a patient with AIDS or HIV infection, any organ system can be the target of life-threatening infections or malignancies; often, several systems are involved. The psychosocial aspects of the disease are also prominent.

Health care professionals need specific training in the care and treatment of AIDS patients to augment the knowledge and clinical expertise of their own medical specialities and subspecialities. Primary care providers in particular need AIDS-specific training to provide better care and to know when to refer patients to specialists. All providers should be capable of taking thorough medical histories that include relevant information on drug use and sexual behavior. They should also be able to recognize the signs and symptoms of HIV infection so that the disease can be diagnosed as early as possible, thus enabling infected individuals or persons at risk to receive prompt care and counseling to reduce transmission.

Several training efforts are currently under way. HHS's Health Resources and Services Administration has provided approximately 10 grants to develop AIDS regional education and training centers. The centers will operate in collaboration with health professions schools, community hospitals, local health departments, and other organizations with an interest in health professions training; their purpose is to prepare community primary care providers to diagnose, counsel, and care for persons with AIDS and other HIV-related conditions. Grantees will also be required to establish a local resource center for disseminating current information about AIDS. In addition, the National Institute of Mental Health has awarded contracts to 21 institutions (universities, professional associations, and volunteer organizations) to provide comprehensive training for health care providers and trainees (medical students and residents) in the medical and psychiatric complications of AIDS, as well as in the ethical, psychosocial, and prevention-related behavioral aspects of the disease.

Such programs begin to fill the gap in AIDS-related provider training and education for health care professionals, but the need for such training far exceeds current efforts. AIDS education has been successfully expanded by many speciality and subspeciality medical societies, and AIDS programs are well attended at society meetings. However, AIDS training has not yet been incorporated into most fellowship and house staff training programs outside of areas with a high prevalence of HIV infection.

In addition to expanded postgraduate AIDS training, medical students and other health professions students would benefit from curricula that incorporate specific information about the diagnosis, prevention, and treatment of HIV infection and AIDS, as well as from clinical experience in the care of HIV-infected patients. Several areas need particular emphasis: (1) the potential risks involved in working in a health care profession in general; (2) confronting death, particularly that of young people; and (3) personal prejudices regarding sexual orientation and discomfort in discussing sexuality.

The committee believes that it is the responsibility of the health professions to stimulate adequate training in HIV infection and AIDS. One way to speed this process is to incorporate questions about AIDS and HIV infection into examinations for medical speciality and subspeciality board certification and state professional licensure; another is to offer continuing medical education courses.

The committee recommends that basic curricula in all medical and health professions education programs be modified to ensure adequate training in the diagnosis, prevention, and treatment of HIV infection and AIDS, as well as in infection control measures.

The Psychological Burden of AIDS Patient Care

The care of AIDS patients has been found to engender severe and chronic emotional and psychological stress in health care providers (Blumenfield et al., 1987; Cooke and Koenig, 1987; Link et al., 1988). Physicians in training who treated many AIDS patients have reported nightmares, preoccupation with the fears of contracting AIDS and of transmitting it to a family member, and other manifestations of marked anxiety (Cooke and Koenig, 1987). Nurses have also reported increased emotional strain in treating AIDS patients as a result of the heavier nursing requirements (approximately 40 percent greater than for other patients, according to Green and coworkers [1987]) and their intense, sustained contact with AIDS patients and family members (Okie and Carton, 1988).* Other factors that contribute to increased stress include the youth of the patients, the stigma attached to the disease, prejudice against high-risk groups, lack of medical knowledge and experience in treating HIV-related conditions, the physical and mental deterioration often associated with the disease, and the frequent fatalities.

Health care workers need opportunities to share and examine the fears they confront daily in caring for AIDS and HIV-infected patients. Family members and friends who usually provide such relief may be unable to offer the necessary emotional support because they too may be concerned about the risks associated with AIDS care and may not understand the motivations for providing it. Structured group sessions led by a trained counselor can help providers learn the necessary coping skills and provide psychological support against the "emotional brutalization" that comes with providing AIDS care. As one physician put it: "I have learned that by naming my fears I can move beyond them; there is no need to recoil . . . the search for understanding releases unexpected possibilities for action" (Shenson, 1988, p. 48).

Despite an increasing awareness of the need for psychological support, there are few, if any, formal support groups in acute care inpatient facilities. Their establishment is often stymied by the twofold difficulty of financing programs that are viewed as luxuries (rather than as essential to the control of the epidemic) and of incorporating such programs into existing health care routines. Yet it is important that providers maintain their own health in order to render effective care. **The committee recommends that research funding be made available to examine the feasibility**

---

*In addition, the AIDS epidemic has come at a time of nursing shortages. The recruitment and retention of nurses for inpatient acute care, even without AIDS, have been difficult, largely because of relatively low salaries and already stressful working conditions that are exacerbated by understaffing (Okun, 1988).

and study the effectiveness of programs to alleviate stress in health workers who care for AIDS patients. In particular, structured group therapy sessions should be evaluated as potential models. If particular approaches can be shown to be effective, funding should be provided to make them widely available. Integrating such services into acute care settings will demand ingenuity and commitment from hospital administrators and staff.

HEALTH CARE COSTS FOR HIV-RELATED CONDITIONS

Concern has been steadily growing over the economic impact of HIV infection and AIDS on the nation's health care system. In certain high-prevalence areas, most notably San Francisco and New York City, the AIDS epidemic is already becoming a considerable financial burden. Data to assess the current situation and project the future economic burden of AIDS are scarce. As in other areas of concern about AIDS, we must rely on the limited power of estimates and projections to describe current circumstances and plan for future health care needs.

Direct Costs of Care for AIDS Patients

The direct costs associated with AIDS include personal medical care expenditures (hospital services, physician inpatient and outpatient services, outpatient ancillary services, and nursing home, home care, and hospice services) and nonpersonal expenditures (biomedical research, health education campaigns, blood screening and testing, and support services) (Scitovsky and Rice, 1987b). The average lifetime medical costs per AIDS case, from diagnosis to death, are estimated to be between $55,000 and $77,000 in 1986 dollars (Seage et al., 1986; Kizer et al., 1987; Scitovsky and Rice, 1987b); in 1987 dollars, these costs are estimated to be between $65,000 and $80,000 (Scitovsky, 1988). All of these estimates suggest that total medical care costs for AIDS patients are considerably lower than the earlier estimate of $147,000 (for lifetime hospital costs) developed by Hardy and colleagues (1986).

Scitovsky and Rice (1987b) went even further in their attempts to understand more fully the economic costs of AIDS in the United States. They estimated total personal medical care costs and nonpersonal costs based on prevalence estimates provided by CDC and relevant cost data derived from various other sources. Their estimate (in current dollars) is that total direct costs for AIDS in 1986 were approximately $1.64 billion, of which $1.1 billion was for personal medical care and $542 million was for nonpersonal costs.

Yet such cost estimates are necessarily uncertain for several reasons. Studies vary considerably in their data sources and in the methods used to estimate the direct medical costs attributable to AIDS. The definition and range of costs that are included also vary. Most studies have been confined to certain hospitals or geographic areas; thus, they may not be representative of all AIDS cases nor generalizable to other parts of the country.* Furthermore, in calculating the medical costs associated with AIDS, studies have excluded individuals with other manifestations of HIV infection and those who are seropositive but clinically asymptomatic. Data on the health care costs of persons in both of these categories are scarce. In particular, there is no information on the number of HIV-infected persons who actually seek medical care or on the costs and types of health services they use. In addition, many studies exclude nonhospital costs such as drugs, ambulatory physician and ancillary services, long-term care, hospice and home health care, counseling, and other community support services. As a result of these shortcomings, the cost estimates to date most likely understate the fiscal consequences of AIDS. Nevertheless, several important trends have been observed.

Hospital treatment costs for patients with AIDS have declined in recent years, apparently because of fewer hospitalizations per patient and shorter lengths of stay (Seage, 1987). Changes in the clinical management of AIDS patients may also have contributed to reductions in inpatient costs. For example, AIDS patients are now less likely to be admitted to intensive care units than they were during the early years of the epidemic (Scitovsky and Rice, 1987b). In some areas of the country, greater reliance on outpatient and community support services allows patients to leave the hospital sooner or avoid hospitalization altogether. Of such areas, San Francisco has been most successful in mobilizing community resources. Its experience has demonstrated that medical care costs for AIDS patients can be significantly reduced when there are community support systems available to provide home health services and hospice care (Arno, 1986; Scitovsky et al., 1986). However, the existence of these community-based organizations usually depends on unpaid labor. As the epidemic grows, it is unlikely that the volunteer pool will grow commensurately (Arno, 1986). If paid personnel must be substituted for volunteers, home care may become as expensive as institutional care (Scitovsky and Rice, 1987a).

Inpatient treatment costs vary by geographic region; they are lower in the West than in the Northeast. Variations are largely caused by differences in average lengths of stay (24 days in the Northeast and 14 days in

---

*In addition, these studies were conducted before CDC's revision of the definition of AIDS to include dementia and wasting syndrome. Hence, the number of AIDS cases on which the cost estimates have been based is probably an underestimation of the actual caseload.

the West) rather than differences in the average charge or cost per hospital day ($633 in the Northeast and $646 in the West) (Andrulis et al., 1987b). Differences in the mix of patients and, consequently, in the presenting or initial diagnosis appear to explain most of the variation in length of hospitalization. For example, a national survey of 169 hospitals that reported treating patients with AIDS found that 45 percent of patients in the Northeast were IV drug abusers and 33 percent were male homosexuals. In the West, the majority of patients, 79 percent, were male homosexuals; only 4 percent were reported to be IV drug abusers (Andrulis et al., 1987a). The principal diagnosis for many IV drug abusers with AIDS is *Pneumocystis carinii* pneumonia (PCP) (Arno and Hughes, 1987). In contrast, Kaposi's sarcoma tends to be the most common presenting diagnosis among male homosexual AIDS patients. Because PCP often requires longer and more frequent hospitalizations than Kaposi's sarcoma, which can be treated to a large extent on an ambulatory basis, the costs of treating patients with PCP are higher than those for treating patients with Kaposi's sarcoma (Scitovsky et al., 1986; Seage et al., 1986; Scitovsky and Rice, 1987b). Apart from their presenting diagnoses, there is some evidence that IV drug abusers with AIDS are more expensive to treat than male homosexual or bisexual AIDS patients; however, currently available data are inconclusive on this point (Scitovsky, 1988).

Indirect Costs of HIV-Related Conditions

Estimates of the economic impact of the AIDS epidemic must also take into account its indirect costs: the loss of wages as a result of illness and disability and the loss of future earnings as a result of premature death. The loss of future productivity is expected to be substantial because the disease mainly strikes young adults in their most productive years.

Two studies have estimated the indirect costs of the epidemic. Their calculations were restricted to persons with AIDS and did not include persons with other HIV-related conditions or asymptomatic seropositive individuals. Hardy and coworkers (1986) estimated the indirect costs of the first 10,000 AIDS cases at $4.8 billion, which is three-and-a-half times their estimate of total hospital expenditures (approximately $1.4 billion) for these cases. More recently, Scitovsky and Rice (1987b) calculated the indirect costs associated with prevalent cases in 1986 at $7 billion, which is approximately seven times their estimate of personal medical care costs ($1.1 billion).

In the absence of hard data on the earnings of people with AIDS, Scitovsky and Rice applied the "human capital" method, which assumes that persons with AIDS have the same average earnings and the same employment patterns as other Americans in their age and gender cohort. This assumption is actually unlikely: there is some evidence that male homosexuals may have above-average earnings, whereas IV drug abusers may have little or no income or may derive it from illegal activity (Scitovsky and Rice, 1987b). These errors may offset one another, however; thus, foregone earnings as a result of disability and premature mortality are still expected to represent a sizable proportion of the total economic costs of the AIDS epidemic.

Cost Implications of Projected AIDS Cases

Total annual costs based on the projection that there will be 172,800 AIDS patients at any one time during the year 1991 (including a 20 percent adjustment for underreporting) are estimated to be $66.5 billion: $8.5 billion for personal medical care expenditures, $2.3 billion for nonpersonal expenditures, and $55.6 billion for indirect costs (Scitovsky and Rice, 1987b). Medical care costs for the 270,000 cumulative AIDS cases projected from 1981 to 1991 should not exceed $22 billion; indirect costs, however, may be as high as $146 billion (extrapolated from Scitovsky and Rice's estimates) (Bloom and Carliner, 1988).

In the context of national health expenditures, the direct costs associated with AIDS in 1986 represented 0.4 percent of total U.S. health expenditures. In 1991 they are expected to account for approximately 1.5 percent of total national health care expenditures (Bloom and Carliner, 1988).

Although the proportion of total health care expenditures devoted to AIDS will continue to be small in 1991, in certain metropolitan areas the economic burden that proportion represents to the health care sector will be great. By the end of 1986 San Francisco and New York City accounted for 34 percent of the nation's live AIDS cases, a caseload that is already straining local health care systems (Green et al., 1987). In such high-prevalence cities, health care facilities are faced with continued financial pressures as the epidemic spreads. For example, in 1986, AIDS patients occupied 3 percent of all medical/surgical beds in hospitals in New York City, 2.7 percent in San Francisco, and 0.4 percent nationally; by 1991 these figures are expected to rise to 8.1 percent, 12.4 percent, and 1.9 percent, respectively (Green et al., 1987). With respect to hospital treatment costs in 1986, AIDS cases accounted for 3.1 percent of total inpatient costs in New York City, 3.5 percent in San Francisco, and 0.6 percent nationally; by 1991 these costs are projected to rise to 8.4 percent, 16.2 percent, and 3 percent, respectively. Future demands on the American health care system appear most striking when the magnitude of the increase in health care resources devoted to AIDS treatment between

1986 and 1991 is considered. In San Francisco alone, projections for 1991 are for nearly a fivefold increase over 1986 in bed utilization and hospital treatment costs. In New York City, anticipated consumption is more than two-and-a-half times that of 1986 (Green et al., 1987).

AIDS will continue to strain health care resources in cities in which cases are now concentrated, but by 1991, 80 percent of those afflicted with AIDS are expected to reside outside New York City and San Francisco. This growth in numbers of cases may pose considerable problems for health care systems in which the small number of AIDS cases now contributes to inadequate preparations for the future (Green et al., 1987).

It is becoming increasingly likely that projections of the economic costs of AIDS for the nation's health care sector underestimate the financial consequences of the epidemic. Such projections suffer from limitations similar to those inherent in the current estimates discussed earlier in this section. In addition, because cost studies are conducted retrospectively, projections are based on the assumption that current patterns of medical expenditures will continue. This is unlikely, but at present there is no way to predict the direction of any change. Several factors contribute to this uncertainty.

Projections of the number of future AIDS cases are of questionable accuracy, particularly in terms of the percentage of seropositive individuals who will eventually develop AIDS. This percentage will probably be adjusted upward (see Chapter 2); in that event, cost estimates based on a lower prediction will understate the resources needed to treat AIDS.

New treatment regimens will undoubtedly influence health care costs or, more specifically, treatment costs. Whether such protocols will ultimately lower or raise medical costs is unclear. Zidovudine (i.e., AZT) is a case in point. There is some evidence that zidovudine may lessen the severity of PCP and thus obviate the need for frequent or prolonged hospitalizations. On the other hand, it may increase treatment costs because (1) zidovudine is expensive (approximately $8,000 to $10,000 per patient per year); (2) close medical monitoring is often required; (3) regular blood transfusions may be necessary for about 30 percent of patients on zidovudine who develop severe anemia; and (4) although zidovudine appears to increase the life expectancy of AIDS patients, they may still die from other AIDS-related (and possibly more expensive) disorders, for example, dementia (Scitovsky, 1988).

Similarly, little is known about the effects on health care costs of new or alternative models of health care delivery. If the trend of avoiding or shortening hospitalization continues, out-of-hospital services will account for a larger part of direct medical costs. More accurate cost estimates of these services are needed to calculate the total medical costs of different approaches to managing AIDS and to analyze fully the cost implications of relying less on hospitalization and more on community support services (Sisk, 1987).

Because the complications resulting from AIDS seem to differ among high-risk groups, changes in incidence patterns could influence the manifestations and hence the cost of the disease (Sisk, 1987). Changes in the demographic profile of AIDS patients will have a profound effect on health resources and medical costs, particularly in certain metropolitan areas. Across the country, there is already an uneven distribution of AIDS patients by risk group. For example, more than 75 percent of U.S. AIDS cases in which IV drug abuse has been the primary risk factor have been in New York City (Des Jarlais et al., 1988); about 40 percent of the nation's pediatric AIDS cases have also occurred there (Arno and Hughes, 1987).

Health care systems that must serve large numbers of patients from these two groups may find their resources overwhelmed. IV drug abusers tend to incur greater medical costs because they are often hospitalized for extended periods as a result of their presenting diagnoses, generally debilitated state, and lack of adequate support systems or a home environment that would permit earlier hospital discharge. Pediatric AIDS patients may also be more expensive to treat because they often remain hospitalized for protracted periods; in fact, a study at Harlem Hospital (Heagarty, 1987) found that one-third of the hospital days and one-fifth of total hospitalization costs for children with AIDS were attributable to unnecessary hospital stays. Because these population groups are often indigent, they are either covered by Medicaid or uninsured and therefore usually receive care in public hospitals. Andrulis and colleagues (1987a) observed that most pediatric AIDS patients were treated in public hospitals. They also noted that nearly twice as many IV drug abusers were treated in public hospitals as were treated in private facilities. In New York City, municipal hospitals are crowded with IV drug abusers, a group that constitutes almost 60 percent of all AIDS patients hospitalized there (Sencer and Botnick, 1985).

Research on Health Care Costs

Confronting AIDS recommended that more information be gathered on all aspects of the costs of care for persons with HIV-related conditions and especially for those with AIDS. Some headway has, indeed, been made in this area. The National Center for Health Services Research and Health Care Technology Assessment has expanded its research agenda for conditions associated with HIV infection. The center has contracted with health economists and statisticians at the Palo Alto Medical Foundation Research Institute to develop research protocols for use by the center in funding studies that are expected to begin this year. In particular, protocols are being developed to determine:

- total direct costs of medical, social, and support services for AIDS patients and patients with other HIV-related conditions;
- the costs of treating AIDS compared with the costs of treating other types of conditions in general;
- the costs of treating AIDS at various stages of the disease;
- the cost-effectiveness of various treatment modalities;
- the cost-effectiveness of various methods of organizing, delivering, and managing services in institutional and noninstitutional settings;
- the costs associated with HIV testing using current methods and current utilization levels, as well as under circumstances of expanded use;
- the costs associated with the introduction of different HIV testing methods; and
- the costs of providing additional training for health professionals in hospital and other settings (NCHSR/HCTA, 1988).

Other research initiatives currently under way should provide useful information regarding the costs and relative effectiveness of providing managed, comprehensive ambulatory and community-based services to people with AIDS and HIV-related illnesses. These studies include an evaluation of the Robert Wood Johnson Foundation's AIDS Health Services Program being conducted by Brown University's Center for Health Care Research with support provided by the foundation. The evaluation is expected to focus on the feasibility of community networks of out-of-hospital services; the appropriateness of such a model as a substitute for inpatient care, particularly in cities with high concentrations of pediatric and IV drug-abusing AIDS patients; and the costs and patterns of health services used by AIDS patients in the varying programs. In addition, HHS's Health Resources and Services Administration has undertaken an evaluation of its AIDS service demonstration projects; this effort will be coordinated with the Brown University study. Such programs are encouraging evidence of serious attention to the cost data deficiencies that now constrain health planning efforts for HIV-infected persons.

FINANCING HEALTH CARE FOR HIV-RELATED CONDITIONS

The problems that are encountered in financing care for persons with AIDS and other HIV-related illnesses are symptomatic of the inequities in the U.S. health care system. The demands AIDS often imposes on the system highlight its limitations: inadequate care for the uninsured, limited access of the poor to care, inadequate funding for preventive health measures, insufficient home health care and other alternatives to institutionalization, and inadequate care for the chronically ill (American College of Physicians, 1988b). **The committee believes that all individuals have a right to equitable access to adequate medical care and that society has an ethical obligation to ensure such access.** Yet the development and implementation of strategies to improve access to care and health coverage are complicated by the pluralism of the health care financing system: private group health insurance for the employed and public sector coverage for the elderly and certain categories of the poor and disabled, supplemented by a patchwork of other public and private payment mechanisms.

This section discusses the major sources of financing for the care of AIDS patients: Medicaid, Medicare, and private insurance. A series of financing strategies is also presented, some or all of which might constitute solutions to the dilemma of financing care, not only for AIDS patients but for all those who suffer from costly life-threatening or chronic illnesses.

Sources of Financing

Medicaid

As noted in *Confronting AIDS,* Medicaid provides health care coverage for a sizable proportion of AIDS patients. HHS's Health Care Financing Administration has estimated that 40 percent of all patients with AIDS are served under Medicaid; in locations such as New York and New Jersey, the proportion may be as high as 65 percent to 70 percent. Medicaid now bears nearly 25 percent of the total medical care costs of AIDS, and this proportion could increase, depending on future epidemiological trends, in particular, the spread of HIV infection among IV drug abusers. Federal and state Medicaid expenditures for patients with AIDS are expected to reach $600 million in 1988; by 1991 expenditures are expected to rise to approximately $1.8 billion (Roper, 1987).

For hospitals providing care to persons with AIDS, Medicaid is the preponderant source of payment. In a national survey of 169 public and private teaching hospitals, 54 percent of AIDS patients were covered by Medicaid, whereas only 17 percent were covered by private insurance. For public hospitals, these differences were even more striking: 62 percent of AIDS patients were covered by Medicaid, as compared with 7 percent who were privately insured (Andrulis et al., 1987b).

Many states, particularly in the South, have Medicaid eligibility criteria that deny coverage to persons who might be covered in other states. Public hospitals in these "restrictive" states face a particular problem in providing AIDS-related care: with less Medicaid coverage, many of their patients with AIDS are classified as "self-paying," which results in a disproportionate amount of unreimbursed care (Andrulis et al., 1987c). Thus, in states with stringent Medicaid eligibility requirements, cities, counties, and private payers are forced to underwrite the cost of AIDS treatment. This policy all too often results in inadequate financing of the total costs of AIDS patient care, thereby leaving public hospitals with insufficient support to cover treatment costs (Andrulis et al., 1987a). Confronted with growing caseloads and increasing levels of uncompensated care, public hospitals may find it impossible to remain solvent without some economic relief or shift in the burden of care.

Medicare

Medicare covers only a small proportion (1 percent) of AIDS patients* and bears an even smaller fraction of the total medical costs of AIDS (Roper, 1987). Given the demographics of HIV infection (most AIDS patients are under the age of 65), Medicare's dramatically lower share of treatment costs is not an unexpected finding. Furthermore, because the disease has a rapidly fatal course, it is unlikely that many AIDS patients will survive the 24-month waiting period to qualify for Medicare benefits. However, with the development of new treatment protocols that prolong the survival of AIDS patients, Medicare could become a significant payment source.

Private Health Insurance

There is some evidence that the proportion of AIDS patients who are covered by private health insurance has declined over time and that payment responsibilities are shifting increasingly to the public sector, primarily to Medicaid (Arno, 1987). Kizer and coworkers (1987) noted that the proportion of AIDS patients covered by Medi-Cal (California Medicaid) rose from 12 percent to 20 percent between 1985 and 1986. This increase is a disturbing trend that may persist as patient demographics continue to change and as private health insurers seek to limit their exposure to financial risk. Almost all insurance companies now refuse to insure individual health insurance applicants with AIDS; 91 percent

---

*As discussed in *Confronting AIDS*, Medicare covers AIDS patients through its disability program, which is tied to the Social Security Disability program. To be eligible, disabled workers must first meet the Social Security requirements for "insured status " and must be considered disabled according to the program's definition. They can then receive Social Security disability benefits for 24 months, after which they may begin to receive benefits under Medicare.

refuse to insure those with antibodies to HIV (Health Insurance Association of America and the American Council of Life Insurance, 1986). Health insurance companies "screen" applicants for individual and small group health insurance policies by including AIDS-related questions on the health history portion of their applications; they do not generally question individuals covered under employment-related group policies.

A recent report by Congress's Office of Technology Assessment (1988), which was based on a survey of commercial insurers, Blue Cross/Blue Shield plans, and health maintenance organizations, found that these insurers plan to reduce their exposure to the financial impact of AIDS. Possible strategies include reducing the amount of individual and small group insurance they sell by using tighter underwriting guidelines, expanding the use of HIV and other testing, adding AIDS questions to enrollment applications, and refusing to insure applicants with a history of sexually transmitted diseases. To maintain a more equitable distribution of AIDS-related medical costs, several states have enacted legislation that prohibits the use of HIV antibody testing to determine health insurability. In these states, private insurance companies can still protect themselves by writing policies that limit AIDS benefits or by refusing to sell health insurance to persons who reside in cities with high concentrations of AIDS cases (Bloom and Carliner, 1988).

Alternative Financing Mechanisms to Improve Health Care Coverage

In February 1988 the Institute of Medicine convened a meeting to examine the special problems associated with financing AIDS care and the inadequacies of the current health care financing system in the face of that task. A number of alternatives emerged from those discussions and are presented in the following sections. These options are not mutually exclusive; in fact, more than one financing scheme may be required to improve health care coverage for persons with AIDS and other HIV-infected individuals.

Ensure Access to and Maintenance of Private Health Insurance Coverage

Earlier sections of this chapter noted how the financial burden of AIDS care is being shifted to the public sector and away from private health insurers. To avoid the collapse of the public system from a weight it was never designed to bear, AIDS and HIV-infected patients must be able to secure private health insurance if they are not already covered or maintain, at least for a time, the coverage they already have. The

American College of Physicians (1988) has suggested a number of possible mechanisms to accomplish this goal:

• Provide incentives through the tax system or through other favorable treatment of insurers to increase the availability of open enrollment policies.

• Subsidize private insurance premiums for lower income persons.

• Protect the financial integrity of insurers from adverse selection in which some insurance companies, because of their more favorable policies, assume a disproportionate share of AIDS-related health insurance costs. Protection could be offered either through direct government assistance or through a system of spreading the costs of insuring HIV-infected persons among insurers.

• Increase the extension-of-coverage period mandated by the 1985 Consolidated Omnibus Budget Reconciliation Act (COBRA) (P.L. 99–272), in which an employee leaving work can continue to pay the group rate premium for up to 18 months of additional coverage. If the 24-month waiting period for Medicare eligibility is not reduced, the COBRA extension should be increased to at least 24 months to prevent a gap in coverage.

• Provide government subsidies, based on income and resources, for any person exercising the COBRA extension option who cannot afford the premium.

Modify Existing Medicaid Programs

There is considerable variation across states with respect to Medicaid eligibility criteria and the scope of services offered to Medicaid recipients. The law requires coverage of certain mandatory services—for example, inpatient and ambulatory hospital care (although the state may limit the number of hospital days covered or the level of services reimbursed), physician services, and skilled nursing facility and home health care for individuals aged 21 and older. Additional services may be offered at the state's discretion, including prescription drugs, intermediate care, hospice care, case management, and personal care services. Currently, 44 states cover zidovudine (AZT) through their Medicaid programs; 2 other states cover zidovudine only during inpatient hospital care (Buchanan, 1988).* Such variation among states raises the issue of fairness to

---

*The Public Health Service administers a $30 million federal emergency fund (the AIDS Drug Reimbursement Program) to cover the costs of zidovudine (AZT) for low-income AIDS patients. Funds are distributed to the states in proportion to their share of all AIDS cases. To be eligible for drug reimbursement, individuals must meet state low-income standards, be ineligible for Medicaid or without private health insurance coverage, or live in a state whose Medicaid program does not cover zidovudine.

beneficiaries of the different plans. Poor states are unlikely to offer the range of services and coverage that wealthier states can provide.

Modifications to make Medicaid more uniform and efficient might include such measures as altering eligibility requirements so that more of the medically indigent are covered. Another possible change is to expand the range of services included in the benefits package, particularly those that are more cost-effective—for example, intermediate care, hospice care, personal care services, and case management services. A third modification involves the determination of reimbursement rates for skilled nursing facility or nursing home care. Reimbursement rates could be adjusted to reflect the costs of the spectrum of patient care.

Several states have attempted to augment the Medicaid services offered to AIDS patients and patients with other HIV-related conditions by using Medicaid waivers for home and community-based care. These waivers allow states to target AIDS patients (especially those who would otherwise require institutional care) for a broad range of community-based services that may be more appropriate for them and less costly to provide. States' applications for waivers, which are subject to federal approval through the Health Care Financing Administration, must document the cost-effectiveness of the proposed configuration of services. To date, seven states have developed community-based service programs through this mechanism.

Establish State Risk Pools

Risk pools have been offered in 15 states, and proposed in 12 others, as a way to provide health insurance for those who are uninsurable because of a preexisting medical condition (e.g., patients with AIDS or those who are seropositive) and for the low-income uninsured. Private health insurers in each state contribute to a risk pool to pay for insurance coverage for those participating in the pool. However, the responsibility for financing the pools has not been equally distributed: much of the burden has fallen on commercial insurers, Blue Cross/Blue Shield plans, and health maintenance organizations. This inequity is largely because of the unanticipated side effects of the Employee Retirement Income Security Act (ERISA) of 1974. The act was originally intended by Congress to ensure that workers received private pension and welfare benefits when they retired and to encourage employers to set up pension plans if they had not already done so. Yet because of the wording in the legislation (in particular, Section 514), state laws relating to employee welfare benefit plans (which generally include medical and hospital benefits) are pre-empted by federal law; state laws governing insured health plans are not. Self-insured employers (those who fund employee health benefits through their own assets) are also exempt from state regulation. In other words, self-insured firms are not required to contribute to state risk pools, comply with state-mandated benefit laws, or pay state-imposed premium taxes (IHPP, 1986). Private insurance companies do not enjoy the same immunity from state regulation.

Aside from the shrinking insurance base for risk pools, several other problems have been encountered with this type of plan. Enrollment has generally been low; available data for six of the fully operational plans in mid-1986 showed that only about 21,000 persons (a small fraction of the 37 million Americans who are uninsured) were participating in risk pools. There are no data on how many persons with AIDS or HIV infection are enrolled in the pools (IHPP, 1987). Most of the pools have high annual premiums and large deductibles, which limit access for the low-income uninsured. To address some of these problems, the Minnesota and Oregon risk pools have granted "presumptive eligibility" status to AIDS patients; Wisconsin has also established a premium subsidy program to assist enrollees (a benefit not limited to AIDS patients) (IHPP, 1987).

Modify Medicare Eligibility Criteria

Pending legislation would eliminate the 24-month disability waiting period for persons with AIDS, a measure the Health Care Financing Administration estimates could cost Medicare an additional $2.1 billion to $8.3 billion over the next 5 years. If this waiting period were eliminated for all disabled individuals, the estimated additional cost would be $35 billion to $42 billion over the next 5 years (Roper, 1987). Although this option has merit in that it would be "disease neutral" (patients with a particular disease would not be treated preferentially), the potential costs to Medicare make it an unlikely alternative.

Develop an AIDS Federal Grant Program

An AIDS federal grant program directing funds to the states allows the federal government to participate in the financing of care for HIV-infected and AIDS patients while also influencing what services are offered and how they are delivered. Such a program would permit the federal government to establish a fixed payment level rather than obligating it to an open-ended financing system. For example, the federal government might agree to provide states with an amount per patient equal to 25 percent of the total annual amount needed for patients who follow an approved treatment protocol. In those states that continued to provide more expensive treatment, the fixed federal contribution rate would effectively be less than 25 percent; for those states that developed a more efficient delivery system, the federal contribution rate would be greater than 25 percent, an incentive for providing care in the most appropriate and cost-effective manner.

An AIDS grant program also enables federal health officials to offer technical assistance to states and local communities in designing appropriate health service delivery patterns. The major advantage of such assistance is that models of care could be transferred across states for possible replication and evaluation, thereby reducing duplication of effort.

Development of a Financing Strategy

The committee recognizes the concerns that have been expressed about singling out AIDS patients and others with HIV-related illnesses for special consideration in the financing of health care. However, because the AIDS crisis is disrupting the health care delivery system (especially in high-prevalence areas), an interim solution to the problem of financing AIDS care is needed. **The committee endorses an AIDS federal grant program as an interim measure to ensure that AIDS patients and those with HIV-related conditions have access to appropriate and cost-effective care.** This approach would offer some financial relief to those states and medical institutions that currently bear a disproportionate burden of AIDS care. It would also remove financial impediments to adequate medical care for HIV-infected persons and persons with AIDS who are presently uninsured or unable to obtain insurance through conventional means.

Another urgent need is to remove the financial barriers that limit access to experimental therapies. The Public Health Service Intragovernmental Task Force on AIDS Health Care Delivery has recommended that all state Medicaid programs and private insurers consider reimbursement for costly AIDS medical therapies once FDA has approved them for treatment under a special investigational new drug (IND) status called treatment IND (see Chapter 6). **The committee would extend the task force recommendation to require such reimbursement.** However, in the future, it may be necessary to develop a mechanism to establish priorities for coverage among potential therapies. Coverage should continue after the therapies have been approved for marketing; however, to limit the burden on public funds, consideration should also be given to copayments, sliding scales, and other cost-sharing mechanisms (PHS, 1988).

An AIDS federal grant program and reimbursement for costly experimental therapies are two relatively limited financing approaches that can nevertheless bring some relief to an overburdened health care system. Yet temporary or piecemeal solutions to the problems of health care financing must not sidetrack or obscure the need for a more comprehensive and equitable scheme. **The committee urges the federal government to take the lead in developing a comprehensive and coherent national plan for delivering and financing care for HIV-infected and AIDS patients.** The following principles should guide the development of such a financing strategy:

• Health care coverage should begin when a person is diagnosed or identified as seropositive, thereby ensuring early access to adequate medical care.
• Consideration should be given to relieving the financial stress of certain localities particularly hard-hit by AIDS.
• Responsibility for financing care should be shared between the public and private sectors, which implies that some balance must be achieved between these sources of funding such that financial risk is equitably distributed.
• The payment mechanism should support and encourage the most cost-effective methods of delivering health care.

The committee concurs with the American College of Physicians (1988) that the current crisis may serve as the crucible in which we can search for and test means of extending health care coverage to all of our citizens.

REFERENCES

Adler, M. 1987. Patient safety and doctors with HIV infection. Brit. Med. J. 295:1297–1298.
AMA (American Medical Association). 1987. Report of the Council on Ethical and Judicial Affairs: Ethical Issues Involved in the Growing AIDS Crisis. Chicago: American Medical Association.
American College of Physicians. 1988. Financing the care of patients with the acquired immunodeficiency syndrome (AIDS). Ann. Intern. Med. 108:470–473.
American College of Physicians and the Infectious Diseases Society of America. 1988. The acquired immunodeficiency syndrome (AIDS) and infection with the human immunodeficiency virus (HIV). Ann. Intern. Med. 108:460–469.
American Nurses' Association, Committee on Ethics. 1986. Statement regarding risk versus responsibility in providing nursing care. American Nurses' Association, Kansas City.
Andrulis, D. P., V. S. Beers, J. D. Bentley, and L. S. Gage. 1987a. The 1985 NAPH/COTH AIDS Survey: Final Report. Washington, D.C.: National Association of Public Hospitals.
Andrulis, D. P., V. S. Beers, J. D. Bentley, and L. S. Gage. 1987b. The provision and financing of medical care for AIDS patients in U.S. public and private teaching hospitals. J. Am. Med. Assoc. 258:1343–1346.
Andrulis, D. P., V. S. Beers, J. D. Bentley, and L. S. Gage. 1987c. State Medicaid policies and hospital care for AIDS patients. Health Affairs 6:110–118.
Arno, P. S. 1986. The nonprofit sector's response to the AIDS epidemic: Community-based services in San Francisco. Am. J. Public Health 76:1325–1330.
Arno, P. S. 1987. The economic impact of AIDS. J. Am. Med. Assoc. 258:1376–1377.

Arno, P. S., and R. G. Hughes. 1987. Local policy responses to the AIDS epidemic: New York and San Francisco. N.Y. State J. Med. 87:264–272.

Baker, J. L., G. D. Kelen, K. T. Sivertson, and T. C. Quinn. 1987. Unsuspected human immunodeficiency virus in critically ill emergency patients. J. Am. Med. Assoc. 257:2609–2611.

Benjamin, A. E. 1988. AIDS and nursing homes. Institute for Health Policy Studies, University of California, San Francisco.

Bloom, D. E., and G. Carliner. 1988. The economic impact of AIDS in the United States. Science 239:604–610.

Blumenfield, M., P. J. Smith, J. Milazzo, S. Seropian, and G. P. Wormser. 1987. Survey of attitudes of nurses working with AIDS patients. Gen. Hosp. Psychiatry 9:58–63.

Boland, M. G. 1987. Management of the child with HIV infection: Implications for service delivery. Pp. 41–43 in Report of the Surgeon General's Workshop on Children with HIV Infection and Their Families. Washington, D.C.: U.S. Public Health Service.

Buchanan, R. J. 1988. State Medicaid coverage of AZT and AIDS-related policies. Am. J. Public Health 78:432–436.

CDC (Centers for Disease Control). 1987a. Recommendations for the prevention of HIV transmission in health-care settings. Morbid. Mortal. Wkly. Rep. 36:3S-18S.

CDC. 1987b. Update: Human immunodeficiency virus infections in health care workers exposed to blood of infected patients. Morbid. Mortal. Wkly. Rep. 36:285–289.

CDC. 1988a. Acquired Immunodeficiency Syndrome Weekly Surveillance Report—United States, May 16, 1988. Atlanta, Ga.: CDC.

CDC. 1988b. Update: Acquired immunodeficiency syndrome and human immunodeficiency virus infection among health-care workers. Morbid. Mortal. Wkly. Rep. 37:229–239.

Cooke, M., and B. Koenig. 1987. Housestaff attitudes towards the acquired immunodeficiency syndrome. P. 154 in Abstracts of the Third International Conference on AIDS, Washington, D.C., June 1–5.

Cotton, D. 1988. Pediatric AIDS: Compelling areas of need in research, treatment, and prevention. Correspondent paper. AIDS Activities Oversight Committee, Washington, D.C.

Curran, J. W., H. W. Jaffe, A. M. Hardy, W. M. Morgan, R. M. Selik, and T. J. Dondero. 1988. Epidemiology of HIV infection and AIDS in the United States. Science 239:610–616.

Des Jarlais, D. C., S. R. Friedman, and R. L. Stoneburner. 1988. HIV infection and intravenous drug use: Critical issues in transmission dynamics, infection outcomes, and prevention. Rev. Infect. Dis. 10:151–158.

DOL/DHHS (Department of Labor/Department of Health and Human Services). 1987. Joint advisory notice: Protection against occupational exposure to hepatitis B virus (HBV) and human immunodeficiency virus (HIV). Fed. Regist. 52(210):41818–41824.

Eisenberg, L. 1986. The genesis of fear: AIDS and the public's response to science. Law Med. Health Care 14:243–249.

Gerberding, J. L., and the University of California at San Francisco Task Force on AIDS. 1986. Recommended infection-control policies for patients with human immunodeficiency virus infection—an update. N. Engl. J. Med. 315:1562–1564.

Gerberding, J. L., C. E. Bryant-LeBlanc, K. Nelson, A. R. Moss, D. Osmond, H. F. Chambers, J. R. Carlson, W. L. Drew, J. A. Levy, and M. A. Sande. 1987. Risk of transmitting the human immunodeficiency virus, cytomegalovirus, and hepatitis B virus to health care workers exposed to patients with AIDS and AIDS-related conditions. J. Infect. Dis. 156:1–8.

Grady, G. F., A. A. Lee, A. M. Prince, G. L. Gitnick, K. A. Fawaz, G. N. Vyas, M. D. Levitt, J. R. Senior, J. T. Galambos, T. E. Bynum, J. W. Singleton, B. F. Clowdus, K.

Akdamar, R. D. Aach, E. I. Winkelman, G. M. Schiff, and T. Hersh. 1978. Hepatitis B immune globulin for accidental exposures among medical personnel: Final report of a multicenter controlled trial. J. Infect. Dis. 138:625–638.

Green, J., M. Singer, N. Wintfeld, K. Schulman, and L. Passman. 1987. Projecting the impact of AIDS on hospitals. Health Affairs 6:19–31.

Gruson, L. 1987. AIDS fear spawns ethics debate as some doctors withhold care. New York Times, July 11, p. A1.

Hardy, A. M., K. Rauch, D. Echenberg, W. M. Morgan, and J. W. Curran. 1986. The economic impact of the first 10,000 cases of acquired immunodeficiency syndrome in the United States. J. Am. Med. Assoc. 255:209–211.

Heagarty, M. C. 1987. Report from the front of medical care for children with AIDS. Correspondent paper. AIDS Activities Oversight Committee, Washington, D.C.

Health Insurance Association of America and the American Council of Life Insurance. 1986. Results of the Health Insurance Association of America and American Council of Life Insurance AIDS survey of member companies. Cited in D. E. Bloom and G. Carliner. 1988. The economic impact of AIDS in the United States. Science 239:604–610.

Henderson, D. K., A. J. Saah, B. T. Zak, R. A. Kaslow, H. C. Lane, T. Folks, W. C. Blackwelder, J. Schmitt, D. J. LaCamera, H. Masur, and A. S. Fauci. 1986. Risk of nosocomial infection with human T-cell lymphotropic virus type III/lymphadenopathy-associated virus in a large cohort of intensively exposed health care workers. Ann. Intern. Med. 104:644–647.

IHPP (Intergovernmental Health Policy Project). 1986. Focus On: ERISA and the States. Washington, D.C.: George Washington University.

IHPP. 1987. AIDS: A Public Health Challenge, M. Rowe and C. Ryan, eds., 3 vols. Washington, D.C.: George Washington University.

Kizer, K., J. Rodriguez, and G. F. McHolland. 1987. An Updated Quantitative Analysis of AIDS in California. Sacramento: California Department of Health Services.

Link, R. N., A. R. Feingold, M. H. Charap, K. Freeman, and S. P. Shelov. 1988. Concerns of medical and pediatric house officers about acquiring AIDS from their patients. Am. J. Public Health 78:455–459.

McCray, E., and the Cooperative Needlestick Surveillance Group. 1986. Occupational risk of the acquired immunodeficiency syndrome among health care workers. N. Engl. J. Med. 314:1127–1132.

McEvoy, M., K. Porter, P. Mortimer, N. Simmons, and D. Shanson. 1987. Prospective study of clinical, laboratory, and ancillary staff with accidental exposures to blood or other body fluids from patients infected with HIV. Br. Med. J. 294:1595–1597.

NCHSR/HCTA (National Center for Health Services Research and Health Care Technology Assessment). 1988. AIDS-related health services research agenda. Draft. Washington, D.C.

Office of Technology Assessment. 1988. AIDS and Health Insurance. Washington, D.C.: Office of Technology Assessment.

Okie, S., and B. Carton. 1988. The stress of treating AIDS. Washington Post, January 19, p. A1.

Okun, S. 1988. Lack of nurses impedes New York AIDS care. New York Times, February 23, p. A1.

Pellegrino, E. D. 1987. Altruism, self-interest and medical ethics. J. Am. Med. Assoc. 258:1939–1940.

PHS (Public Health Service). 1987. Report of the Surgeon General's Workshop on Children with HIV Infection and Their Families. Washington, D.C.: U.S. Public Health Service.

PHS. 1988. Report of the Intragovernmental Task Force on AIDS Health Care Delivery. Washington, D.C.: U.S. Public Health Service.

President's Commission for the Study of Ethical Problems in Medicine and Biomedical and Behavioral Research. 1983. Securing Access to Health Care. 3 vols. Washington, D.C.: Government Printing Office.

Roper, W. L. 1987. From the Health Care Financing Administration. J. Am. Med. Assoc. 258:3489.

Scitovsky, A. A. 1988. Review of current state of knowledge regarding the personal medical care costs of persons with AIDS. Correspondent paper. AIDS Activities Oversight Committee, Washington, D.C.

Scitovsky, A. A., and D. P. Rice. 1987a. The cost of AIDS. Issues Sci. Technol. 4:61–66.

Scitovsky, A. A., and D. P. Rice. 1987b. Estimates of the direct and indirect costs of acquired immunodeficiency syndrome in the United States, 1985, 1986, and 1991. Public Health Rep. 102:5–17.

Scitovsky, A. A., M. Cline, and P. R. Lee. 1986. Medical care costs of patients with AIDS in San Francisco. J. Am. Med. Assoc. 256:3103–3106.

Seage, G. R. 1987. Cost of medical care for AIDS in Massachusetts: Trends over a two-year period. P. 145 in Abstracts of the Third International Conference on AIDS, Washington, D.C., June 1–5.

Seage, G. R., S. Landers, A. Barry, J. Groopman, G. A. Lamb, and A. M. Epstein. 1986. Medical care costs of AIDS in Massachusetts. J. Am. Med. Assoc. 256:3107–3109.

Seeff, L. B., E. C. Wright, H. J. Zimmerman, H. J. Alter, A. A. Dietz, B. F. Felsher, J. D. Finkelstein, P. Garcia-Pont, J. L. Gerin, H. B. Greenlee, J. Hamilton, P. V. Holland, P. M. Kaplan, T. Kiernan, R. S. Koff, C. M. Leevy, V. J. McAuliffe, N. Nath, R. H. Purcell, E. R. Schiff, C. C. Schwartz, C. H. Tamburro, Z. Vlahcevic, R. Zemel, and D. S. Zimmon. 1978. Type B hepatitis after needle-stick exposure: Prevention with hepatitis B immune globulin. Ann. Intern. Med. 88:285–293.

Sencer, D. J., and V. E. Botnick. 1985. Report to the Mayor: New York City's response to the AIDS crisis. Cited in P. S. Arno and R. G. Hughes. 1987. Local policy responses to the AIDS epidemic: New York and San Francisco. N.Y. State J. Med. 87:264–272.

Shenson, D. 1988. When fear conquers: A doctor learns about AIDS from leprosy. New York Times Magazine, February 28, p. 35.

Sisk, J. E. 1987. The costs of AIDS: A review of the estimates. Health Affairs 6:5–21.

Vlahov, D., and B. F. Polk. 1987. Transmission of human immunodeficiency virus within the health care setting. Occup. Med. 2:429–450.

Zuger, A., and S. H. Miles. 1987. Physicians, AIDS, and occupational risk: Historic traditions and ethical obligations. J. Am. Med. Assoc. 258:1924–1928.

6

The Biology of HIV and Biomedical Research Needs

Since the publication of *Confronting AIDS* in October 1986, there has been appreciable progress in elucidating certain structural and functional attributes of HIV. Early research efforts were productive in defining the HIV genetic structure and important aspects of viral replication in vitro. Less progress has been made in understanding the behavior of HIV in vivo and the interaction of the virus with its human host.

This chapter describes new knowledge gained from AIDS research efforts, ways in which that knowledge may be used against HIV infection, the difficulties of developing drugs and vaccines to combat the epidemic, and the variety of resources needed for the task.

HIV BIOLOGY

Viral Taxonomy and Disease

Over the past 2 years, researchers have begun to appreciate more fully the nature and diversity of HIV, especially following the discovery in 1986 and subsequent characterization of a second human retrovirus, HIV-2. The first retrovirus found to cause AIDS, now referred to as HIV-1, is responsible for the vast majority of AIDS cases reported to date, and it accounts for the most prevalent and geographically dispersed occurrences of human retroviral infection now known (IOM/NAS, 1986). HIV-2 is most prevalent in certain regions of West Africa, where its transmission and pathogenesis mirror those of HIV-1 (Clavel et al., 1986a,

123

1987; Kanki et al., 1986); it has been linked to a growing number of cases of immunodeficiency diseases that are clinically indistinguishable from HIV-1-associated AIDS (Clavel et al., 1986a, 1987; Kanki et al., 1986, 1987). It is not known whether HIV-2 infection leads to AIDS at the same rate or with the same frequency as HIV-1 infection, but it is clearly a pathogenic retrovirus. HIV-2 is not as effectively detected as HIV-1 by the screening tests now available.

Through morphologic and genetic analyses of HIV-1 and HIV-2, their taxonomic assignment has been further defined as the subfamily of retroviruses known as lentiviruses (Gonda et al., 1985; Sonigo et al., 1985; Clavel et al., 1986b; Guyader et al., 1987). Lentiviruses are the causative agents of a number of diseases in other mammalian species that are characterized by persistence of infection, the effective impotence of the host immune response to clear the infection, long incubation periods, and protracted symptomatic phases.

Although HIV-1 was the first lentivirus to be described with profoundly immunosuppressive properties, a growing number of retroviruses of this type have since been discovered. Shortly after the isolation of HIV-1, a related lentivirus, simian immunodeficiency virus, or SIV, was identified in a variety of monkey species (Daniel et al., 1985; Kanki et al., 1985). HIV-2, in fact, is more closely related in its genetic structure to this simian virus than to HIV-1 (Chakrabarti et al., 1987; Franchini et al., 1987; Guyader et al., 1987; Hirsch et al., 1987). Recently, researchers have identified other lentiviruses as potential agents of immunodeficiency disease in cows (bovine immunodeficiency virus) and cats (feline immunodeficiency virus) (Gonda et al., 1987; Pederson et al., 1987). The continued study of these simian, bovine, and feline lentiviruses may provide valuable models of the pathogenesis and therefore potential treatment of HIV infection in humans. In April 1988 scientists from Gabon announced the isolation of a newly identified virus from chimpanzees that appears to be closely related to HIV-1 (R. Widdus, World Health Organization, personal communication, 1988).

Using molecular cloning and nucleotide sequence analysis of multiple isolates of HIV-1, researchers have defined an exceptionally complex retroviral genome with characteristics not previously seen in retroviruses (Muesing et al., 1985; Ratner et al., 1985; Sanchez-Pescador et al., 1985; Wain-Hobson et al., 1985). Studies have shown that the HIV-1 genome contains a number of novel genes in addition to those that encode the usual structural and enzymatic functions required for retroviral replication. These studies have identified the protein products of HIV-1's unusual genes, and, as they do not appear to be present in mature virus particles, it has been postulated that these gene products have regulatory rather than structural roles in viral replication. The importance of such findings lies in our improved understanding of the mechanisms of action of the HIV regulatory genes, an understanding that could speed the development of specific, effective means to inhibit HIV replication.

The nucleotide sequences of independent isolates of HIV-1 are also notable for their degree of variation and the patterns of these variations (Alizon et al., 1986; Coffin, 1986; Starcich et al., 1986). As discussed in *Confronting AIDS*, a fuller understanding of the origin and immunologic significance of variations in the nucleotide sequences of HIV is central to efforts to engender protective immunity through vaccination. Work in this area has brought improved definition of conserved and variable domains in the envelope glycoproteins, but little is known as yet about the biological processes that may give rise to and possibly select for sequence divergence (Coffin, 1986; IOM/NAS, 1986). Several independent isolates of HIV-2 have now been molecularly cloned and sequenced, and they appear to demonstrate a similar degree of variation (Clavel et al., 1986b; Guyader et al., 1987).

Molecular studies of the HIV-1 genome have delineated the basic structure of the genes that encode the necessary replicative functions provided by the viral core proteins (*gag*), polymerase (*pol*), and surface glycoproteins (*env*). They have also defined the structure of the genetic regulatory sequences in the retroviral long terminal repeats (LTRs). In addition to these expected retroviral genes, the studies have shown that HIV-1 contains genes that are without known counterparts in other retroviruses: the so-called open reading frames, referred to as *sor* and 3'-*orf*. These open reading frames give rise to proteins that are produced during the course of HIV infection in vitro and in vivo (Allan et al., 1985; Lee et al., 1985; Kan et al., 1986). Recently, Alizon and coworkers (1986) and Wong-Staal and colleagues (1987) have demonstrated that another conserved open reading frame, *R*, also encodes a protein product. Functional studies and mutagenic analyses of biologically active molecular clones of HIV-1 have resulted in the discovery of two additional viral genes, *tat*-III and *art/trs* (Sodroski et al., 1984; Arya et al., 1985; Dayton et al., 1986; Feinberg et al., 1986; A. G. Fisher et al., 1986b; Sodroski et al., 1986a).

Thus, whereas many other naturally occurring, replication-competent retroviruses have only three genes, HIV-1 contains at least eight (Figure 2). Of these, the *tat*-III and *art/trs* genes are known to be essential for HIV-1 replication, and the *sor* gene product appears to be important for efficient viral transmission; the *R* and 3'-*orf* genes appear to be dispensable for replication in vitro (A. G. Fisher et al., 1986a, 1987; Luciw et al., 1987; Strebel et al., 1987). All of the structural (*gag*, *pol*, and *env*) and what are presumed to be the regulatory (*tat*-III, *art/trs*, *sor*, *R*, and 3'-*orf*) genes encode proteins that are recognized by sera from infected individuals, indicating that the proteins are produced in vivo and are immunogenic (Allan et al., 1985; Lee et al., 1985; Aldovini et al., 1986; Knight et al., 1987; Wong-Staal et al., 1987).

126

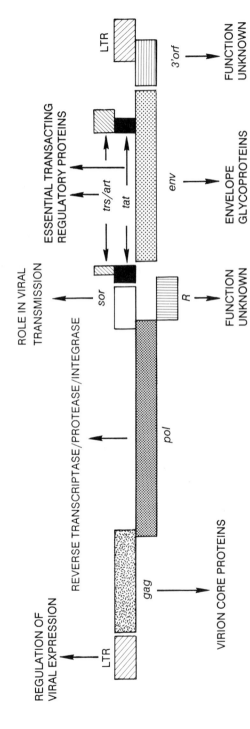

FIGURE 2   The HIV-1 genome. Source: Courtesy of Mark Feinberg, Whitehead Institute for Biomedical Research, Cambridge, Massachusetts.

The genome of HIV-2 has now been molecularly cloned and studied in detail (Guyader et al., 1987). In addition to the requisite *gag, pol, env*, and regulatory genes, HIV-2 encodes an additional centrally located open reading frame (*X*) that is not found in the genome of HIV-1.

Control of Viral Gene Expression

Like all other retroviruses, HIV uses double-stranded DNA copies of the viral genome as templates for the synthesis of viral RNA molecules. The transcription of retroviral RNA uses the host cell's synthetic machinery, but it is regulated by genetic elements resident in the viral long terminal repeats, or LTRs. The complex behavior of HIV is thought to include mechanisms that facilitate both the amplification and attenuation of viral expression (production). Although there is still much to be learned about these regulatory processes, it appears likely that they are mediated in large part through specific nucleotide sequences in the HIV LTRs.

Studies have shown that HIV production in vitro is enhanced by a variety of immunologic stimuli and specific cytokines (proteins produced by host cells) (Hoxie et al., 1985; Zagury et al., 1986; Folks et al., 1987). Whether or not increased production follows similar stimulation in vivo is unknown; if so, such stimuli (other infections, perhaps) might be important factors mediating the pace of progression of immunocompromise and disease following initial HIV infection. The basic mechanisms regulating gene expression in human (and other eukaryotic) cells are only beginning to be understood. Early studies have clearly shown, however, that the cellular transcription apparatus may be preferentially activated to express specific subsets of cellular genes within the context of a given cell's differentiation program. Recently, evidence has been presented suggesting that the activation of HIV production by cellular stimulation is mediated by the activation of a host regulatory protein binding to the genetic regulatory elements of the viral LTR, which previously had been shown to function as transcriptional enhancer elements. Additional studies have identified a number of other host cell proteins that bind to specific sequences in the HIV LTR and that may also play important roles in controlling the transcription of HIV RNA (Jones et al., 1986; Franza et al., 1987; Garcia et al., 1987).

Regulation and Production of HIV

As discussed in the previous section, the double-stranded DNA (proviral) form of HIV residing in the nucleus of an infected cell serves as the template for synthesizing full-length viral RNA transcripts. Some of the transcripts remain intact and enter the cytoplasm for incorporation into virus particles and transmission to other cells. Researchers also believe that the full-length transcripts are used in the translation of HIV *gag* and *pol* proteins, which derive from proteolytic cleavage of a large polyprotein precursor (IOM/NAS, 1986). Because the reading frames of *gag* and *pol* are adjacent but discontinuous, until recently it was unclear how the precursor protein was produced. Now, studies have described the process, called ribosomal frameshifting, that HIV uses to generate the precursor of the mature *gag* and *pol* proteins (Jacks et al., 1988). Researchers have also recently identified a virally encoded protease responsible for the proteolytic cleavage of the *gag-pol* precursor into its mature functional constituents. The constituents include the viral core structural proteins and the reverse transcriptase, endonuclease, and RNase H activities of the HIV polymerase complex (Debouck et al., 1988).

The remaining HIV proteins, including the *env* glycoproteins and the regulatory proteins, are all translated from subgenomic RNA transcripts derived by an unusually complicated pattern of RNA splicing (Muesing et al., 1985). What is yet unknown are the mechanisms by which retroviruses achieve an appropriate balance between sufficient unspliced RNA transcripts to provide new genomic RNA molecules for additional cycles of infection and spliced mRNAs to encode the requisite viral structural and regulatory proteins. It appears that HIV may encode a specific, novel gene to regulate the pattern of spliced RNAs produced in infected cells and, consequently, the amount of virus particles produced (Feinberg et al., 1986).

HIV envelope glycoproteins play an essential role in the replication of HIV and may be responsible for many of the cytopathic consequences of viral infection (Lifson et al., 1986a; Sodroski et al., 1986a; Somasundaran and Robinson, 1987; McCune et al., 1988). The envelope protein is translated from a spliced mRNA and synthesized as a large precursor protein; this precursor protein is then heavily glycosylated (sugar residues are added) to a form known as gp160 and proteolytically cleaved into two associated subunits, gp120 and gp41 (IOM/NAS, 1986). Recent work has shown definitively that the gp120 molecule mediates viral attachment to the cellular receptor, the host cell surface protein CD4 (Dalgleish et al., 1984; Klatzmann et al., 1984; Maddon et al., 1986). The gp41 anchors the envelope glycoprotein complex in the lipid bilayer of the viral membrane. The glycosylation and proteolytic processing of the gp160 envelope precursor are host cell enzymatic functions (IOM/NAS, 1986). Now, researchers also understand that glycosylation of the HIV envelope protein is necessary for receptor binding and infectivity, and may play an additional role in masking critical envelope domains from host immunologic attack (Matthews et al., 1987). Proteolytic cleavage of the envelope precursor has been shown to be essential for the generation of infectious, cytopathic HIV particles.

The protein products of the HIV genes *sor*, *R*, *tat*-III, *art/trs*, and *3'-orf* (and *X* in the case of HIV-2) are synthesized from multiply spliced viral mRNA transcripts. These regulatory proteins have been identified, but a good deal of uncertainty and controversy surrounds any definition of their exact functions. For example, early studies have demonstrated that the *tat*-III and *art/trs* proteins play roles in HIV replication and appear to involve genetic processes that are without known precedents in human cells. It is likely that the *R*, *3'-orf*, and *X* genes also play important roles in the biology of HIV-1 and HIV-2, but a more thorough understanding of these genes has been limited by the lack of in vitro assays of their functions.

The *tat*-III protein greatly amplifies (or transactivates) the level of replication of HIV-1 (Sodroski et al., 1984; Arya et al., 1985). Studies have shown that this enhancement requires specific nucleotide sequences (the transactivation response element, or TAR) that are contained within the viral LTR; following transcription, these sequences are included at the 5'-end of all viral RNA transcripts (Rosen et al., 1985; Muesing et al., 1987). Whether the *tat*-III protein directly binds to the TAR regions is not yet known, but researchers have concluded that the TAR region assumes a complex RNA secondary structure whose specific topology is essential for proper functioning (Hauber and Cullen, 1988). Reportedly, the *tat*-III protein enhances both the transcription and translation of HIV-1 RNA (Cullen, 1986; Feinberg et al., 1986; Peterlin et al., 1986; Rosen et al., 1986; Wright et al., 1986; Hauber et al., 1987; Kao et al., 1987; Muesing et al., 1987). Defining the relative importance of several proposed mechanisms of *tat*-III action awaits additional experimental evaluation. Nevertheless, although the function of the *tat*-III protein is still poorly defined, it has been shown to assume a predominantly nuclear localization in infected cells (a possible clue to its function), and important aspects of its molecular structure are emerging (Hauber et al., 1987; Frankel et al., 1988).

The *art/trs* protein of HIV-1 also has an essential although poorly understood function in viral replication (Feinberg et al., 1986; Sodroski et al., 1986b; Knight et al., 1987). The *art/trs* gene appears to control, directly or indirectly, the pattern of HIV-1 RNA transcripts seen in infected cells. In the absence of *art/trs* expression, the smaller, multiply spliced mRNA species that encode the viral regulation proteins predominate, at the expense of the full-length and singly spliced *env* transcripts that provide viral genomes and specify translation of the HIV-1 virion structural components (Feinberg et al., 1986; Sadaie et al., 1988). The *art/trs* function may specifically affect the splicing of viral RNA and thus permit important differential regulation of HIV expression; additional *art/trs* effects on the translation of specific viral mRNAs have also been suggested. Rosen and colleagues (1988) have postulated that the *art/trs* protein acts through specific, incompletely defined sequences contained in HIV-1 RNA transcripts. Like the *tat*-III protein, the *art/trs* protein is localized in the nucleus of HIV-1-infected cells, consistent with its postulated role in the splicing of viral RNA.

It has been reported that the *sor* gene of HIV-1 is required for efficient replication. This finding is based on studies of viruses with experimentally induced mutations in the *sor* gene. The studies show that the viruses spread poorly and only through cell-to-cell contact in in vitro lymphocyte cultures (A. G. Fisher et al., 1987; Strebel et al., 1987). The nature of this handicap is not well understood, however. It is thought that the *sor* protein is not incorporated in HIV virus particles.

The 3'-*orf* gene of HIV-1 is not needed for replication in vitro, and recent reports have suggested that viruses that lack a functional 3'-*orf* gene may, in fact, replicate more efficiently than wild-type viruses (A. G. Fisher et al., 1986a; Luciw et al., 1987). Whether the 3'-*orf* protein specifically inhibits HIV-1 production is not yet known. It has been suggested that the 3'-*orf* protein influences the expression of certain host cellular genes.

The role of the *R* gene of HIV-1 has only recently begun to be scrutinized, but preliminary results (Wong-Staal et al., 1987) indicate that it may not be required for HIV-1 replication in vitro. Also in need of direct evaluation are the roles of HIV-2 regulatory genes, although these are assumed to be analogous to those of HIV-1. The significance and function of the distinctive *X* gene of HIV-2 await elucidation. Because SIV's genetic structure is closely related to that of HIV-2, it will permit experimental analyses of the in vivo function of the unusual regulatory genes of the immunodeficiency-inducing lentiviruses—analyses that are not possible with the human AIDS viruses (Chakrabarti et al., 1987; Franchini et al., 1987; Hirsch et al., 1987).

Interrupting Infection by HIV

The HIV replicative cycle presents a number of opportunities for interruption by antiviral interventions. Since 1986 a good deal of progress has been made; however, much of the information that emerges from ongoing studies highlights the difficulties that must be overcome before effective prophylactic or therapeutic interventions are feasible.

The earliest event in the establishment of HIV infection is the binding of the virus particle through its envelope glycoprotein (gp120) to a specific receptor on the host cell's surface. This CD4 cell receptor is found on the surface of certain members of the T lymphoid and macrophage-monocyte cell lineages (IOM/NAS, 1986; Maddon et al., 1986; Sattentau and Weiss,

1988). The range of cells that are susceptible to HIV-1 infection, both in vitro and in vivo, appears to parallel those that display the CD4 surface receptor. HIV-2 also uses the CD4 molecule as its receptor in the initiation of infection.

Current studies are defining the interaction between the HIV-1 gp120 envelope protein and the CD4 receptor with increasing resolution. The region of the gp120 molecule that interacts with the CD4 molecule recently has been defined; the identification of the corresponding binding domain of CD4 is being actively pursued (Lasky et al., 1987). Potential strategies to inhibit the gp120-CD4 interaction, and thus HIV infection, include vaccination to elicit antibodies that recognize and bind to the critical receptor-binding domain of the HIV envelope and the inhibition of cell surface binding through competition with appropriate exogenously added fragments of the CD4 protein. Recent studies have shown the feasibility of the latter approach by successfully inhibiting HIV infection in vitro with a soluble form of the CD4 molecule produced through recombinant DNA methods (Smith et al., 1987; Deen et al., 1988; R. A. Fisher et al., 1988; Traunecker et al., 1988). It is hoped that small fragments of CD4 may soon be identified that will prevent HIV infection but that will not interfere with the critical immunologic functions of the CD4 molecule in vivo. Experimental clinical trials of the soluble CD4 preparation in HIV-positive persons are expected to begin shortly; however, this approach may be limited by the inability of such preparations to cross the blood–brain barrier and thus reach the important reservoir of infection within the central nervous system (Ho et al., 1985; Shaw et al., 1985; Gartner et al., 1986b; Koenig et al., 1986).

After HIV binds to the CD4 receptor, it appears to enter the host target cell by direct fusion of the viral and cellular plasma membranes (Stein et al., 1987; McClure et al., 1988). It is thought that this process requires a hydrophobic domain on the HIV gp41 that assumes an active fusogenic conformation following cleavage of the gp160 precursor molecule (McCune et al., 1988). One important manifestation of the cytopathic consequence of HIV infection in vitro involves a specific interaction between the HIV envelope glycoprotein complex and the CD4 molecule that results in the fusion and subsequent death of cells that have CD4 receptors (Lifson et al., 1986a,b; Sodroski et al., 1986a). This process, which is known as syncytia formation, may also involve the fusogenic domain of gp41 (McCune et al., 1988). The development of approaches to inhibit envelope-mediated membrane fusion may lead to novel ways of preventing HIV infection and its consequences.

Once the virus is inside the host target cell, the HIV RNA genome is copied into a double-stranded DNA form by the viral reverse transcriptase. If reverse transcriptase could be inhibited, the lack of it would disrupt an essential stage of HIV replication, and this antiviral strategy is being actively pursued (IOM/NAS, 1986). The drug zidovudine (i.e., AZT) acts to interrupt this stage of the infection. Zidovudine is a nucleoside analog that, once it has been phosphorylated by host cell kinases, is preferentially used by the HIV reverse transcriptase to synthesize the complementary strand of retroviral DNA. Once zidovudine is incorporated into the nascent DNA copy of HIV RNA, however, DNA polymerization stops, prematurely, and the DNA strand cannot be extended (Yarchoan and Broder, 1987). Zidovudine effectively inhibits HIV-1 replication in vitro, and early clinical trials have shown that it improves survival in persons with severe manifestations of HIV-1 infection (Fischl et al., 1987; Yarchoan et al., 1987). Although the clinical utility of zidovudine may be limited by its untoward side effects, which include anemia and neutropenia, it provides a hopeful precedent for future drug development efforts (Richman et al., 1987). A related chain-terminating nucleoside analog, 2',3'-dideoxycytidine (ddC), is an even more potent inhibitor of HIV replication in vitro and is now the subject of clinical trials (Yarchoan and Broder, 1987).

Another area of potential inhibition involves the processes that control the transcription and translation of HIV RNA. Much remains to be learned about these processes, although the requirements of the *tat*-III and *art/trs* genes in the HIV replicative cycle are clear. Still, a much better understanding of their functions is needed before studies can explore the specific inhibition of their activities. Similarly, researchers need an improved definition of the replicative role of the *sor, R, X,* and 3'-*orf* genes before they can evaluate their candidacy as targets for antiviral interventions.

The processing and assembly of the HIV structural components offer a range of potential points for inhibiting HIV replication. The necessary proteolytic cleavage of the *gag-pol* polyprotein precursor is one possible target, and its mechanism is currently undergoing active analysis (Debouck et al., 1988). Likewise, the proteolytic processing of the envelope polyprotein gp160, which is necessary for HIV infectivity, is a susceptible stage for inhibition. The glycosylation of the HIV envelope protein also appears to be necessary for viral infectivity, and drugs that interfere with this process have demonstrated antiviral activity in vitro (Gruters et al., 1987). Further studies of the pathways of viral assembly and maturation may identify additional promising antiviral targets.

Natural History of HIV Infection

Studies of HIV-infected persons have demonstrated the presence and expression of the virus in a number of host tissues, including peripheral blood cells, lymph nodes, bone marrow, spleen, lung, retina, brain, cerebrospinal fluid, semen, cervical and vaginal secretions, saliva, and tears of infected individuals (IOM/NAS, 1986). Epidemiological analyses provide evidence that the essentially exclusive modes of HIV transmission are sexual intercourse, blood and blood products, and perinatal transmission (see Chapter 2). As in the case of other lentiviruses, studies have detected very little cell-free virus in HIV-seropositive persons. Perhaps in keeping with the lentivirus analogy, HIV may also be spread by virally infected cells carried in secretions rather than by cell-free virus. The factors that determine whether an HIV-infected person will transmit the viral infection to another individual are poorly understood (see Chapter 2). For instance, it appears that HIV-infected persons differ in their degree of infectiousness over time. Similarly, the factors that may influence an individual's susceptibility to HIV infection following a given exposure are incompletely defined.

Other aspects of HIV infection are somewhat better understood, for example, which cells are targets of the virus in an infected human host. In addition to the CD4 helper-inducer cell population that is progressively depleted in the clinical development of AIDS, researchers now recognize that cells of the macrophage-monocyte lineage are important targets in the establishment, dissemination, and persistence of the infection (Gartner et al., 1986a; Ho et al., 1986; Koenig et al., 1986). Because macrophages permit HIV replication, are capable of wide-ranging migration, and are relatively resistant to the cytopathic consequences of viral infection, they probably play a major role in the pathogenesis of HIV-induced disease. Studies have found infected macrophage populations within the lymphatics, the central nervous system, and a variety of peripheral tissues, frequently at sites manifesting local pathology (Koenig et al., 1986). Interestingly, recent evidence suggests that different HIV isolates may replicate preferentially in either CD4-positive T lymphocytes or in macrophage populations derived from a variety of host tissues (Gartner et al., 1986a; Koyanagi et al., 1987). It is not known whether viruses with different cytotropisms give rise to specific clinical manifestations of HIV infection, nor what genetic differences account for the biological diversity of HIV isolates. Further hypotheses awaiting examination involve the possible in vivo interactions among populations of HIV in an individual or the evolution of HIV in an infected individual, either of which might result in altered cytotropism or enhanced virulence during the course of disease progression.

Once HIV infection is established, it persists throughout the lifetime of the infected person, avoiding clearance by the host immune response. The means by which HIV is able to avoid clearance is not known. Although HIV is found only in rare cells in the peripheral bloodstream, it can be more readily detected within the central nervous system (Shaw et al., 1985; Harper et al., 1986; Koenig et al., 1986), where it is less accessible to immune clearance. The number and types of infected cells in HIV-positive persons remain incompletely defined. The persistence of HIV infection in vivo, which is often imprecisely called a latent infection (because there is no evidence as yet that the HIV genome is integrated and not expressed), undoubtedly involves a complex interaction between host and virus. Lentiviruses, including HIV, are characterized by a low level of expression in vivo (Haase, 1986), and the mechanisms by which HIV infection may be activated are not understood.

Studies have shown that antibodies present in the sera of HIV-infected persons recognize and bind to the viral envelope glycoprotein. Because the glycoprotein mediates binding of the virus to host cells, it might be expected to provide a target for the neutralization of infectivity by the immune system. Yet although such neutralizing antibodies can be demonstrated in the sera of HIV-positive persons using in vitro assays, they do not appear to be protective in vivo (Robert-Guroff et al., 1985; Weiss et al., 1985; Weber et al., 1987). A possible explanation for this lack of efficacy is the requirement, and the apparent failure, of the less avid antienvelope antibodies to overcome the extremely high-affinity interaction between the HIV gp120 and the cellular CD4 receptor (Lasky et al., 1987). The possible contribution of HIV's extensive genomic diversity to a resistance to immune clearance is also poorly defined. Such diversity has been observed in patients during the course of an infection (Hahn et al., 1986), but a process of immunologic selection for viral variation has yet to be demonstrated. Researchers have noted a number of correlations between the loss of host antibody response to specific HIV components and progression to AIDS (Laurence et al., 1987; Weber et al., 1987). It is not known, however, whether the change in serologic reactivity in these persons is the cause or consequence of their evolving immunodeficiency.

The extent to which the host cellular immune system may recognize HIV infection and limit its spread is an area of great interest, although little is known about the role of cellular immunity in modulating the course of HIV infection. Some HIV-seropositive persons carry cytotoxic T lymphocytes that specifically recognize determinants on the viral envelope, *gag,* and polymerase proteins (Plata et al., 1987; Walker et al., 1987, 1988). These cytotoxic T lymphocytes may play a role in the host's containment of HIV infection, but they may also contribute to the inflammatory and sometimes deleterious reactions seen in HIV-infected persons (Plata et al., 1987). Researchers have also observed antibody-dependent, cell-mediated cytotoxic recognition and destruction of HIV-infected cells, but thus far they have been unable to determine their contribution to the protection of an infected person or, alternatively, to the progression to clinical disease (Lyerly et al., 1987). Improved understanding of the cell-mediated immune response to HIV infection becomes even more critical if HIV-1 is transmitted through infected cells rather than in free viral form.

Research has produced little information as yet about the pathogenesis of HIV-induced disease. In addition, studies have yet to define the in vivo mechanism by which HIV destroys or inhibits cells of the immune system. Although it has been shown that HIV-induced cell fusion, or syncytia formation, exerts a dramatic cytopathic effect in vitro, its contribution to the immunologic consequences of HIV infection in vivo has yet to be demonstrated (Lifson et al., 1986b; Sodroski et al., 1986a; Somasundaran and Robinson, 1987). Researchers have also suggested that autoimmune phenomena may contribute to the immune compromise that develops following HIV infection, but there are currently too few data to evaluate these suggestions (Stricker et al., 1987). Likewise, little is known about the role of host and viral factors in the development of HIV-1-induced neurologic disease, although its prevalence and severity have generated increased research attention over the past few years.

Another important unresolved question is whether there are genetic or environmental cofactors that may modulate the tempo or course of disease development in HIV-infected persons. Studies have identified a variety of agents, both host immunoregulatory and other exogenous, infectious pathogens, that appear to enhance HIV-1 production in vitro, but claims of their in vivo relevance find little support in the available epidemiological data (IOM/NAS, 1986). Unfortunately, as the estimates of the percentage of HIV-infected persons who will progress to AIDS are revised upward, the likely importance of essential cofactors for disease progression—and the possibilities they offer for ameliorative intervention—diminish.

The Importance of Basic Research

Understanding the processes and consequences of HIV infection described in the preceding pages is crucial to the development of therapies and vaccines against HIV. This understanding, in turn, is rooted in all basic research in the areas of cellular biology, virology, immunology, and genetics. As often happens in scientific investigation, serendipitous developments that initially are unrelated to HIV may unexpectedly contribute to progress in AIDS research. For example, many of the techniques that have been used to study HIV were developed during research in other fields. For this reason, increasing the amount of funds devoted to AIDS without a concomitant strengthening of all basic biomedical research is shortsighted. **The committee recommends that**

funding for basic research in all areas of biology should continue to grow rather than be curtailed in favor of AIDS-targeted research.

DRUG DEVELOPMENT AND TESTING

The difficulties and consequent challenges of developing drugs that alleviate the symptoms or slow the course of HIV infection lie in the complex virus–host interactions and the multiple pathologies to which immune deficiency gives rise. Yet despite these complexities, there is cause for cautious optimism. Current knowledge of the HIV proteins and their functions offers several potential targets for rational drug design. Several novel and worthwhile approaches to antiviral therapy also deserve consideration. In addition, our understanding of the immune system continues to grow, fueled in part by recent technical improvements in monoclonal antibody development, cell cloning, and growth factor isolation and characterization.

Recent accomplishments in basic research on HIV and AIDS were described earlier in this chapter. Yet applying the results of these efforts to drug development requires coordinated action. For example, molecular virologists who describe a novel viral inhibitor active in cells in tissue culture should have ready access to pharmacologists or toxicologists who can begin to develop an agent that will function at tolerable levels in a human being. These kinds of partnerships are vital for rapid progress in drug development, but they do not occur naturally in most research or medical centers.

The National Institute of Allergy and Infectious Diseases (NIAID), through its National Cooperative Drug Discovery Groups (NCDDG) program, has sought to encourage such cooperation among bench scientists and pharmaceutical companies with experience in drug development and evaluation. The members of each group share information, thus profiting from complementary expertise. In addition, the NCDDGs have formed an intergroup information network for the rapid exchange of news of progress in a particular strategy or agent. Individual scientists and drug companies have established similar partnerships.

The search for therapeutic agents for HIV-infected persons must also encompass the screening of existing compounds. Scientists and industry leaders who are experienced in drug development predict that screening existing compounds rather than designing or attempting to discover new drugs to treat HIV infection and AIDS may prove more successful, at least in the immediate future (IOM, 1987). A screening program is now under way at the National Cancer Institute involving the use of automated tests to determine the potential antiviral activity of compounds. When fully operational, this program will have the capacity to screen tens of thousands of compounds yearly.

An extensive discussion of particular antiviral agents is beyond the scope of this report (interested readers are referred to the *AmFAR Directory of Experimental Treatments for AIDS and ARC* [Abrams et al., 1987]). Yet several approaches to treatment that are currently being tested deserve mention. One is the combination of an antiviral agent such as zidovudine (i.e., AZT) with a biological response modifier such as granulocyte macrophage colony-stimulating factor. Another combination of therapies under evaluation is the alternate administration of zidovudine and a different reverse transcriptase inhibitor, ddC. The logic for this design is that zidovudine and ddC have similar intended sites of action but different side effects. Alternate dosing may keep adverse side effects to a minimum while maintaining high levels of reverse transcriptase inhibition.

Other protocols of particular note involve tests of the treatment of asymptomatic HIV-infected people with zidovudine. In these trials, zidovudine is being evaluated for its ability to prolong the asymptomatic phase of HIV infection or reduce the severity of disease.

Once a drug appears to be a candidate substance for the treatment of HIV infection or AIDS (or both), it begins the long journey toward licensure. The United States has the most rigorous review process for new drug approval of any country in the world. The development of any new drug is regulated by FDA and begins with preclinical testing of its activity and safety, a stage that generally requires 1 to 2 years. In the next step of the process, the drug sponsor files an investigational new drug (IND) application that includes the results of all animal testing and how the drug is made. Once the application is approved, promising drugs begin clinical (human) testing, which consists of three phases of activity. Phase I measures safety (i.e., toxicity) and establishes pharmacological profiles of (in this case) the antiviral agent. Tests during this phase involve a small number of healthy people (not patients) and are completed usually in less than 1 year. Phase II trials, which generally last 1 to 2 years, assess the drug's effectiveness using controlled studies with 200 to 300 volunteer patients. Phase III tests involve large numbers of volunteer patients in clinics and hospitals. These latter trials are necessary to confirm early efficacy studies and identify low-incidence adverse reactions; they generally last about 3 years.

After the completion of phase III trials, the drug sponsor files a new drug application (NDA). After FDA approves the application and authorizes the marketing of the drug, the drug sponsor must continue to file periodic reports of adverse reactions. For some drugs, FDA also requires postmarketing monitoring or additional studies to evaluate long-term effects (phase IV). Thus, for the average pharmaceutical, the process of preclinical development, clinical testing, and new drug application takes approximately 7 to 10 years.

The FDA drug approval process has been constantly evolving since its establishment. Although the process has been criticized for being slow and cumbersome, it has also been credited, rightly, with protecting the American public from the harmful effects of inadequately tested drugs. Yet the urgent need for antiviral agents to treat increasing numbers of AIDS patients has placed pressure on the system to change. In the committee's view, FDA has responded with commitment and energy. The agency has agreed to complete its reviews of new drug applications in 6 months or less rather than the 2 to 3 years normally required. Review of IND applications (prior to clinical trials) has also been speeded up. In addition, FDA has proposed new procedures to facilitate patients' access to promising new drugs as early as possible in the drug development process (Young, 1987). Drug sponsors may now apply for a special treatment status for their investigational new drug when the following conditions are met:

- the drug will treat an immediately life-threatening or otherwise serious disease;
- no satisfactory alternative drug or therapy exists to treat the disease;
- the drug is already under investigation in a controlled clinical trial under a standard IND process; and
- the sponsor of the controlled trial is pursuing marketing approval of the investigational drug with due diligence.

Treatment IND status allows the drug sponsor to sell the drug at cost (no profit making is allowed) for treatment purposes. Trimetrexate, a drug to treat *Pneumocystis carinii* pneumonia, was granted treatment IND status in February 1988. It was the first AIDS-related drug to be approved under the new regulations.

Zidovudine (AZT), which was approved in September 1986 under a prototype treatment IND mechanism, received the fastest evaluation that has ever occurred within FDA. It remains the only drug proven to prolong the life of some AIDS patients. Yet the diversion of FDA personnel from other areas that was necessary to approve zidovudine resulted in a backlog of applications in FDA's Division of Anti-Infective Drug Products. As the number of applications for treatment IND status grows, these personnel problems may become more severe.

At present, FDA is not a "bottleneck" in the availability of new drugs to treat HIV infection and AIDS. The paucity of new drugs is related more to shortcomings in the science of antiviral agents than to the drug approval process. However, as more promising new drugs are discovered or designed, FDA, without additional resources, could become an impediment to speedy availability. **The committee believes that FDA resources for new drug approval should be commensurate with the task.** The need to borrow personnel from other parts of the agency should be relieved; the need for space, which appears to be particularly acute, should also be addressed.

The committee applauds FDA's ingenuity in instituting new regulations for investigational new drugs. Nevertheless, it also believes a note of caution is warranted. The availability of treatment INDs could interfere with the ability to execute conclusive clinical trials. For example, the pharmaceutical industry has expressed concern that the use of the treatment IND mechanism may make it more difficult to enroll sufficient numbers of patients in clinical trials: people who know that the drug under investigation could be offered to them as treatment in the near future may be reluctant to participate in tests (Cooper, 1988). There is also concern about potential issues of legal liability on the part of drug manufacturers and individual physicians: for instance, when patients who are receiving investigational new drugs under the treatment IND mechanism develop adverse reactions or when patients fail to receive an investigational drug because their physicians are unaware of its availability. **In light of these concerns, the committee recommends that an outside evaluation of the treatment IND process be conducted after enough time has elapsed to determine its possible unanticipated consequences for any new drugs.**

HIV infection and AIDS have generated a pressing need to develop and test experimental drugs for treatment and to make effective drugs widely available as soon as possible. The committee recognizes the frustration, fear, and anger of people with HIV infection, who may feel a lack of urgency in the drug development process. However, **the committee believes that once drugs are through phase I testing for toxicity, carefully controlled trials are still the fastest, most efficient way to determine what treatments work.** In asymptomatic or mildly ill patients, trials should be placebo controlled (until an effective therapy is discovered for these patients); in patients with severe symptoms of HIV infection or AIDS, experimental drugs should be compared to zidovudine (AZT). Conducting well-designed trials from the beginning will benefit more patients, sooner, than any other approach. Poorly designed trials, or administering drugs without controls and "observing" the course of disease, risk being inconclusive or drawing incorrect conclusions. The wide distribution of untested drugs makes it impossible to determine whether or not they are effective, especially if the benefits are real but small. The end result of these approaches could include the continued prescribing of useless or harmful therapies.

More than other diseases, AIDS has brought forth calls to include large numbers of people in clinical trials, both for humanitarian reasons (access to potentially effective therapy as soon as possible) and to offer HIV-infected persons a chance to contribute to the solution of the problem. Yet the distinction between making proven, effective treatments widely available and enrolling as many people as possible in clinical trials is an important one. In fact, the best-designed trial enrolls the smallest number of people needed to show a significant difference between the experimental and the control drugs, thereby minimizing the possibility of doing harm. **The committee believes that, following scientifically sound guidelines, wider access to clinical trials can be gained by broadening their geographic base, by extending trials to previously untapped populations including women, IV drug abusers, and pediatric patients, and by testing all compounds that appear to have a possibility of effectiveness.** The budget for pediatric trials in particular must be increased. It is the responsibility of those conducting trials to communicate with the public about their availability and to encourage wide participation.

In particular, NIAID, through its AIDS clinical trial units (ACTUs), has opportunities for such communication and encouragement, in part because of the role of ACTUs in the clinical evaluation of new drugs. The ACTUs, a component of the newly organized AIDS Clinical Trials Cooperative Group, are located at 35 sites around the country. Formerly called AIDS treatment evaluation units or clinical study groups, the units enlist clinical investigators and patients for large-scale, standardized collaborative clinical trials. The ACTU program is designed to evaluate promising drugs efficiently by coordinating protocol design, data collection and analysis, and subject recruitment. An important goal of the program is to speed the transfer of therapies, once they are proven effective, to physicians and their patients. Research scientists or pharmaceutical companies' may submit drugs for evaluation at ACTU sites. The current test roster of the ACTUs includes agents to treat HIV infection, immune deficiency, opportunistic infection, and combinations of these conditions. In addition to the obvious advantages of drug trial coordination and standardization, the ACTUs have a special utility in their capacity to test combined therapies involving compounds from different sources. The pharmaceutical industry also conducts clinical trials through its system of privately sponsored testing.

The committee believes that, to the greatest extent possible, trials should take place within well-established sites for drug testing. Community-based trials need to be carefully supervised to yield useful results. Phase IV postmarketing surveillance for already approved drugs may be the most appropriate role for community-based studies.

Finally, the committee abhors the exploitation of people with HIV infection and AIDS by those promoting and selling "effective" therapies that are in fact unproven.

VACCINE DEVELOPMENT AND TESTING

Although research findings afford hope for successful antiviral treatments, the prevention of HIV infection by vaccination continues to pose fundamental difficulties. Researchers have pursued sound experimental approaches, but so far they have been unable to prevent H!V infection in primates or humans. Nonetheless, innovative research continues and may produce more promising results in the future.

The appeal of a vaccine to prevent HIV infection is straightforward. Vaccination prevents the infection of a healthy person by priming the immune system to respond rapidly to inactivate an infectious organism. A successful vaccine is a nonpathogenic derivative of the infectious organism that induces a protective immune response. When a person is exposed again to the pathogen after vaccination, the protective response is triggered and amplified to prevent infection. So far, vaccination has only succeeded when the pathogen itself induces some protective immunity during natural infection.

Today's vaccine design exploits the many technical advances in biology that have occurred in recent years. Earlier vaccines were prepared by killing or weakening the infectious organism or by extracting some immunogenic component from it. Modern techniques of genetic engineering now allow researchers to identify a likely immunogenic protein and isolate the gene that encodes it. The protein can then be produced separately for use as a vaccine. This approach eliminates the possibility that the vaccine itself will be infectious, although other potential toxicities remain. Proteins that are often selected for this purpose are outer surface components of the organism, such as cell wall constituents, or viral envelope proteins.

With this general strategy in mind, researchers have looked to the HIV envelope glycoprotein gp120 and its precursor gp160 as promising vaccine candidates. For one thing, these envelope glycoproteins induce antibody production during the course of natural HIV infection; in addition, humans generate cytotoxic T-cell responses directed toward gp120 (Shearer, 1987). What may be even more important is that not only does gp120 appear on the outer surface of HIV, but it is through gp120 binding to the cell surface protein CD4 that HIV attaches to and enters T lymphocytes. The ability to bind the CD4 molecule is a characteristic that is retained across serologically distinct strains of HIV, which suggests that some HIV gp120 epitopes will also be conserved among all HIV strains. Interference with viral entry seems a possible means of antibody-mediated prevention of infection. When tested in tissue culture, antibodies that bind either CD4 or gp120 molecules prevent the infection of T cells (McDougal, 1987).

Accordingly, investigators have cloned the gene that codes for gp160 (the gp120 precursor), inserted it into a baculovirus vector, and used the construct to produce gp160 in insect cells. The protein is then prepared as a vaccine that, not surprisingly, induces antibody synthesis in mice and chimpanzees (Francis, 1987). Neutralizing antibodies (i.e., those that block HIV infection in tissue culture) are among the antibodies detected. However, it appears that the production of neutralizing antibodies may be irrelevant to protection from HIV infection in vivo. When immunized chimpanzees were infected with HIV, they continued to produce antibodies but became persistently infected. Currently, the baculovirus-derived gp160 is being tested in humans for safety and immunogenicity. FDA has also approved a different construct of gp160 for clinical evaluation; in this vaccine the gene for gp160 is inserted into a vaccinia virus genome, and the vaccinia expresses gp160 on its outer surface. So far, this vaccine does not appear to alter the course of HIV infection in chimpanzees when a challenge is presented.

Another test of vaccination in chimpanzees has used immunization with purified gp120, which induced neutralizing antibodies, followed by infection with a virus of the same strain in a low dose but of sufficient strength to infect each of the three animals being tested. Viremia developed in all of the animals. Thus, neutralizing antibodies were not able to block infection by even a small quantity of infective HIV (Nara, 1988).

Other experiments are consistent with these negative findings. For example, in a study using passive immunization (the transfer of antibodies) to test the general principle that the human response to HIV infection can be protective, researchers injected human sera containing neutralizing antibodies into chimpanzees that were then inoculated with HIV. The chimpanzees became infected with HIV even in the presence of human neutralizing antibodies (Fultz, 1987b).

Another result that calls into question the ability of the body's immune responses to prevent HIV infection comes from a superinfection experiment with chimpanzees. The procedure tested whether immune responses or other interference phenomena established by infection with one strain of HIV inhibit infection by a second, serologically distinct strain. Superinfection did occur, indicating that no protective mechanism was fully effective (Fultz, 1987a).

Finally, researchers have seen no correlation between the level of neutralizing antibodies and the progress of natural infection in humans. Total HIV antibody levels drop in AIDS patients in very late stages of the disease, a drop that may be the result of antigen excess. Thus, it appears that HIV infection proceeds in the presence of neutralizing antibodies and cytotoxic T cells that are capable of killing HIV-infected cells in vitro. Because naturally occurring immune responses to HIV are insufficient to prevent infection, it is apparent that HIV has evolved a way to coexist with the immune response of its host.

Several mechanisms may explain why an HIV-infected person is unable to generate sustained protective immunity (Seligmann et al., 1987). First, HIV may escape what would ordinarily be an adequate immune response by antigenic drift (i.e., the viral structures that are recognized by the immune system may change into an unrecognizable form). Second, several serological types of HIV may infect one person, and, as the immune system attacks one type, another type may take its place. Third, although cell-mediated responses of the immune system may be responsible for lysing those cells that are actively producing new viral particles, if there are cells in which HIV exists in a latent form, they may escape immune detection. The frequent activation of these latently infected cells could result in persistent viral replication and infection. Fourth, as in the case of measles, HIV-infected cells may avoid immune detection by not displaying their HIV-encoded antigens. Fifth, some of the body's immune responses to HIV mask viral antigens so that protective mechanisms cannot be stimulated. Finally, the production of HIV antibodies may actually make infection more likely if a person already has circulating HIV antibodies when he or she becomes infected. The HIV particles that are bound in complexes to the HIV antibodies may be phagocytized (engulfed) by macrophages; if the particles remain infectious, they may establish infection in the macrophages when they enter these cells (Halstead, 1987).

Despite these obstacles, researchers continue to search for protective vaccines. Further analysis of earlier results has suggested new approaches. Particular regions of gp120, such as the conserved residues that contact the CD4 receptor, are being cloned and displayed in a highly immunogenic form. Normally, these residues are buried in the native gp120 molecule and may not be immunogenic, but it is possible that antibodies against them, once produced, could block the initial gp120 binding to CD4 and thus prevent infection from being established (Moreine, 1987).

Other research efforts have included the use of an antibody that binds gp120 as an antigen to induce an anti-idiotypic response that in turn can form the basis of an idiotype-anti-idiotype network in which anti-gp120 is endogenously induced (Kennedy, 1987). This approach has a potential side effect, however, in that a broadly specific anti-gp120 antibody may mimic CD4 structure and thus induce anti-CD4 responses. Different kinds of antigens—for instance, gp120 and viral core proteins—can also be combined in a vaccine that may be more effective than one composed of either alone. In addition, these antigens can be mixed with a highly immunogenic carrier, such as tetanus toxoid, for vaccine delivery.

Another approach that is currently being tested involves a vaccine composed of whole killed HIV (Salk, 1987). This sort of vaccine may be useful for primary prevention, but it differs from the protective vaccines discussed earlier in that it has another intended use. Its "immunotherapeutic" effect would be to boost the responses already induced by natural HIV infection in seropositive patients rather than to protect individuals against infection. In this case, a beneficial effect may be the alleviation of symptoms or prolongation of life in HIV-infected persons.

All of these approaches require long-term, large-scale testing and evaluation before candidate vaccines are available to the public. The process by which a vaccine is tested and approved for general use is similar to that for drugs. The sponsor or developer of the vaccine generally tests it first in animal models and, if the vaccine appears promising, applies to FDA for investigational new drug (IND) status to begin clinical testing. Once the application is approved, the sponsor begins three phases of human trials. Phase I tests the vaccine in a small number of persons for safety and immunogenicity at various dose levels and by various routes of administration. Phase II involves administering the vaccine to larger numbers of people to obtain further data. These two phases often overlap. Phase III consists of large-scale, controlled field trials with a sufficiently large number of subjects (at sufficiently high risk of infection) to determine whether the vaccine protects people (at a statistically significant level) against disease. It is this third phase of testing that confirms or disproves the efficacy of the vaccine in preventing infection.

FDA standard practice has generally been that a vaccine must show protective efficacy in an accepted animal model before tests can progress to human volunteers. However, given the urgency surrounding the potentially disastrous effects of the AIDS epidemic, FDA has approved (to date) the precedent-setting initiation of human trials for two vaccine candidates in the absence of proof of protective efficacy in animals. It is unclear whether any future vaccine candidate will be required to demonstrate protection.

There has been substantial controversy about the wisdom of proceeding to human trials for vaccines in the absence of evidence for efficacy in animal tests. The move's supporters offer several rationales for the departure from standard procedure. One, of course, is the pressing need for a protective vaccine against HIV. Another is the knowledge to be gained about the relationship between human and chimpanzee responses to HIV antigens, which could prove applicable to future HIV vaccine trials. Furthermore, testing vaccines composed of viral envelope antigens for safety in humans will provide information, in general, about both humoral and cell-mediated human immune responses to HIV antigens.

Another rationale offered for human trials is that with further information about dosages, immunogenicity, and toxicity, some of the steps of clinical evaluation might be accelerated.

Yet there are potential risks in a phase I trial that cannot be ignored. Some HIV proteins themselves have immunoregulatory activity, and a vaccine derived from such a protein may interfere with the normal operation of the immune system. In addition, it is unclear whether a vaccine might increase the severity of a subsequent, naturally acquired infection. As mentioned earlier in this chapter, antibody-HIV complexes may enter macrophages, but it is not known whether HIV retains its infectivity at this point. If it remains infectious, vaccination could facilitate the initial infection of macrophages or promote the later spread of the virus throughout the body. Furthermore, nonneutralizing antibodies induced by a vaccine that are capable of binding to key sites on HIV without inhibiting it might interfere with the subsequent recognition of the virus by other components of the immune system. Finally, with little hope (considering their negative protective results in animals) that the vaccines now being tested for safety will prove effective, public expectations may be raised unrealistically.

The committee believes that human trials of HIV vaccine candidates should proceed only when (1) protection against infection has been demonstrated in chimpanzees (HIV), in macaques (SIV), or in another suitable animal model, or (2) the vaccine candidate rests on fundamental new knowledge of the relevant human response that cannot be adequately modeled in animals.

The committee also believes that planning should begin now for large-scale human efficacy trials of as yet undeveloped vaccines. Such trials are complex to design, and their results are difficult to evaluate. The trials must enroll sufficiently large numbers of subjects at sufficiently high risk of infection that any decrease in the number of infected persons attributable to the experimental vaccine will be statistically significant. For this reason, the sites for large-scale vaccine efficacy trials will most likely include African and other developing countries. A process should be agreed on for joint decision making among the countries involved. The World Health Organization (WHO) is developing guidelines for the conduct of these trials. In general, the same criteria used in the United States for human vaccine trials should be applied to trials conducted in any other country. Ethical considerations also dictate that those who receive the vaccine must be counseled about behavior changes that diminish the chance for HIV infection. This counseling will have to be taken into consideration in calculating the required number of trial participants.

The question of legal liability may be even more pressing for vaccines than for drugs. Typically, vaccine manufacturers are protected by insurance to cover liability-associated damages. AIDS is so visible and so controversial, however, that vaccine manufacturers are concerned that their standard liability coverage may be inadequate for an AIDS vaccine. At the same time, clinical investigators and manufacturers are now also questioning whether liability insurance may not be needed even for experimental vaccines, which a subject has traditionally taken at his or her own risk after being fully informed of the potential problems. Fears of liability and subsequent damages may impede manufacturers from further developmental work on any vaccine.

To encourage companies to continue the production of vaccines for other diseases, Congress recently established a childhood vaccine compensation schedule. A surcharge to vaccine costs will go toward a fund to pay medical costs and some limited damages for people injured by vaccines. Standards will be set in the near future for determining injury and compensation. This plan could serve as a model for a federal program to protect the rights of recipients of an AIDS vaccine while sheltering manufacturers from impossibly high legal damages.

The pessimism expressed in *Confronting AIDS* about the likelihood of a licensed vaccine becoming available within the next 5 to 10 years has not been mitigated by the accomplishments of the past 2 years. The vaccine development effort has been characterized by a series of animal experiments that have yielded universally negative results. Future animal experiments should use cloned viruses and standardized neutralization tests.

ROUNDTABLE ON DRUGS AND VACCINES

The Institute of Medicine Conference on Promoting Drug Development Against AIDS and HIV Infection (August 31–September 1, 1987) and the Conference on the Development of Vaccines Against HIV Infection and AIDS (December 14–15, 1987) brought together biomedical scientists, clinicians, drug manufacturers, and policymakers to consider ways in which to speed the availability of effective therapy for HIV infection. The participants found the conferences so valuable in fostering a productive exchange of views and information that they recommended that IOM consider convening more conferences and invitational workshops on these issues. In response, IOM plans to establish the Roundtable on the Development of Drugs and Vaccines Against AIDS. The roundtable will have approximately 15 members representing government, the pharmaceutical industry, academia, the legal community, clinical medicine, and the public. Its goal is to facilitate progress in drug and vaccine development by providing a neutral forum in which developmental barriers can be addressed, problems can be aired, and opportunities can be identified and pursued. **The committee endorses the establishment of the Roundtable on** the Development of Drugs and Vaccines Against AIDS and encourages active participation by all sectors.

ANIMAL MODELS OF AIDS

Research on AIDS and HIV infection requires the development of model systems in which an animal infected with HIV develops the same symptoms and exhibits the same course of disease progression found in human patients with HIV infection. Such models not only enable investigators to better understand HIV infection and AIDS but also provide them with a tool for initially testing antiviral agents and vaccines for biological activity and safety. Indeed, one of the key problems currently facing AIDS investigators is the lack of a suitable animal model.

Current animal models are based on animal viruses, which can be divided into four categories of increasing relevance to human HIV infection: (1) retroviruses such as feline leukemia virus and type D retrovirus that have no obvious, close relationship to HIV but that can induce chronic disease in cats and other animals with manifestations that include immunologic abnormalities; (2) lentiviruses such as maedi-visna virus, caprine arthritis-encephalitis virus, and equine infectious anemia virus, all of which induce disease in hoofed animals; (3) HIV-related viruses of Old World primates (i.e., simian immunodeficiency virus, or SIV); and (4) HIV infection of chimpanzees (Desrosiers and Letvin, 1987).

Some of the HIVs that infect humans can also infect some primates. Recent studies, for example, indicate that baboons can be infected with a human AIDS virus isolate, although the infection is transient (Letvin et al., 1987). In addition, both gibbons (Desrosiers, 1987) and rhesus macaques (Gardner and Luciw, 1987) can become persistently infected with HIV-1 and HIV-2, respectively. None of the animals in either of these studies developed a disease suggestive of AIDS, however, nor did any infected animal die.

Chimpanzees can also become persistently infected with HIV, although to date they show minimal clinical or laboratory evidence of disease. Studies with chimpanzees have also demonstrated the transmission of HIV from an infected chimpanzee to an uninfected animal. To try to induce disease in HIV-infected chimpanzees, researchers use various approaches including superinfecting the animal with the same or a different virus or suppressing its immune system (Fultz, 1987a,b). Another approach focuses on isolating a strain of HIV that may become modified when it is deliberately passed from one infected chimpanzee to another. Investigators plan to test whether using such a viral preparation to infect smaller nonhuman primates and rodents can lead to a suitable animal model.

The chimpanzee is now the animal of choice when HIV is used to challenge vaccinated animals to determine whether a vaccine provides safe, effective protection. Tests with chimpanzees are also being used to determine the number of different strains of HIV that must be included in a vaccine. Nevertheless, as discussed earlier in this chapter, experiments to date with vaccines in chimpanzees have failed to show that any vaccine candidate confers protection against HIV infection.

The use of SIV to infect Old World primates such as rhesus macaques results in an animal model that quickly develops an AIDS-like disease with a subsequent high death rate. As described earlier in this chapter, the protein products and the organization of the SIV genome generally resemble those of HIV. **The committee believes that SIV infection in macaques and the resulting disease are the best parallels at this time to human HIV infection and should be vigorously exploited.**

Studies of AIDS pathogenesis, the development of AIDS vaccines, and analyses of drug therapies will require tens of thousands of research animals (Weissman, 1988). The lack of adequate numbers of chimpanzees and other primates for AIDS-related research is a serious problem. Currently, there are only about 1,200 chimpanzees in biomedical research colonies in the United States; another 80 are kept in pharmaceutical industry colonies in the United States (Desrosiers and Letvin, 1987). Although approximately 300 of these animals are available for breeding, current reproductive predictions indicate an annual increase of only about 35 chimpanzees for research use.

Without significant increases in our understanding of primate reproduction and conservation, there will be inadequate numbers of these animals available for AIDS-related research. Furthermore, the unregulated use for medical research of chimpanzees shipped from countries in which the animals exist in the wild could lead to their extinction. Sufficient lead time and funding must also be provided for the production of macaques in large numbers (Desrosiers and Letvin, 1987).

The use of chimpanzees and other primates for AIDS research and, in particular, efforts to increase the available numbers of animals through breeding demand national-level coordination. Present programs for the conservation, population expansion, and optimal use of these animals appear inadequate (Gardner and Luciw, 1987). **The committee recommends that plans for breeding, conserving, and otherwise expanding the present stock of chimpanzees be examined. This expansion may require increased funding.** The committee is concerned that poorly designed studies will waste previously unexposed chimpanzees. The assistant secretary for health should ensure that this does not occur.

Small animals can also be used in HIV infection research and efforts to develop animal models for AIDS. A mouse model, for example, would be a crucial breakthrough in AIDS research, as laboratory mice are plentiful and well understood as research animals. In some studies, investigators have constructed transgenic mice by introducing DNA from other organisms (humans or viruses) into the genomes of individual mice, which then express the foreign genetic instructions. The gene encoding the CD4 molecule, the essential regulatory elements of HIV that control viral expression, and the entire HIV genome have each been used to produce transgenic mice. If such efforts are successful, the transgenic mouse model could be valuable for determining which agents influence the expression of discrete genetic regions of HIV (M. Martin, NIAID, personal communication, 1988).

In another model of HIV infection, researchers have transplanted all elements of the human blood-forming and immune systems into genetically immunodeficient mice. Investigators hope this mouse strain will prove susceptible to HIV infection and possibly to the development of AIDS (I. Weissman, Stanford University, personal communication, 1988).

Whatever its final form, the development of a small animal model for AIDS is of utmost importance. A completely analogous animal model of HIV-induced human disease, especially in a small, plentiful, and well-understood animal such as the mouse, would greatly enhance vaccine and drug development. If efforts to develop a small animal model are carried out under carefully regulated, safe laboratory conditions, the committee strongly supports further work in this area.

RESOURCES

Facilities

One of the major obstacles to further advances in research on HIV and AIDS remains the lack of adequate facilities—in particular, the shortage of laboratories that are equipped to handle HIV safely and of centers for housing and studying infected research animals. The paucity of such facilities is a problem in both the public and private sectors: it was estimated in the fall of 1987 that fewer than five pharmaceutical companies have containment facilities suitable for work with live HIV (IOM, 1987). Even some institutions that are generally in the forefront of research technology are underequipped for AIDS research (Weissman, 1988).

Similar problems are apparent at the various primate centers located throughout the United States. Despite the emergence of significant data on simian retroviruses and AIDS, actual funding for primate research decreased during the several years prior to 1986 (Weissman, 1988). Currently, five of the country's seven regional primate centers have active AIDS research programs, and the federal government has provided additional funding to these facilities for their AIDS activities. Yet the extent to which the centers can use these funds to further increase their research output is limited by available laboratory space and resources. A case in point is the small number of biological containment facilities that are currently available in the United States for macaques inoculated with hazardous viruses (e.g., SIV) (Desrosiers and Letvin, 1987).

In response to these needs, the federal government has authorized additional funds to be available beginning in 1988. About $24 million has been provided to the Division of Research Resources at the National Institutes of Health (NIH) to support infrastructure improvements at extramural research sites around the country and to purchase related equipment (letter from J. B. Wyngaarden, NIH, to T. Cooper, 1988). Of this amount, $2.8 million will be reserved for grants to the regional primate research centers for similar uses. Congress has also appropriated an additional $19 million to address NIH intramural facility needs. Plans are under way to use this money for renting office and off-campus laboratory space and for other improvements.

Yet despite these encouraging funding developments, the two congressional allocations for renovations and infrastructure improvements are only a modest beginning to the facility upgrading necessary for productive AIDS research. More funds are needed to develop high-containment facilities at existing labs, and money for new laboratory construction is still a critical need. Such facilities are by no means inexpensive. Office space for personnel is another essential underpinning of a successful research effort. Additional funds are also needed to provide housing for experimental animals such as large primates.

The committee recommends that the director of NIH, in consultation with research scientists from within and without the institutes, assess the need for and costs of new intramural and extramural facilities for AIDS research. This information should be forwarded to Congress for evaluation and subsequent action.

Reagent Distribution Center

To support AIDS research and provide the scientific community with the necessary biological materials for this work, NIAID has established the AIDS Research and Reference Reagent Program asking investigators to contribute appropriate materials that are needed for AIDS research. Reagents to be offered by the center include antisera, monoclonal antibodies, biological response modifiers, proteins derived from HIV and other related retroviruses, cellular proteins, bacterial and eukaryotic cell lines, HIV-related retroviruses, and other opportunistic infectious agents associated with HIV infections. The committee supports this development. Currently, however, the success of the reagent center depends entirely on voluntary participation. **The committee recommends that NIH stipulate that all investigators receiving NIH funds must make their AIDS-related reagents available to the distribution center, and thereby to all qualified investigators, after publication of their research.** Industry is also urged to participate after the establishment of any patent rights. The committee plans to review the experience of the NIAID AIDS Research and Reference Reagent Program after it has been in operation for 1 year.

Finally, **the committee supports the development by NIH, perhaps through the reagent program, of an HIV/SIV research "starter kit" that would enable qualified new investigators to begin research more easily.** The kit would contain sensitive cell lines, infectious virus, cloned DNAs, specific antibodies, and initial protocols for maintaining and infecting cell lines.

FUNDING FOR RESEARCH

Confronting AIDS recommended that federal appropriations for research on AIDS and HIV infection reach at least $1 billion annually by 1990. At the present rate of increase, it appears that this goal will be met. The 1988 NIH budget for AIDS research is $467.8 million, and the proposed 1989 budget is $587.6 million. The 1989 budget includes an additional $300 million (approximately) for AIDS research expenditures by CDC, HHS's Alcohol, Drug Abuse, and Mental Health Administration, and FDA.

The committee believes that when federal research expenditures for AIDS reach $1 billion annually, an assessment of the need for further increases should be made. It is important to ensure that other federal research programs are not penalized by a long-term disproportionate growth in the AIDS budget.

REFERENCES

Abrams, D., M. Gottlieb, M. Grieco, M. Speer, and S. Bernstein, eds. 1987. AmFAR Directory of Experimental Treatments for AIDS and ARC. Vol. 1. New York: Mary Ann Liebert, Inc.

Aldovini, A., C. Debouck, M. B. Feinberg, M. Rosenberg, S. K. Arya, and F. Wong-Staal. 1986. Synthesis of the complete *trans*-activation gene product of human T-lymphotropic virus type III in *Escherichia coli*: Demonstration of immunogenicity in vivo and expression in vitro. Proc. Natl. Acad. Sci. USA 83:6672–6676.

Alizon, M., S. Wain-Hobson, L. Montagnier, and P. Sonigo. 1986. Genetic variability of the AIDS virus: Nucleotide sequence analysis of two isolates from African patients. Cell 46:63–74.

Allan, J. S., J. E. Coligan, T.-H. Lee, M. F. McLane, P. J. Kanki, J. E. Groopman, and M. Essex. 1985. A new HTLV-III/LAV encoded antigen detected by antibodies from AIDS patients. Science 230:810–813.

Arya, S. K., C. Guo, S. F. Josephs, and F. Wong-Staal. 1985. *Trans*-activator gene of human T-lymphotropic virus type III (HTLV-III). Science 229:69–73.

Chakrabarti, L., M. Guyader, M. Alizon, M. D. Daniel, R. C. Desrosiers, P. Tiollais, and P. Sonigo. 1987. Sequence of simian immunodeficiency virus from macaques and its relationship to other human and simian retroviruses. Nature 328:543–547.

Clavel, F., D. Guétard, F. Brun-Vézinet, S. Chamaret, M.-A. Rey, M.-O. Santos-Ferreira, A. G. Laurent, C. Dauguet, C. Katlama, C. Rouzioux, D. Klatzmann, J.-L. Champalimaud, and L. Montagnier. 1986a. Isolation of a new human retrovirus from West African patients with AIDS. Science 233:343–346.

Clavel, F., M. Guyader, D. Guétard, M. Sallé, L. Montagnier, and M. Alizon. 1986b. Molecular cloning and polymorphism of the human immune deficiency virus type 2. Nature 324:691–695.

Clavel, F., K. Mansinho, S. Chamaret, D. Guétard, V. Favier, J. Nina, M.-O. Santos-Ferreira, J.-L. Champalimaud, and L. Montagnier. 1987. Human immunodeficiency virus type 2 infection associated with AIDS in West Africa. N. Engl. J. Med. 316:1180–1185.

Coffin, J. M. 1986. Genetic variation in AIDS viruses. Background paper. Committee on a National Strategy for AIDS, Washington, D.C.

Cooper, T. M. 1988. Treatment IND: Making investigational new drugs available to the desperately ill. Address at the American Medical Association-Food and Drug Administration Conference, Washington, D.C., February 17.

Cullen, B. R. 1986. *Trans*-activation of human immunodeficiency virus occurs via a bimodel mechanism. Cell 46:973–982.

Dalgleish, A. G., P. C. L. Beverley, P. R. Clapham, D. H. Crawford, M. F. Greaves, and R. A. Weiss. 1984. The CD4 (T4) antigen is an essential component of the receptor for the AIDS retrovirus. Nature 312:763–767.

Daniel, M. D., N. L. Letvin, N. W. King, M. Kannagi, P. K. Sehgal, R. D. Hunt, P. J. Kanki, M. Essex, and R. C. Desrosiers. 1985. Isolation of T-cell tropic HTLV-III-like retrovirus from macaques. Science 228:1201–1204.

Dayton, A. I., J. G. Sodroski, C. A. Rosen, W. C. Goh, and W. A. Haseltine. 1986. The *trans*-activator gene of the human T cell lymphotropic virus type III is required for replication. Cell 44:941–947.

Debouck, C., J. G. Gorniak, J. E. Strickler, T. D. Meek, B. W. Metcalf, and M. Rosenberg. 1988. Human immunodeficiency virus protease expressed in *Escherichia coli* exhibits autoprocessing and specific maturation of the gag precursor. Proc. Natl. Acad. Sci. USA 84:8903–8906.

Deen, K. C., J. S. McDougal, R. Inacker, G. Folena-Wasserman, J. Arthos, J. Rosenberg, P. J. Maddon, R. Axel, and R. W. Sweet. 1988. A soluble form of CD4 (T4) protein inhibits AIDS virus infection. Nature 331:82–84.

Desrosiers, R. C. 1987. Simian and feline models of AIDS. Paper presented at the Institute of Medicine Conference on the Development of Vaccines Against HIV Infection and AIDS, Washington, D.C., December 14–15.

Desrosiers, R. C., and N. L. Letvin. 1987. Animal models for acquired immunodeficiency syndrome. Rev. Infect. Dis. 9:438–446.

Feinberg, M. B., R. F. Jarrett, A. Aldovini, R. C. Gallo, and F. Wong-Staal. 1986. HTLV-III expression and production involve complex regulation at the levels of splicing and translation of viral RNA. Cell 46:807–817.

Fischl, M. A., D. D. Richman, M. H. Grieco, M. S. Gottlieb, P. A. Volberding, D. L. Laskin, J. M. Leedom, J. E. Groopman, D. Mildvan, R. T. Schooley, G. G. Jackson,

D. T. Durack, D. King, and the AZT Collaborative Working Group. 1987. The efficacy of azidothymidine (AZT) in the treatment of patients with AIDS and AIDS-related complex: A double-blind, placebo-controlled trial. N. Engl. J. Med. 317:185–191.

Fisher, A. G., M. B. Feinberg, S. F. Josephs, M. E. Harper, L. M. Marselle, G. Reyes, M. A. Gonda, A. Aldovini, C. Debouk, R. C. Gallo, and F. Wong-Staal. 1986a. The *trans*-activator gene of HTLV-III is essential for virus replication. Nature 320:367–371.

Fisher, A. G., L. Ratner, H. Mitsuya, L. M. Marselle, M. E. Harper, S. Broder, R. C. Gallo, and F. Wong-Staal. 1986b. Infectious mutants of HTLV-III with changes in the 3' region and markedly reduced cytopathic effects. Science 233:655–659.

Fisher, A. G., B. Ensoli, L. Ivanoff, M. Chamberlain, S. Petteway, L. Ratner, R. C. Gallo, and F. Wong-Staal. 1987. The *sor* gene of HIV-1 is required for efficient virus transmission in vitro. Science 237:888–893.

Fisher, R. A., J. M. Bertonis, W. Meier, V. A. Johnson, D. S. Costopoulos, T. Liu, R. Tizard, B. D. Walker, M. S. Hirsch, R. T. Schooley, and R. A. Flavell. 1988. HIV infection is blocked in vitro by recombinant soluble CD4. Nature 331:76–78.

Folks, T. M., J. Justement, A. Kinter, C. A. Dinarello, and A. S. Fauci. 1987. Cytokine-induced expression of HIV-1 in a chronically infected promonocyte cell line. Science 238:800–802.

Franchini, G., C. Gurgo, H.-G. Guo, R. C. Gallo, E. Collalti, K. A. Fargnoli, L. F. Hall, F. Wong-Staal, and M. S. Reitz, Jr. 1987. Sequence of simian immunodeficiency virus and its relationship to the human immunodeficiency viruses. Nature 328:539–543.

Francis, D. 1987. Current U.S. attempts at vaccine development. Paper presented at the Institute of Medicine Conference on the Development of Vaccines Against HIV Infection and AIDS, Washington, D.C., December 14–15.

Frankel, A. D., D. S. Bredt, and C. O. Pabo. 1988. Tat protein from human immunodeficiency virus forms a metal-linked dimer. Science 240:70–73.

Franza, B. R., S. F. Josephs, M. Z. Gilman, W. Ryan, and B. Clarkson. 1987. Characterization of cellular proteins recognizing the HIV enhancer using a microscale DNA-affinity precipitation assay. Nature 300:391–395.

Fultz, P. 1987a. Conspectus on primate models for AIDS. Correspondent paper. AIDS Activities Oversight Committee, Washington, D.C.

Fultz, P. 1987b. Responses of chimpanzees to HIV immunization. Paper presented at the Institute of Medicine Conference on the Development of Vaccines Against HIV Infection and AIDS, Washington, D.C., December 14–15.

Garcia, J. A., F. K. Wu, R. Mitsuyasu, and R. B. Gaynor. 1987. Interactions of cellular proteins involved in the transcriptional regulation of the human immunodeficiency virus. EMBO J. 6:3761–3770.

Gardner, M. B., and P. Luciw. 1987. Nonhuman primate models for AIDS. Correspondent paper. AIDS Activities Oversight Committee, Washington, D.C.

Gartner, S., P. Markovits, D. M. Markovitz, M. H. Kaplan, R. C. Gallo, and M. Popovic. 1986a. The role of mononuclear phagocytes in HTLV-III/LAV infection. Science 233:215–219.

Gartner, S., P. Markovits, D. M. Markovitz, R. F. Betts, and M. Popovic. 1986b. Virus isolation from and identification of HTLV-III/LAV-producing cells in brain tissue from a patient with AIDS. J. Am. Med. Assoc. 256:2365–2371.

Gonda, M. A., F. Wong-Staal, R. C. Gallo, J. E. Clements, O. Narayan, and R. V. Gilden. 1985. Sequence homology and morphologic similarity of HTLV-III and visna virus, a pathogenic lentivirus. Science 227:173–177.

Gonda, M. A., M. J. Braun, S. G. Carter, T. A. Kost, J. W. Bess, L. O. Arthur, and M. J. Van Der Maaten. 1987. Characterization and molecular cloning of a bovine lentivirus related to human immunodeficiency virus. Nature 330:388–391.

Gruters, R. A., J. J. Neefjes, M. Tersmette, R. E. Y. de Goede, A. Tulp, H. G. Huisman, F. Miedema, and H. L. Ploegh. 1987. Interference with HIV-induced syncytium formation and viral infectivity by inhibitors of trimming glucosidene. Nature 330:74–77.

Guyader, M., M. Emerman, P. Sonigo, F. Clavel, L. Montagnier, and M. Alizon. 1987. Genome organization and transactivation of the human immunodeficiency virus type 2. Nature 326:662–669.

Haase, A. T. 1986. Pathogenesis of lentivirus infections. Nature 322:130–136.

Hahn, B. H., G. M. Shaw, M. E. Taylor, R. R. Redfield, P. D. Markham, S. Z. Salahuddin, F. Wong-Staal, R. C. Gallo, E. S. Parks, and W. P. Parks. 1986. Genetic variation in HTLV-III/LAV over time in patients with AIDS or at risk for AIDS. Science 232:1548–1553.

Halstead, S. 1987. Immuno-enhancement of disease. Paper presented at the Institute of Medicine Conference on the Development of Vaccines Against HIV Infection and AIDS, Washington, D.C., December 14–15.

Harper, M. E., L. M. Marselle, R. C. Gallo, and F. Wong-Staal. 1986. Detection of lymphocytes expressing human T-lymphotropic virus type III in lymph nodes and peripheral blood from infected individuals by in situ hybridization. Proc. Natl. Acad. Sci. USA 83:772–776.

Hauber, J., and B. R. Cullen. 1988. Mutational analysis of the *trans*-activation-responsive region of the human immunodeficiency virus type I long terminal repeat. J. Virol. 62:673–679.

Hauber, J., A. Perkins, E. P. Heimer, and B. R. Cullen. 1987. Trans-activation of human immunodeficiency virus gene expression is mediated by nuclear events. Proc. Natl. Acad. Sci. USA 84:6364–6368.

Hirsch, V., N. Riedel, and J. I. Mullins. 1987. The genome organization of STLV-3 is similar to that of the AIDS virus except for a truncated transmembrane protein. Cell 49:307–319.

Ho, D. D., T. R. Rota, R. T. Schooley, J. C. Kaplan, J. D. Allan, J. E. Groopman, L. Resnick, D. Felsenstein, C. A. Andrews, and M. S. Hirsch. 1985. Isolation of HTLV-III from cerebrospinal fluid and neural tissues of patients with neurologic syndromes related to the acquired immunodeficiency syndrome. N. Engl. J. Med. 313:1493–1497.

Ho, D. D., T. R. Rota, and M. S. Hirsch. 1986. Infection of monocyte/macrophages by human T lymphotropic virus type III. J. Clin. Invest. 77:1712–1715.

Hoxie, J. A., B. S. Haggarty, J. L. Rackowski, N. Pillsbury, and J. A. Levy. 1985. Persistent noncytopathic infection of normal human T lymphocytes with AIDS-associated retrovirus. Science 229:1400–1402.

IOM (Institute of Medicine). 1987. An Agenda for AIDS Drug Development. Report of the Conference on Promoting Drug Development Against AIDS and HIV Infection. Washington, D.C.: National Academy Press.

IOM/NAS (Institute of Medicine/National Academy of Sciences). 1986. Future research needs. Pp. 177–259 in Confronting AIDS: Directions for Public Health, Health Care, and Research. Washington, D.C.: National Academy Press.

Jacks, T., M. D. Power, F. R. Masiarz, P. A. Luciw, P. J. Barr, and H. E. Varmus. 1988. Characterization of ribosomal frameshifting in HIV-1 *gag-pol* expression. Nature 331:280–283.

Jones, K. A., J. T. Kadonaga, P. A. Luciw, and R. Tjian. 1986. Activation of the AIDS retrovirus promoter by the cellular transcription factor, Sp1. Science 232:755–759.

Kan, N. C., G. Franchini, F. Wong-Staal, G. C. DuBois, W. G. Robey, J. A. Lautenberger, and T. S. Papas. 1986. Identification of HTLV-III/LAV *sor* gene product and detection of antibodies in human sera. Science 231:1553–1555.

Kanki, P. J., J. Alroy, and M. Essex. 1985. Isolation of T-lymphotropic retrovirus related to HTLV-III/LAV from wild-caught African green monkeys. Science 230:951–954.

Kanki, P. J., F. Barin, S. M'Boup, J. S. Allen, J. L. Romet-Lemonne, R. Marlink, M. F. McLane, T.-H. Lee, B. Arbeille, F. Denis, and M. Essex. 1986. New human T-lymphotropic retrovirus related to simian T-lymphotropic virus type III (STLV-III$_{AGM}$). Science 232:238–243.

Kanki, P. J., S. M'Boup, D. Ricard, F. Barin, F. Denis, C. Boye, L. Sangare, K. Travers, M. Albaum, R. Marlink, J.-L. Romet-Lemonne, and M. Essex. 1987. Human T-lymphotropic virus type 4 and the human immunodeficiency virus in West Africa. Science 236:827–831.

Kao, S.-Y., A. F. Calman, P. A. Luciw, and B. M. Peterlin. 1987. Anti-termination of transcription within the long terminal repeat of HIV-1 by *tat* gene product. Nature 330:489–493.

Kennedy, R. 1987. Correspondent paper (untitled). AIDS Activities Oversight Committee, Washington, D.C.

Klatzmann, D., E. Champagne, S. Chamaret, J. Gruest, D. Guétard, T. Hercend, J.-C. Gluckman, and L. Montagnier. 1984. T-lymphocyte T4 molecule behaves as the receptor for human retrovirus LAV. Nature 312:767–768.

Knight, D. M., F. A. Flomerfelt, and J. Ghrayeb. 1987. Expression of the art/trs protein of HIV and study of its role in viral envelope synthesis. Science 236:837–840.

Koenig, S., H. E. Gendelman, J. M. Orenstein, M. C. Dal Canto, G. H. Pezeshkpour, M. Yungbluth, F. Janotta, A. Aksamit, M. A. Martin, and A. S. Fauci. 1986. Detection of AIDS virus in macrophages in brain tissue from AIDS patients with encephalopathy. Science 233:1089–1093.

Koyanagi, Y., S. Miles, R. T. Mitsuyasu, J. E. Merrill, H. V. Vinters, and I. S. Y. Chen. 1987. Dual infection of the central nervous system by AIDS viruses with distinct cellular tropisms. Science 236:819–822.

Lasky, L. A., G. Nakamura, D. H. Smith, C. Fennie, C. Shimasaki, E. Patzer, P. Berman, T. Gregory, and D. J. Capon. 1987. Delineation of a region of the human immunodeficiency virus type 1 gp120 glycoprotein critical for interaction with the CD4 receptor. Cell 50:975–985.

Laurence, J., A. Saunders, and J. Kulkosky. 1987. Characterization and clinical association of antibody inhibitory to HIV reverse transcriptase activity. Science 235:1501–1504.

Lee, T. H., J. E. Coligan, J. S. Allan, M. F. McLane, J. E. Groopman, and M. Essex. 1985. A new HTLV-III/LAV protein encoded by a gene found in cytopathic retroviruses. Science 236:1546–1549.

Letvin, N. L., M. D. Daniel, P. K. Sehgal, J. M. Yetz, K. R. Solomon, M. Kannagh, D. K. Schmidt, D. P. Silva, L. Montagnier, and R. C. Desrosiers. 1987. Infection of baboons with human immunodeficiency virus-2 (HIV-2). J. Infect. Dis. 156:406–407.

Lifson, J. D., G. R. Reyes, M. S. McGrath, B. S. Stein, and E. G. Engleman. 1986a. AIDS retrovirus induced cytopathology: Giant cell formation and involvement of CD4 antigen. Science 232:1123–1127.

Lifson, J. D., M. B. Feinberg, G. R. Reyes, L. Rabin, B. Banapour, S. Chakrabarti, B. Moss, F. Wong-Staal, K. S. Steimer, and E. G. Engleman. 1986b. Induction of CD4-dependent cell fusion by the HTLV-III/LAV envelope glycoprotein. Nature 323:725–728.

Luciw, P. A., C. Cheng-Mayer, and J. A. Levy. 1987. Mutational analysis of the human immunodeficiency virus: The *orf-B* region down-regulates virus replication. Proc. Natl. Acad. Sci. USA 84:1434–1438.

Lyerly, H. K., T. J. Matthews, A. J. Langlois, D. P. Bolgonesi, and K. J. Weinhold. 1987. Human T-cell lymphotropic virus III$_B$ glycoprotein (gp120) bound to CD4 determinants on normal lymphocytes and expressed by infected cells serves as target for immune attack. Proc. Natl. Acad. Sci. USA 84:4601–4605.

Maddon, P. J., A. G. Dalgleish, J. S. McDougal, P. R. Clapham, R. A. Weiss, and R. Axel. 1986. The T4 gene encodes the AIDS virus receptor and is expressed in the immune system and the brain. Cell 47:333–348.

Matthews, T. J., K. J. Weinhold, H. K. Lyerly, A. J. Langlois, H. Wigzell, and D. P. Bolognesi. 1987. Interaction between the human T-cell lymphotropic virus type III$_B$ envelope glycoprotein gp120 and the surface antigen CD4: Role of carbohydrate in binding and cell fusion. Proc. Natl. Acad. Sci. USA 84:5424–5428.

McClure, M. O., M. Marsh, and R. A. Weiss. 1988. Human immunodeficiency virus infection of CD4-bearing cells occurs by a pH-independent mechanism. EMBO J. 7:513–518.

McCune, J. M., L. B. Rabin, M. B. Feinberg, M. Lieberman, J. C. Kosek, G. R. Reyes, and I. L. Weissman. 1988. Endoproteolytic cleavage of gp160 is required for the activation of human immunodeficiency virus. Cell 53:55–67.

McDougal, J. S. 1987. The immune response to HIV. Correspondent paper. AIDS Activities Oversight Committee, Washington, D.C.

Moreine, B. 1987. Adjuvants and presentation of antigens. Paper presented at the Institute of Medicine Conference on the Development of Vaccines Against HIV Infection and AIDS, Washington, D.C., December 14–15.

Muesing, M. A., D. H. Smith, C. D. Cabradilla, C. V. Benton, L. A. Lasky, and D. J. Capon. 1985. Nucleic acid structure and expression of the human AIDS/lymphadeno-pathy retrovirus. Nature 313:450–458.

Muesing, M. A., D. H. Smith, and D. J. Capon. 1987. Regulation of mRNA accumulation by a human immunodeficiency virus *trans*-activator protein. Cell 48:691–701.

Nara, P. 1988. Introductory remarks at the Public Health Service Workshop on AIDS Vaccines, Bethesda, Maryland, April 25.

Pederson, N. C., E. W. Ho, M. L. Brown, and J. K. Yamamoto. 1987. Isolation of a T-lymphotropic virus from domestic cats with an immunodeficiency-like syndrome. Science 235:790–793.

Peterlin, B. M., P. A. Luciw, P. J. Barr, and M. D. Walker. 1986. Elevated levels of mRNA can account for the trans-activation of human immunodeficiency virus. Proc. Natl. Acad. Sci. USA 83:9734–9738.

Plata, F., B. Autran, L. P. Martins, S. Wain-Hobson, M. Raphaël, C. Mayaud, M. Denis, J.-M. Guillon, and P. Debré. 1987. AIDS virus-specific cytotoxic T lymphocytes in lung disorders. Nature 328:348–351.

Ratner, L., W. Haseltine, R. Patarca, K. J. Livak, B. Starcich, S. F. Josephs, E. R. Doran, J. Antoni Rafalski, E. A. Whitehorn, K. Baumeister, L. Ivanoff, S. R. Petteway, M. L. Pearson, J. A. Lautenberger, T. S. Papas, J. Ghrayeb, N. T. Chang, R. C. Gallo, and F. Wong-Staal. 1985. Complete nucleotide sequence of the AIDS virus, HTLV-III. Nature 313:277–284.

Richman, D. D., M. A. Fischl, M. H. Grieco, M. S. Gottlieb, P. A. Volberding, O. L. Laskin, J. M. Leedom, J. E. Groopman, D. Mildvan, M. S. Hirsch, G. G. Jackson, D. T. Durack, S. Nusinoff-Lehrman, and the AZT Collaborative Working Group. 1987. The toxicity of azidothymidine (AZT) in the treatment of patients with AIDS and AIDS-related complex: A double-blind, placebo-controlled trial. N. Engl. J. Med. 317:192–197.

Robert-Guroff, M., M. Brown, and R. C. Gallo. 1985. HTLV-III-neutralizing antibodies in patients with AIDS and AIDS-related complex. Nature 316:72–74.

Rosen, C. A., J. G. Sodroski, and W. A. Haseltine. 1985. The location of *cis*-acting regulatory sequences in the human T cell lymphotropic virus type III (HTLV-III/LAV) long terminal repeat. Cell 41:813–823.

Rosen, C. A., J. G. Sodroski, W. C. Goh, A. I. Dayton, J. Lippke, and W. A. Haseltine. 1986. Post-transcriptional regulation accounts for the *trans*-activation of the human T-lymphotropic virus type III. Nature 319:555–559.

Rosen, C. A., E. Terwilliger, A. Dayton, J. G. Sodroski, and W. A. Haseltine. 1988. Intragenic cis-acting *art* gene-responsive sequences of the human immunodeficiency virus. Proc. Natl. Acad. Sci. USA 85:2071–2075.

Sadaie, M. R., T. Benter, and F. Wong-Staal. 1988. Site-directed mutagenesis of two trans-regulatory genes (*tat*-III, *trs*) of HIV-1. Science 239:910–913.

Salk, J. 1987. Prospects for the control of AIDS by immunizing seropositive individuals. Nature 327:473–476.

Sanchez-Pescador, R., M. D. Power, P. J. Barr, K. S. Steimer, M. M. Stempien, S. L. Brown-Shimer, W. W. Gee, A. Renard, A. Randolph, J. A. Levy, D. Dina, and P. A. Luciw. 1985. Nucleotide sequence and expression of an AIDS-associated retrovirus (ARV-2). Science 227:484–492.

Sattentau, Q. J., and R. A. Weiss. 1988. The CD4 antigen: Physiological ligand and HIV receptor. Cell 52:631–633.

Seligmann, M., A. J. Pinching, F. S. Rosen, J. L. Fahey, R. K. Khaitov, D. Klatzmann, S. Koenig, N. Luo, J. Ngu, G. Rietmuller, and T. J. Spira. 1987. Immunology of human immunodeficiency virus infection and the acquired immunodeficiency syndrome. Ann. Intern. Med. 107:234–242.

Shaw, G. M., M. E. Harper, B. H. Hahn, L. G. Epstein, D. C. Gajdusek, R. W. Price, B. A. Navia, C. K. Petito, C. J. O'Hara, J. E. Groopman, E.-S. Cho, J. M. Oleske, F. Wong-Staal, and R. C. Gallo. 1985. HTLV-III infection in brains of children and adults with AIDS encephalopathy. Science 227:177–182.

Shearer, G. 1987. Immune responses to HIV. Correspondent paper. AIDS Activities Oversight Committee, Washington, D.C.

Smith, D. H., R. A. Byrn, S. A. Marsters, T. Gregory, J. E. Groopman, and D. J. Capon. 1987. Blocking of HIV-1 infectivity by a soluble, secreted form of the CD4 antigen. Science 238:1704–1707.

Sodroski, J. G., C. A. Rosen, and W. A. Haseltine. 1984. *Trans*-acting transcriptional activation of the long terminal repeat of human T lymphotropic viruses in infected cells. Science 225:381–385.

Sodroski, J., W. C. Goh, C. Rosen, K. Campbell, and W. A. Haseltine. 1986a. Role of HTLV-III/LAV envelope in syncytium formation and cytopathicity. Nature 322:470–474.

Sodroski, J. G., W. C. Goh, C. Rosen, A. Dayton, E. Terwilliger, and W. Haseltine. 1986b. A second post-transcriptional *trans*-activator gene required for HTLV-III replication. Nature 321:412–417.

Somasundaran, M., and H. L. Robinson. 1987. A major mechanism of human immunodeficiency virus-induced cell killing does not involve cell fusion. J. Virol. 61:3114–3119.

Sonigo, P., M. Alizon, K. Staskus, D. Klatzmann, S. Cole, O. Danos, E. Retzel, P. Tiollais, A. Haase, and S. Wain-Hobson. 1985. Nucleotide sequence of the visna lentivirus: Relationship to the AIDS virus. Cell 42:369–382.

Starcich, B. R., B. H. Hahn, G. M. Shaw, P. D. McNeeley, S. Modrow, H. Wolf, E. S. Parks, W. P. Parks, S. F. Josephs, R. C. Gallo, and F. Wong-Staal. 1986. Identification and characterization of conserved and variable regions in the envelope gene of HTLV-III/LAV, the retrovirus of AIDS. Cell 45:637–648.

Stein, B. S., S. D. Gowda, J. D. Lifson, R. C. Penhallow, K. G. Bensch, and E. G. Engleman. 1987. pH-Independent HIV entry into CD4-positive T cells via virus envelope fusion to the plasma membrane. Cell 49:659–668.

Strebel, K., D. Daugherty, K. Clouse, D. Cohen, T. Folks, and M. A. Martin. 1987. The HIV "A" (*sor*) gene product is essential for virus infectivity. Nature 328:728–730.

Stricker, R. B., T. M. McHugh, D. J. Moody, W. J. W. Morrow, D. P. Stites, M. A. Shuman, and J. A. Levy. 1987. An AIDS-related cytotoxic autoantibody reacts with a specific antigen on stimulated CD4$^+$ T cells. Nature 327:710–713.

Traunecker, A., W. Luke, and K. Karjalainen. 1988. Soluble CD4 molecules neutralize human immunodeficiency virus type 1. Nature 331:84–86.

Wain-Hobson, S., P. Sonigo, O. Danos, S. Cole, and M. Alizon. 1985. Nucleotide sequence of the AIDS virus, LAV. Cell 40:9–17.

Walker, B. D., S. Chakrabarti, B. Moss, T. J. Paradis, T. Flynn, A. G. Durno, R. S. Blumberg, J. C. Kaplan, M. S. Hirsch, and R. T. Schooley. 1987. HIV-specific cytotoxic T lymphocytes in seropositive individuals. Nature 328:345–348.

Walker, B. D., C. Flexner, T. J. Paradis, T. C. Fuller, M. S. Hirsch, R. T. Schooley, and B. Moss. 1988. HIV-1 reverse transcriptase is a target for cytotoxic T lymphocytes in infected individuals. Science 240:64–66.

Weber, J. N., P. R. Clapham, R. A. Weiss, D. Parker, C. Roberts, J. Duncan, I. Weller, C. Carne, R. S. Tedder, A. J. Pinching, and R. Cheingsong-Popov. 1987. Human immuno-deficiency virus infection in two cohorts of homosexual men: Neutralizing sera and association of anti-*gag* antibody with prognosis. Lancet 1:119–122.

Weiss, R. A., P. R. Clapham, R. Cheingsong-Popov, A. G. Dalgleish, C. A. Carne, I. V. D. Weller, and R. S. Tedder. 1985. Neutralization of human T-lymphotropic virus type III by sera of AIDS and AIDS-risk patients. Nature 316:69–72.

Weissman, I. L. 1988. AIDS research funding. Report presented to the President's Commission on the Human Immunodeficiency Virus Epidemic, New York, February 18.

Wong-Staal, F., P. K. Chanda, and J. Ghrayeb. 1987. Human immunodeficiency virus: The eighth gene. AIDS Res. Hum. Retrovir. 3:33–39.

Wright, C. M., B. K. Felber, H. Paskalis, and G. N. Pavlakis. 1986. Expression and characterization of the *trans*-activator of HTLV-III/LAV virus. Science 234:988–992.

Yarchoan, K., and S. Broder. 1987. Development of antiretroviral therapy for the acquired immunodeficiency syndrome and related disorders: A progress report. N. Engl. J. Med. 316:557–564.

Yarchoan, K., G. Berg, P. Brouwers, M. A. Fischl, A. R. Spitzer, A. Wichman, J. Grafman, R. V. Thomas, B. Safai, A. Brunetti, C. F. Perno, P. J. Schmidt, S. M. Larson, C. E. Myers, and S. Broder. 1987. Response of human-immunodeficiency-virus-associated neurological disease to 3'-azido-3'-deoxythyminine. Lancet 1:132–135.

Young, F. E. 1987. Treatment use of experimental drugs. Address to the Council on Health Care Technology, Institute of Medicine, Washington, D.C., March 20.

Zagury, D., J. Bernard, R. Leonard, R. Cheynier, M. Feldman, P. S. Sarin, and R. C. Gallo. 1986. Long-term cultures of HTLV-III-infected cells: A model of cytopathology of T-cell depletion in AIDS. Science 231:850–853.

7

International Aspects of AIDS and HIV Infection

As of March 1988, 133 of the 158 countries or territories reporting to the World Health Organization (WHO) had listed one or more cases of AIDS. A total of more than 81,000 cases has been reported from countries on all continents. However, AIDS case reporting to WHO is incomplete. In the United States, for example, the reporting system is estimated to capture approximately 80 percent of AIDS cases, a proportion that probably applies to other industrialized nations. Countries whose reporting systems are less well established or nonexistent capture a much smaller percentage of cases. A further complication in data collection is the considerable lag in reporting in many countries. In light of these considerations, a more accurate estimate of the number of AIDS cases worldwide is at least 150,000 as of April 1988.

Because of the relatively long interval between infection and the appearance of AIDS, increasing reliance is being placed on seroepidemiology to assess the spread of the epidemic. On the basis of seroprevalence surveys or estimates that have been made in a wide variety of countries, WHO currently estimates that the number of infected persons worldwide is at the lower end of the earlier range of estimates, which was 5 to 10 million. Considering the data that have accumulated in the past 2 years, this estimate can now be viewed as much more reliable than it was when it was first offered in 1986.

Three different patterns of AIDS can be seen in the various countries, and although these patterns are necessarily generalizations, they nevertheless describe the worldwide epidemiology of the disease (Piot et al.,

1988). The first pattern, in which most AIDS cases have occurred among homosexual or bisexual men and urban IV drug abusers, is found in North America, many Western European countries, Australia, New Zealand, and parts of South America. In these areas, heterosexual transmission of the infection is responsible for only a small percentage of cases, but it is increasing, as is perinatal transmission. Transmission through HIV-contaminated blood and blood products has now been largely controlled by routine screening for HIV antibodies and a campaign to encourage persons with known risk factors to refrain from donating blood. The male-to-female ratio in countries with this pattern of AIDS cases ranges from 10:1 to 15:1. The prevalence of HIV infection in their overall populations is estimated to be less than 1 percent, but it has been reported to exceed 50 percent in some high-risk groups (e.g., homosexual men with multiple sexual partners who practice receptive anal intercourse, and IV drug abusers).

The second pattern applies to some areas of southern, central, and eastern Africa and some areas of the Caribbean, where most AIDS cases occur among heterosexuals and the male–female ratio is approximately 1:1. As a consequence, perinatal transmission is relatively common, but transmission through IV drug abuse and homosexual activity appears to be infrequent. In a number of these countries, it is estimated that the prevalence of HIV infection in the overall population is more than 1 percent; in some urban areas, the prevalence of infection may be as high as 15 percent in the young and early middle-aged population (15 to 40 years of age). Transmission of the infection through contaminated blood remains a significant problem in countries that have not yet begun nationwide blood screening, and the possibility of HIV transmission through the medical use of unsterilized needles and syringes or other skin-piercing instruments is thought to be substantial.

The third pattern is found in Eastern Europe, the eastern Mediterranean area, Asia, and most of the Pacific, where HIV appears to have been introduced in the early to mid-1980s and only small numbers of cases have been reported thus far. Both homosexual and heterosexual transmission paths have been documented in cases that, in general, have occurred in persons who traveled to or had sexual contact with persons from endemic areas. In these countries, some AIDS cases are also attributed to the use of imported blood or blood products. The prevalence of infection has not been estimated.

THE WHO GLOBAL PROGRAMME ON AIDS

The WHO Global Programme on AIDS has worked extensively during the past year in two general directions: (1) providing support to various national AIDS control and prevention programs and (2) conducting global AIDS-related activities such as surveillance; biomedical, social, behavioral, and epidemiological research; forecasting; and impact assessment. In addition, the Global Programme and the United Nations Development Programme (UNDP) recently concluded an agreement whereby UNDP country resident representatives will provide additional support to national AIDS control and prevention programs in accordance with the general scientific and technical strategies laid out by WHO.

To launch a global blood safety initiative, WHO has drawn together various organizations such as the International Society for Blood Transfusion, UNDP, the International League of Red Cross and Red Crescent Societies, and its own Global Programme on AIDS and Health Laboratory Technology Units. The blood safety initiative is intended to reduce the risks of transmission of HIV and other pathogens by establishing or strengthening blood transfusion systems in all countries. The goal is to establish a system in each country that is capable of employing quality control procedures, including screening, on a sustained, routine basis.

National AIDS committees have been established in over 150 countries; WHO has provided technical assistance to at least 115 of them. Of the countries to which WHO has given assistance, 78 have established short-term AIDS control and prevention programs and 22 have medium-term plans (3 to 5 years) in place. Nearly $30 million has been raised for these medium-term plans through meetings convened to elicit support from bilateral development funds and international agencies. In addition, WHO's Global Programme on AIDS has provided an amount approximately equal to that raised by national efforts thus far. WHO anticipates that two-thirds of the Global Programme's 1988 budget of $66 million will be spent on direct assistance to countries. More than 30 consensus meetings were held during 1987 by the program to provide guidance to national efforts in such areas as criteria for HIV screening and HIV in relation to breastfeeding and breastmilk, contraceptive methods, routine childhood immunizations, and HIV testing of international travelers.

RATIONALE FOR U.S. INTERNATIONAL INVOLVEMENT

The past year has seen an appreciable increase in information that confirms or strengthens the rationale for U.S. involvement in international AIDS activities. The rationale is threefold, involving foreign policy considerations, health improvement assistance issues, and opportunities for mutually beneficial research.

• *Foreign Policy Considerations*—Recent economic analyses conducted by the World Bank and others (Over et al., 1988) indicate that combating AIDS will impose a considerable economic burden on a large number of substantially affected countries. The adverse economic effects of AIDS are clearly unavoidable in certain countries of central, eastern, and southern Africa, and there is likewise a potential for significant economic impacts in those countries in which HIV infection is established or is becoming established in the heterosexual population (e.g., countries of the Caribbean and Latin America). In industrialized countries, the economic burden of AIDS will continue to be heavy in such high-risk groups as male homosexuals and IV drug abusers. For young and middle-aged adults in certain developing countries, it is estimated that, by 1991, AIDS-related deaths will double the mortality rates (from 500 to 1,000 deaths per 100,000 inhabitants). In addition to the toll exacted by the large numbers of casualties, the many deaths among young, highly educated urban dwellers who are normally very productive members of the society will exacerbate the disease's economic impact. The increase in AIDS-related deaths undoubtedly will adversely affect development in such countries, toward whose welfare the United States contributes.

• *Health Improvement Assistance*—It has become increasingly apparent during the last year that perinatal transmission of HIV has the potential to raise infant and child mortality to such a level that recent advances in child survival may well be reversed in some countries (Mann, 1988). Such reverses are particularly feared in those countries in which heterosexual transmission is the predominant mode of spreading the infection.

• *Opportunities for Mutually Beneficial Research*—As the epidemic spreads, the need for international collaboration in pursuing biomedical, epidemiological, and behavioral research opportunities in relation to AIDS becomes more apparent. Important research directions include aspects of perinatal and heterosexual transmission, as well as the influence of cofactors for the acquisition or progression of HIV infection and the pathogenicity of related viruses (e.g., HIV-2) that are not prevalent in the United States (see Chapter 6).

THE U.S. CONTRIBUTION TO INTERNATIONAL EFFORTS

The United States contributes to international AIDS activities through a variety of agencies. Specific international activities are part of the programs of CDC, various agencies of NIH (e.g., the National Institute of Allergy and Infectious Diseases, the National Cancer Institute, and the Fogarty International Center), and the Department of Defense. The U.S. Agency for International Development (USAID), part of the State Department, has provided considerable technical and financial support to the WHO Global Programme on AIDS. U.S. contributions to the WHO program totaled $1 million in 1986 and $5 million in 1987; they are anticipated to be $15 million in 1988. In addition, funds have been provided through USAID country missions in support of specific national AIDS efforts. Recently, a number of philanthropic foundations (e.g., the Rockefeller and Ford Foundations) have also begun to fund AIDS-related activities outside the United States or have indicated their intention to consider such support.

In addition to these contributions, however, the United States has a special responsibility in international health efforts to control AIDS because of our exceptional resources in public health specialists and biomedical scientists, the large number of infected persons in the United States, and our relative affluence. Cooperation with other countries should occur both through WHO and in bilateral arrangements, making full use of the expertise of the U.S. Public Health Service. Emphasis should be given to helping severely affected countries in central Africa implement educational efforts, test and counsel sexually active persons, conduct serologic screening of blood donors, eliminate inappropriate or unnecessary blood transfusions, improve indigenous epidemiological and surveillance capabilities, and prepare for consequent increases in the incidence of tuberculosis.

U.S. responsibility also extends to less direct aspects of support for AIDS prevention and control activities. WHO's Global Programme on AIDS is mainly funded by extrabudgetary monies, those contributed in addition to the regular assessed contributions of each nation. Yet the AIDS program is also supported, in a sense, by regular budget contributions to WHO in that the program interacts to a considerable extent with other WHO units—for example, the divisions of mental health and communicable diseases. The AIDS program also draws on the administrative structures of WHO as a whole. As of May 1988 the United States was in arrears on its regular WHO budget assessment—approximately $38 million for 1987 and $75 million for 1988. Although the United States has indicated its intention to honor those assessments, payment delays are having severely deleterious effects on WHO's capacity to support the Global Programme on AIDS. **The committee strongly urges that the United States pay its assessed contributions to WHO in total as soon as possible.**

Finally, U.S. commitment to the long-term support of international AIDS activities is essential. Although the future course of the AIDS epidemic is not known, the death toll thus far and its rate of increase identify the disease as a major global health problem that will require sustained international efforts in the search for a solution and substantial U.S. support of those efforts. Some predictions (Anderson et al., 1988) are that it may be at least several decades before the full effects of AIDS and HIV infection are seen, even in those countries in which the disease currently is most prevalent. Politicians and policymakers should plan now to provide a substantial increase in resources over the next few years, or perhaps over the next few decades, to be devoted to AIDS prevention and control. Funds will also be needed to ensure that today's predominantly educational methods for preventing HIV transmission can be supplemented with appropriate vaccines and drugs when and if they become available.

The committee is encouraged by the United States' response to the needs of the international campaign against AIDS and HIV infection. U.S. support at present is adequate to the requirements of well-planned programs; future support should be based on demonstrated needs. The committee urges policymakers to be sensitive to the public concern about the AIDS epidemic elsewhere in the world and its relevance to U.S. interests.

Effective planning for U.S. participation requires that we know the detail and extent of international AIDS research activities in which we are already engaged. The committee responsible for *Confronting AIDS* could find no such data base 2 years ago. The present committee has also failed to find such a source. These data are crucial to the coordination of U.S. endeavors worldwide. **The committee urges that a data base for international AIDS research activities be established and maintained.**

REFERENCES

Anderson, R. M., R. M. May, and A. R. McLean. 1988. Possible demographic consequences of AIDS in developing countries. Nature 332:228–234.

Mann, J. 1988. Global AIDS: Epidemiology, impact, projections, and the global strategy. Paper presented at the World Summit of Ministers of Health on Programs for AIDS Prevention, London, January 26–28.

Over, M., S. Bertozzi, J. Chin, B. N'Galy, and K. Nyamuryekung'e. 1988. The direct and indirect costs of HIV infection in developing countries: The cases of Zaire and Tanzania. Paper presented at the International Conference on the Global Impact of AIDS, London, March 8–10.

Piot, P., F. A. Plummer, F. S. Mhalu, J.-L. Lamboray, J. Chin, and J. M. Mann. 1988. AIDS: An international perspective. Science 239:573–579.

8

A National Commission on HIV Infection and AIDS

In *Confronting AIDS,* the IOM/NAS Committee on a National Strategy for AIDS highlighted deficiencies in the efforts being directed against the AIDS epidemic and in the use of the nation's resources in that task. The 1986 report also identified as a major concern a lack of cohesiveness and strategic planning throughout the national endeavor and recommended the creation of a national commission on AIDS.

In reviewing the events and progress of the last 20 months, the present committee considered the areas of public health, health care, and research. In addition, the committee carefully weighed the question of whether or not the IOM/NAS recommendation to establish a national commission on AIDS should be reaffirmed. In its deliberations, the committee evaluated the quality of leadership provided by various individuals and components of government. Some of those considerations are presented below.

The Presidential Commission on the Human Immunodeficiency Virus Epidemic was established in June 1987 and will conclude its work in June 1988. In the committee's view the commission has made major contributions to the public's understanding of HIV infection and AIDS and to the development of a compassionate and informed response to the epidemic. Guided by Admiral James D. Watkins's strong leadership and open-minded approach, the commission's focused attention has been effective in bringing diverse public and private resources to bear on a national problem. Yet the Presidential Commission's mandate, although well executed, was short term. A commission with a long-term mandate to

165

formulate and sustain a coherent national policy could capitalize on the momentum created by the current body.

The obligation to formulate AIDS policy spans a variety of federal government departments and touches, in addition to the Department of Health and Human Services, the Departments of Justice, Education, Defense, Energy, and other components of the executive branch. The HHS assistant secretary for health chairs the Federal Coordinating Committee on Information, Education, and Risk Reduction on AIDS, which is intended to coordinate the activities of HHS and other departments, agencies, and executive branch offices. In the committee's view, this body has operated to facilitate communication and coordinate activity rather than to set policy. The lack of guidance in federal policymaking is manifested by false starts and misguided efforts; some illustrations include interdepartmental disputes over the proper educational approach, the administration's advocacy of screening for certain low-risk populations, the failure to move rapidly to reduce the risk of HIV transmission among IV drug abusers, and the announcement by the military services in December 1987 that they would remove service personnel who tested positive for HIV antibodies from aircraft pilot duties and other sensitive positions (a policy that is now under review by the Department of Defense).

Within HHS, the Public Health Service Executive Task Force on AIDS, also under the direction of the assistant secretary for health, coordinates AIDS activities within the Public Health Service. (A new office, the National AIDS Program Office, has been proposed to replace and expand the task force.) At the NIH level, the new Office of AIDS Research will direct and coordinate AIDS research activities among the institutes. These efforts should streamline progress within the Public Health Service, but they are not meant to have the broader, overarching responsibility for setting national policy directions that the committee feels is lacking.

In the absence of strong federal leadership, a variety of private organizations, foundations, volunteer groups, professional organizations, and state and local governments have taken the initiative to create educational programs, formulate laws and regulations, and address other facets of the epidemic. These efforts are an enormous contribution to the progress that has been made thus far against AIDS and HIV infection; nevertheless, the absence of coherent national direction condemns many localities to "reinvent the wheel" when it comes to setting local policy and increases the likelihood that failed experiments will be repeated from place to place. Ill-conceived public policy (e.g., HIV antibody testing for marriage license applicants, described in Chapter 4) is doubly harmful: besides the damage that may be caused by the action itself, it redirects energies and resources that might have been better spent elsewhere.

Finally, the lack of a coherent national policy dooms areas unblessed with energetic private groups, generous foundations, or strong local governments to face heavy economic burdens.

These considerations helped to shape the committee's thinking in its review of various ways to achieve optimal federal direction of efforts to control the epidemic of HIV infection and AIDS. The committee considered a separate AIDS agency but concluded that such a body, cutting as it would across already well-established and effective agencies in many federal departments, would cause unnecessary disruptions. In light of the positive strides that have been made, the committee also considered whether the status quo is satisfactory. There have been many areas of progress: biomedical research, some improvements in public education evidenced by the recent all-household mailing planned by CDC and the continuing superb leadership of Surgeon General C. Everett Koop, improvements in the FDA drug approval process, and the ongoing CDC surveillance efforts. The committee has concluded, however, that the federal response has been too uneven. Where direction has been reasonable, the lack of forceful policymaking may have done little harm. But where public policy has been clearly inadequate—for instance, in the provision and financing of health care, in setting standards for antibody testing and antidiscrimination, in addressing IV substance abuse, and in furnishing overarching direction for all components of the government and the private sector—the nation has suffered from the absence of strong federal leadership.

The Institute of Medicine and the National Academy of Sciences are generally reluctant to recommend that a new government entity be established; however, in this case, the committee feels that such a body is needed to inform policy and provide sustained, coherent advice to the nation. In the past, the creation of a commission has achieved the successful resolution of difficult and important national issues, most notably in the case of the Social Security Commission. Furthermore, the nature of the epidemic is such that controversies will continue to arise, demanding an informed, timely response. Therefore, **the committee reaffirms the 1986 recommendation that a national commission on AIDS and HIV infection be established.** The commission would assume an advisory rather than an operating role and be responsible for:

• adopting as its scope a broad view of the epidemic that spans all components of the public and private sectors;
• monitoring the course of the epidemic;
• evaluating research, health care, and public health needs;
• formulating recommendations for altering the direction or intensity of health care, public health, and research efforts as the problem evolves;

- setting the tone for educational campaigns;
- assuming an advisory and catalytic role in stimulating appropriate action by federal, state, and local government bodies, industry, the academic scientific community, and private foundations and organizations;
  - encouraging greater U.S. contributions to international efforts;
  - monitoring and advising on related legal and ethical issues;
- reporting to the American public to clarify points of possible confusion such as the extent and danger of heterosexual spread or the effectiveness of condoms; and
  - providing a forum for all involved and interested parties.

To carry out these responsibilities, the commission must have certain attributes. It should:

- be endorsed at the highest levels of government—both by the President and Congress;
- have sufficient national and international stature and credibility for its advice to influence all participants in the struggle against AIDS; and
- be able to engage all of the diverse public and private resources that can be brought to bear on AIDS and its associated problems.

Considering these responsibilities and attributes, the committee proposes the establishment of a national commission on AIDS with a 5-year, renewable term. The commission chair should be a senior, recognized leader, engaged full time in this capacity and reporting directly to the President. In addition to the chair, the commission should consist of eight other members, each of whom is a senior expert of national stature in one of the areas of particular relevance to AIDS. Each commissioner should in turn head a panel of experts to explore such topics as research (biomedical, health care services, and social sciences), the provision and financing of health care, public health and education, epidemiology and modeling, law and ethics, and the United States' international role in combating AIDS. The commission should have ample professional staff and a sufficient budget. In addition, consideration should be given to establishing a $10 million discretionary fund that would be spent through existing agencies to allow quick responses to new, unforeseen opportunities.

The establishment of a national commission signals a major commitment to national leadership for preventing and controlling HIV infection and AIDS. Such a commission would move beyond the mere tracking of relevant AIDS activities and take the lead in setting clear policies for the nation. HIV infection is a rapidly moving target; a sustained, well-guided effort is needed if we are to remain attentive to its course and thwart its effects.

Appendixes

A

Summary and Recommendations from *Confronting AIDS: Directions for Public Health, Health Care, and Research*

STATUS OF THE EPIDEMIC

The first cases of the disease now known as acquired immune deficiency syndrome (AIDS) were identified in 1981. Since then the disease has become an epidemic—as of September 1986 more than 24,500 cases had been reported in the United States, and between 1 million and 1.5 million people in the United States probably are infected with the virus that causes AIDS. In the same five years, great progress has been made in understanding AIDS. Much is known about the virus that causes it, about the ways in which the virus is transmitted, about the acute and chronic manifestations of infection, and about its impact on society. Although this knowledge is incomplete, it is extensive enough to permit projections of a likely 10-fold increase in AIDS cases over the next five years, to provide a basis for planning the provision of health care, to guide policy decisions on public health, and to envisage strategies for drug and vaccine development.

Early in the epidemic the diversity of diseases observed in patients was explained by the discovery that the common thread was damage to the patient's immune system. For this reason patients succumb to infections with usually harmless microorganisms or to unusual cancers that individuals with normal immune systems are able to ward off. The damage to the immune system results primarily from the destruction of certain crucially important white blood cells known as T lymphocytes. The death of these blood cells is a consequence of their infection with human immunodefi-

Confronting AIDS: Directions for Public Health, Health Care, and Research. Copyright © 1986 by the National Academy of Sciences. National Academy Press, Washington, D.C.

ciency virus (HIV), also known as lymphadenopathy-associated virus (LAV), human T-cell lymphotropic virus type III (HTLV-III), and AIDS-associated retrovirus (ARV). The geographic and biologic origins of HIV are not clear, but there is little doubt that this is the first time in modern history that it has spread widely in the human population.

Infection and Transmission

A test has been developed to detect the presence in a person's blood of antibodies that specifically recognize HIV and that serve as a marker for viral infection. The virus can be isolated from most persons who test positive for the presence of these antibodies. Anyone who has antibodies to the virus must be assumed to be infected and probably capable of transmitting the virus. Use of the test has greatly improved the safety of the banked blood supply by enabling elimination of donated blood that tests positive.

A person infected with HIV may not show any clinical symptoms for months or even years but apparently never becomes free of the virus. This long, often unrecognized period of asymptomatic infection, during which an infected person can infect others, complicates control of the spread of the virus.

The virus spreads from infected persons either by anal or vaginal intercourse or by the introduction of infected blood (or blood products) through the skin and into the bloodstream, which may occur in intravenous (IV) drug use, blood transfusion, or treatment of hemophilia. In addition, it can spread from an infected mother to her infant during pregnancy or at the time of birth. Studies show no evidence that the infection is transmitted by so-called casual contact—that is, contact that can be even quite close between persons in the course of daily activities. Thus, there is no evidence that the virus is transmitted in the air, by sneezing, by shaking hands, by sharing a drinking glass, by insect bites, or by living in the same household with an AIDS sufferer or an HIV-infected person. Male-to-male transmission of virus during anal intercourse and male-to-female and female-to-male transmission during vaginal intercourse have been well documented, but the relative efficiency of various types of sexual transmission is not known.

The risk of infection with HIV is directly related to the frequency of exposure to the virus. Groups now at highest risk of infection are homosexual men, IV drug users, persons likely to have heterosexual intercourse with an infected person, and the fetuses or newborn infants of infected mothers. The risk of infection to recipients of blood or blood products is now greatly reduced, although persons in this group already infected may progress to disease.

Clinical Manifestations of the Disease

HIV infection can result in a wide range of adverse immunologic and clinical conditions. The opportunistic infections (those caused by micro-organisms that seldom cause disease in persons with normal defense mechanisms) and cancers resulting from immune deficiency are generally the most severe of these, but neurologic problems, such as dementia resulting from HIV infection of the brain, can also be disabling and ultimately fatal. Other clinical consequences of HIV infection include fevers, diarrhea, and swollen lymph nodes. Such cases, if not meeting the criteria for AIDS, are termed ARC (AIDS-related complex). It is not yet fully clear that asymptomatic HIV infection and ARC are stages of an irreversible progression to AIDS, but many investigators suspect this to be so.

The Public Health Service's Centers for Disease Control (CDC) has established a set of criteria to define cases of AIDS based on the presence of certain opportunistic infections and/or other conditions such as cancer. Opportunistic infections in AIDS patients are serious, difficult to treat, and often recurring. Among these infections, a type of pneumonia caused by a protozoan, *Pneumocystis carinii,* is the most common cause of death. Cures for any one of the host of opportunistic infections associated with AIDS, with the possible exception of *P. carinii* pneumonia, would not prolong survival much, because it is the HIV infection that causes the immune system damage and thus, ultimately, the death of AIDS patients. There have been no recorded cases of prolonged remissions of AIDS. Most patients die within two years of the appearance of clinical disease; few survive longer than three years.

Statistical Dimensions of the Epidemic

Because of the long symptom-free period between infection and clinical disease, HIV has spread unnoticed and widely in some population groups. Studies have shown that infection with the virus is far more common than is AIDS or ARC, and suggest that at least 25 to 50 percent of infected persons will progress to AIDS within 5 to 10 years of infection. The possibility that the percentage is higher cannot be ruled out.

As of September 1986, approximately 24,500 cases of AIDS had been reported to the Centers for Disease Control. The number of ARC cases—which is somewhat uncertain, depending on the definition adopted—is probably between 50,000 and 125,000. Among homosexual and bisexual men in some cities, as many as 70 percent may be infected. Substantial numbers of IV drug users also are infected, although precise figures are lacking.

HIV infection is a major and growing problem in some developed countries besides the United States, and it is nearing catastrophic proportions in certain developing countries, particularly in parts of sub-Saharan Africa. Worldwide, as many as 10 million persons may be infected.

There is no satisfactory treatment now for HIV infection. Prospects are not promising for at least five years and probably longer for a vaccine against HIV. One drug has recently shown benefits in the treatment of AIDS, but agents that are acceptably safe for possible long-term treatment and that effectively halt or cure the disease may also not be available for at least five years.

THE FUTURE COURSE OF THE EPIDEMIC

Estimates of the future course of the epidemic are important to the planning of health care, public health measures, and research. Following a June 1986 planning conference at Coolfont, Berkeley Springs, West Virginia, the Public Health Service (PHS) issued projections of the course of the epidemic through 1991. Among the most important PHS estimates are the following:

- By the end of 1991 there will have been a cumulative total of more than 270,000 cases of AIDS in the United States, with more than 74,000 of those occurring in 1991 alone.
- By the end of 1991 there will have been a cumulative total of more than 179,000 deaths from AIDS in the United States, with 54,000 of those occurring in 1991 alone.
- Because the typical time between infection with HIV and the development of clinical AIDS is four or more years, most of the persons who will develop AIDS between now and 1991 already are infected.
- The vast majority of AIDS cases will continue to come from the currently recognized high-risk groups.
- New AIDS cases in men and women acquired through heterosexual contact will increase from 1,100 in 1986 to almost 7,000 in 1991.
- Pediatric AIDS cases will increase almost 10-fold in the next five years, to more than 3,000 cumulative cases by the end of 1991.

Projections of the future incidence and prevalence of AIDS and HIV infection derived from empirical models such as those used by the PHS pose several difficulties, not the least of which is the assumption that past trends—such as the distribution of cases by age, sex, geographic location, and risk group—will not change with time.

Uncertainties notwithstanding, **the Institute of Medicine-National Academy of Sciences Committee on a National Strategy for AIDS believes** that the PHS estimates are reasonable, and the committee supports their use for planning purposes. This acceptance does not, however, obviate the need to acquire information that will facilitate the construction of better models that will lead to more reliable estimates. Data are needed on many aspects of the virus, its infectivity, the natural history and pathogenesis of disease, the size of the groups at risk, and the epidemiology of the epidemic.

The populations at highest risk for HIV infection in the near future will continue to be homosexual men and IV drug users. HIV infection will probably continue to spread in homosexual males, although possibly at a slower rate than in the past because of increased avoidance of anal intercourse and greater use of condoms. Continuing spread of HIV in IV drug users throughout the United States is also expected. Infected bisexual men and IV drug users of both sexes can transmit the virus to the broader heterosexual population where it can continue to spread, particularly among the most sexually active individuals. Although there is a broad spectrum of opinion on the likelihood of further spread of HIV infection in the heterosexual population, there is a strong consensus that the surveillance systems and studies presently in place have very limited ability to detect such spread. Better approaches to tracking this spread can be instituted, but general population surveys are probably neither practical nor ethical. **The committee believes** that over the next 5 to 10 years there will be substantially more cases of HIV infection in the heterosexual population and that these cases will occur predominantly among the population subgroups at risk for other sexually transmitted diseases.

In view of the numbers of people now infected, it is extremely unlikely that the rising incidence of AIDS will soon reverse itself. Disease and death resulting from HIV infection are likely to be increasing 5 to 10 years from now and probably into the next century. But the opportunity does exist to avert an increase in this burden by preventing the further spread of infection.

OPPORTUNITIES FOR ALTERING THE COURSE OF THE EPIDEMIC

Neither vaccines nor satisfactory drug therapies for HIV infection or AIDS are likely to be available in the near future, but actions can be taken now to reduce the further spread of HIV infection and thus to alter the course of the epidemic.

Public Education

For at least the next several years, the most effective measure for significantly reducing the spread of HIV infection is education of the public, especially those individuals at higher risk. (In fact, education will be a central preventive public health measure for this disease under any circumstances.) People must have information on ways to change their behavior and encouragement to protect themselves and others. "Education" in this context is not only the transfer of knowledge but has the added dimension of inducing, persuading, or otherwise motivating people to avoid the transmission of HIV. Education also is needed for those who are in a position to influence public opinion and for those who interact with infected persons. The present federal effort is woefully inadequate in terms of both the amount of educational material made available and its clear communication of intended messages. **The committee recommends** a major educational campaign to reduce the spread of HIV.

If an educational campaign is to change behavior that spreads HIV infection, its message must be as direct as possible. Educators must be prepared to specify that intercourse—anal or vaginal—with an infected or possibly-infected person and without the protection of a condom is very risky. They must be willing to use whatever vernacular is required for that message to be understood. Admonitions to avoid "intimate bodily contact" and the "exchange of bodily fluid" convey at best only a vague message.

In addition to knowing which sexual activities are risky, people also need reassurance that there are sexual practices that involve little or no risk. For example, unprotected sexual intercourse between individuals who have maintained a sexual relationship exclusively with each other for a period of years can be considered essentially free of risk for HIV transmission, assuming that other risk factors are absent. An integral aspect of an education campaign must be the wide dissemination of clear information about those behaviors that do not transmit the disease.

Condoms have been shown under laboratory conditions to obstruct passage of HIV. They should be much more widely available and more consistently used. Young people, early in their sexually active lives and thus less likely to have been infected with HIV, have the most protection to gain from the use of condoms.

Because in the United States the majority of AIDS patients are men, the implications of HIV infection in women have often been overlooked. Women need to know that if they are infected with HIV they may transmit the virus to their sexual partners and possibly to their future offspring. This message is particularly important for IV drug users and their sexual partners.

The most obvious targets for a campaign of education about AIDS are persons whose behavior puts them at special risk—for example, male homosexuals who practice anal intercourse without a condom. Education directed at this group could exploit the fact that although HIV infection prevalence higher than 50 percent occurs in male homosexuals in some urban centers, the much larger proportion of male homosexuals *not* infected outside these areas could protect themselves.

Many other groups, including health care professionals, public officials, and opinion makers, must receive education about AIDS. In addition, special educational efforts must be addressed to teenagers, who are often beginning sexual activity and also may experiment with illicit drugs. Sex education in the schools is no longer only advice about reproductive choice, but has now become advice about a life-or-death matter. Schools have an obligation to provide sex and health education, including facts about AIDS, in terms that teenagers can understand.

In planning the needed education programs for various groups, cultural traditions and practices should be taken into account, because blacks and Hispanics make up a disproportionately high percentage of AIDS cases. Because so many different groups must be educated in this campaign, its early activities must include the instruction of trainers suitable to each of the groups.

Not only must education about AIDS take many forms, but also it must have financial support from many sources. The most fundamental obligation for AIDS education rests with the federal government, which alone is in a position to develop and coordinate a massive campaign. **The committee recommends** consideration of the establishment of a new office or appointment that would be devoted exclusively to education for the prevention of HIV infection, possibly within the Office of the Assistant Secretary for Health. The office should be responsible for implementing and assessing a variety of innovative educational programs and for encouraging the involvement of state and local governments and private organizations.

The committee recognizes that the reluctance of governmental authorities to address issues of sexual behavior reflects a societal reticence regarding open discussions of these matters. However, the committee believes that governmental officials charged with protection of the public's health have a clear responsibility to provide leadership when the consequences of certain types of behavior have serious health outcomes.

If government agencies continue to be unable or unwilling to use direct, explicit terms in the detailed content of educational programs, contractual arrangements should be established with private organizations that are not subject to the same inhibitions.

A massive, coordinated educational program against HIV infection will not be cheap. Although there was an increase in funding by the federal government in Fiscal Year (FY) 1986 for such activities, many times the amount budgeted could be spent usefully.

The committee recommends that substantially increased educational and public awareness activities be supported not only by the government but also by foundations, by experts in advertising, by the information media, and by other private sector organizations that can effectively campaign for health. Legal and administrative barriers to the use of paid television for these educational purposes should be removed.

Preventing HIV Infection Among IV Drug Users

As a group, IV drug users have incurred the second-largest number of AIDS cases in the United States. IV drug users are also the primary source of heterosexual HIV transmission (via their sexual partners) and of perinatal transmission to newborn children. The large differences in the prevalence of HIV infection in IV drug users in different parts of the country is heartening, because it indicates an opportunity to halt the further spread of infection by changing behavior.

Preventing AIDS among the sexual partners of IV drug users may be a more difficult matter. The behavior changes required to prevent heterosexual and *in utero* transmission can entail disruption of sexual relationships and decisions to forgo having children. These behavior changes require intensive efforts with persons who are generally distrustful of authority and unlikely to be responsive to the mere dissemination of information. Sexual partners of IV drug users who do not themselves use drugs may also be difficult to reach, because they do not necessarily come in contact with treatment centers or with the criminal justice system.

There is no doubt that the best way of preventing HIV infection among IV drug users would be to stop the use of illicit IV drugs altogether. The United States' experience in curbing use of such drugs has not been wholly promising, however. The fear of AIDS will probably lead some IV drug users to seek treatment for their addictions. But in the United States as a whole, the availability of treatment for IV drug use was less than the demand even before the AIDS epidemic. Thus, a major possibility for reducing illicit IV drug use and the transmission of HIV is expansion of the system for treating IV drug use. Through treatment, users who have not been infected with HIV could greatly reduce their chances of being infected, and users who have already been infected would be less likely to infect others. At a purely economic level, treating AIDS costs from $50,000 to $150,000 per case, whereas drug abuse treatment costs as little as $3,000 per patient per year in nonresidential programs. **The committee believes** that more methadone and other treatment programs, detoxification programs, and testing and counseling services are needed.

In general, the life-styles and the frequent involvement of IV drug users in unlawful activity make it difficult to apply traditional public health measures in an effort to control the spread of infection in this population. It will not be possible to persuade all IV drug users to abandon drugs or to switch to noninjectable drugs. Many may wish to reduce their chances of exposure to HIV but will neither enter treatment nor refrain from all drug injection. Increasing the legal availability of hypodermic needles has received some support among public health officials but has generally been opposed by law enforcement officials, who predict that it would lead to greater IV drug use. However, if drugs are available and clean needles and syringes are not, IV drug users will probably use available unsterile equipment. **The committee concludes** that trials to provide easier access to sterile, disposable needles and syringes are warranted. Results of such trials should be measured both in incidence of HIV infection and in drug use.

Public Health Measures

The use of public health methods such as contact tracing is complicated in HIV infection by the frequently long lag between infection and identification of disease, the lack of satisfactory treatment for contacts, the impracticality of follow-up in some circumstances, and the potentially adverse social consequences for those identified (such as discrimination in housing or employment).

In 1983-1984, researchers discovered a way to culture the causative agent of AIDS and thus provided the basis for the HIV antibody test used to screen blood. Two years later, this test is used more than 20 million times a year, or about 80,000 times per working day. Although not 100 percent sensitive or specific, the test is at least as accurate as most serologic tests in routine use, and it has made the nation's blood supply much safer.

The use of the test remains controversial because of public perceptions about AIDS, the technical limitations of the test, and the sheer magnitude and diversity of the test's present and projected applications. Important questions about the use of the test relate to uncertainties over the long-term implications of positive results. As more data become available from longitudinal studies of the health of seropositive persons—those who test positive for HIV antibodies—the implications of a positive result will become clearer, and the significance of the test can be better explained to those tested.

Screening tests are of paramount importance in the context of blood, plasma, and tissue banking. The ability to screen blood rather than donors obviates some of the potential for discrimination arising with programs that depend on identifying individuals at risk. The small fraction of false-negative test results and the length of time between infection with the virus and the appearance of antibodies underscore the continuing need for those who have engaged in high-risk behaviors to refrain from donation. **The committee urges** that blood and plasma collection centers also establish administrative systems to further encourage self-deferral of donations and diversion of suspect blood to research while maintaining donor privacy.

Surveillance

Surveillance, which involves both the passive reporting and the active seeking of information, provides data on the prevalence, incidence, and distribution of disease or infection in the population. Such data can be used to monitor the spread of a disease, to shed light on the mechanisms of transmission of infectious agents, to help in designing public health measures to prevent the spread of a disease, to evaluate the effectiveness of interventions, and to guide planning for the provision of facilities. Data on HIV infection and related disease are critical to all aspects of coping with the epidemic.

All states require that AIDS cases be reported promptly to local and state health authorities, who then report the cases to the Centers for Disease Control. Unfortunately, anecdotal accounts suggest that the stigma associated with AIDS may have led to some underreporting of new cases and fatalities. Prompt reporting of individual AIDS cases, the disease's manifestations, the cause of death, and underlying risk factors is essential. **The committee supports** a vigorous program of early reporting of both AIDS and ARC cases (as soon as acceptable definitions for reporting ARC can be formulated) to local and state public health agencies under strict policies of confidentiality.

Surveillance of the general population for HIV infection presents ethical, logistic, and practical problems. Specific epidemiologic research is therefore needed to ascertain the spread of infection in certain populations, such as heterosexuals.

Mandatory Screening

Mandatory screening of the entire U.S. population for HIV infection would be impossible to justify now on either ethical or practical grounds. Mandatory screening of selected subgroups of the population—for example, homosexual males, IV drug users, prostitutes, prisoners, or pregnant women—raises serious problems of ethics and feasibility. People whose private behavior is illegal are not likely to comply with a mandatory screening program, even one backed by assurances of confidentiality. Mandatory screening based on sexual orientation would appear to discriminate against or to coerce entire groups without justification.

The committee is generally opposed to the mandatory screening now of population subgroups, but recognizes that arguments can be made for its application in the military.

Voluntary Testing

In the context of personal health services, the HIV antibody test enables a physician to identify an infected patient. But it should be the patient's decision to be tested, and only after being informed of the implications of a reaffirmed positive test and assured of strict confidentiality. The importance of confidentiality should perhaps be emphasized through the establishment of punitive measures against persons who make unauthorized disclosure of antibody test results.

Voluntary, confidential testing should be encouraged, because individual and aggregate antibody test results enable epidemiologists to assemble baseline data for longitudinal studies of the incidence, prevalence, and natural history of the disease. Such studies can be used to monitor the spread of the virus and to provide the data needed for changing control strategies.

Many persons in high-risk groups are already aware of the dangers their behavior poses to themselves or others. Yet screening programs possibly could identify many seropositive persons who had no reason to suspect they were at risk of infection—for instance, someone unaware of a sexual partner's infection or IV drug use. Persons who test positive in any circumstance have a right to know the results. No testing should be undertaken without adequate pre-test and post-test counseling. If situations arise in which the testing agency has no mandate to provide counseling—as by the military with applicants rejected because they test seropositive—counseling programs by third parties should be established.

The Role of Coercive Measures in Public Health Efforts

Proposals have been made to use coercive measures to control AIDS and HIV infection. Newspaper editorials and legislative bodies have discussed measures such as isolation and quarantine traditionally used to contain contagious disease. However, those diagnosed with AIDS do not usually pose great danger in the further spread of the epidemic. Rather, the greater danger lies with the hundreds of thousands of people who are already infected but asymptomatic. These individuals could not be identified without universal screening programs that would infringe on civil liberties in a manner unacceptable in this society.

The active voluntary cooperation of individuals who are at risk will be needed to curtail the epidemic. Coercive measures will not solicit this cooperation and could prevent it. Believing that coercive measures would not be effective in altering the course of the epidemic, **the committee recommends** that public health authorities use the least-restrictive measures commensurate with the goal of controlling the spread of infection.

Most state health authorities already have laws and regulations that could be applied in unusual situations, such as in the case of a seropositive person who refuses to obey reasonable public health directives. However, the public health statutes concerning infectious disease are outmoded in some states, may not afford civil rights protections adopted by the American courts, and should be reviewed accordingly.

Compulsory actions taken to deal with AIDS have largely affected closed populations, such as prisoners, psychiatric inpatients, and the institutionalized mentally retarded. The public authorities who administer these facilities have a legal obligation to care for residents by taking precautions to prevent the spread of diseases. However, although special precautions against the spread of HIV may be necessary in closed populations, coercive measures should be applied only as necessary for the protection of health. Such measures should not be regarded as models for compulsory programs among the general population.

Questions have previously arisen about admitting children with HIV infection to school classrooms. An accumulation of evidence about the transmission of the virus has now made it apparent that risk from contact with an infected child is negligible, and has made possible the establishment of guidelines for school attendance.

The committee recommends that, as a general policy, children with HIV infection be admitted to the same primary and secondary school classes they would attend if not infected. Guidelines published by the Centers for Disease Control are recommended for special circumstances.

Funding for Education and Other Public Health Measures

The committee did not attempt to work out in detail the cost of the education and other public health measures needed to stem the spread of HIV infection, but it estimated the general magnitude of the funds needed over the next few years. Resources are needed for education, serologic screening, surveillance, increased drug use treatment, and experiments designed to test the effects of greater availability of sterile needles and syringes to drug users. Present expenditures are inadequate.

Federal funds for AIDS education and other public health measures are appropriated to the Centers for Disease Control and also via that agency to states through a variety of arrangements, including cooperative agreements, contracts, and grants for activities such as establishing alternative serologic testing sites (independent of blood donation centers) and demonstration projects for risk-reduction education. The total funds allocated to the Centers for Disease Control for all AIDS education and public health measures are estimated to have been $64.9 million in FY 1986. The Public Health Service budget request to the U.S. Department of Health and Human Services for FY 1988 includes $68.8 million for all AIDS public health and education efforts within a total request of $471.1 million for AIDS-related activities.

Expenditures by states for AIDS-related prevention efforts have grown markedly in the last few years. For FY 1986-1987, a total of $65 million in state expenditures is projected. Five states (California, New York, Florida, New Jersey, and Massachusetts) account for 85 percent of the total spent since July 1, 1983 ($117.3 million), with California and New York jointly accounting for 66 percent.

If efforts to stop the spread of HIV infection are to be effective, they must start (or be expanded) immediately, not only in areas where there are reported AIDS cases but also in areas where there are few or no cases. Delaying such efforts until cases occur increases the likelihood that the problem of AIDS in those areas will subsequently be much greater. The opportunity to forestall the further spread of infection must not be lost.

Some examples illustrate the magnitude of funding needs:

- Testing at alternative test sites, including counseling, is estimated to cost $40 per person, and more than 10 million individuals may be candidates for testing.
- The most successful education programs to date (exemplified by the experience in San Francisco) have occurred within small geographic areas where there are educated homosexuals. Programs for other groups, such as IV drug users, will face more difficult problems of access and motivation; they will therefore probably require more resources per capita. In addition, large groups such as sexually active heterosexuals who have had a number of partners will need to be reached and motivated to adopt risk-reducing behaviors.
- Newspaper, radio, and particularly television advertising are influential means of communicating information, but the use of these media is expensive. One page of advertising in a major newspaper can cost around $25,000 per day, and a minute of national television time can cost between $60,000 and $400,000. Consequently, to influence the behaviors affecting HIV transmission, policymakers must begin to contemplate expenditures similar to those made by private sector companies to influence behaviors—for instance, $30 million to introduce a new camera, or $50 million to $60 million to advertise a new detergent. Furthermore, advertising

campaigns are judged successful even when they produce relatively modest shifts in behavior. The efforts needed to influence the behaviors that spread HIV will have to be greater and more sustained.

California has moved earlier than most states to provide funds for AIDS prevention, undoubtedly because the need for such actions has been reinforced by the occurrence of large numbers of AIDS cases. (It is hoped that other states will not delay launching prevention efforts until they have the same stimulus.) Current annual state expenditures for AIDS prevention efforts in California average 65 cents per capita, and in San Francisco such expenditures approximate $5 per capita. Extrapolated on a population basis for the entire United States, these figures would amount to state expenditures nationwide of approximately $150 million and $1 billion, respectively. The committee believes that the desirable level of state expenditures probably falls between these two figures. It bases this conclusion on the fact that, although San Francisco has a sizable concentration of homosexual men, this group does not unduly bias the California population as a whole. In addition, the need for active prevention of spread among heterosexuals is only now becoming recognized, and efforts need to be directed to this group. The risk to heterosexuals is greater in areas of high prevalence, but prevention efforts will need to be relatively uniform nationwide.

The committee also believes that expenditures just from the states of the size mentioned above will be inadequate for a number of reasons. For one, the effectiveness of the educational message will be reinforced if it is delivered from a variety of agencies in a variety of settings. Thus, federal efforts should complement those of the states, which in turn should complement the local efforts of employers and private groups. Funds should be provided for these efforts at each level.

For these reasons, **the committee believes** that a necessary goal is a total national expenditure based on per capita prevention expenditures roughly similar to those made in San Francisco by the state of California. This suggests the need for approximately $1 billion annually for education and other public health expenditures by 1990. A major portion of this total should come from federal sources, because only national agencies are in position to launch coordinated efforts commensurate with the potential size of the problem.

The process of designing and implementing educational interventions to reduce the risk of HIV transmission, followed by evaluations of their effectiveness, will enable policymakers to evaluate over the next year or two the magnitude of effort needed to bring about a drastic reduction in the spread of HIV infection. It is possible that the amounts envisaged by the committee will not be sufficient to stem increases in the prevalence of infection, especially since some of the groups at risk are difficult to reach with conventional approaches and since, despite the expenditures noted above, the infection continues to spread in areas such as San Francisco, though at a reduced rate. More funding for prevention measures will be necessary if those projected here for 1990 do not prove sufficiently great to slow the epidemic.

Discrimination and AIDS

The stigma associated with AIDS has led to instances of discrimination in employment, housing, and access to social services. Sometimes AIDS or ARC sufferers are discriminated against by those who misunderstand the modes of transmission and fear infection from mere casual contact. Improved public awareness resulting from educational efforts may decrease this problem. In other instances, discrimination is rooted in prejudices against the behavior of those presently most at risk for AIDS or HIV infection.

The committee is of the opinion that discriminating against those with AIDS or HIV infection because of any health risk they may pose to others in the workplace or in housing is not justified and should not be tolerated. Laws prohibiting discrimination in employment and housing are encouraged and supported as formal expressions of public policy. Any form of discrimination against groups at high risk for AIDS should be prohibited by state legislation and, where appropriate, by federal laws and regulations. Participation by representatives of high-risk groups in policymaking bodies should be encouraged when appropriate and practicable, and the help of organizations representing high-risk groups should be enlisted for public service programs such as health education, personal counseling, and hospital and home treatment services.

CARE OF PERSONS INFECTED WITH HIV

The provision of care for persons with AIDS or other HIV-related conditions will place an increasing burden on the health care system of the United States for years to come. Based on experience to date, **the committee believes** that if the care of these patients is to be both comprehensive and cost-effective, it must be conducted as much as possible in the community, with hospitalization only when necessary. The various requirements for the care of patients with asymptomatic HIV infection, ARC, or AIDS (i.e., community-based care, outpatient care, hospitalization) should be carefully coordinated.

AIDS patients need an array of services that can prove difficult for hospitals to accommodate if they have not organized for the task. **The committee recommends** that, for provision of hospital inpatient care, AIDS units or teams should be established in high-incidence areas, with a nursing and psychosocial support staff trained in AIDS care and integrated with outpatient and community-based staff. Furthermore, for high-incidence areas, where HIV infection puts the greatest logistic and financial stress on health care systems, the development of multidisciplinary outpatient clinics dedicated to treating AIDS and other HIV-related conditions should be considered.

Systems of community-based care should be able to provide these patients with attendant or homemaking services up to 24 hours daily, as needed; nursing staff able to provide necessary specialized medical intervention; and social support, including small-group housing. The use of volunteer groups to assist in patient care and counseling should be encouraged. Also, representatives of existing agencies and health care providers should organize AIDS care groups to coordinate efforts toward community-based care.

Special systems of care may be required to meet the particular needs of certain AIDS patients, such as IV drug users.

All physicians should be alerted to the signs and symptoms of HIV infection; opportunities to train in the care of HIV-infected patients should be provided to physicians less familiar with the disease; and medical education programs should include academic and practical training related to HIV infection and disease.

Many AIDS patients, being young, have not previously considered the reality of severe illness and death. Therefore, it is important that psychiatric care and psychosocial support be provided to patients with AIDS and ARC, to individuals infected with HIV but asymptomatic, to members of risk groups, and to health care providers for these persons.

Various ethical issues pertain to HIV-related disease: society has an ethical obligation to provide an adequate level of health care to all of its members, and health professionals have an ethical obligation to care for all persons infected with HIV. Additionally, persons who may be infected have ethical obligations to protect others from possible infection. They may do this by avoiding unprotected sexual intercourse and by not sharing needles; by refraining from donating blood, sperm, or other tissues or organs; and by notifying care providers of their status so that recommended precautions against the spread of infection can be used during treatment.

Implicit in society's obligation to provide appropriate care for persons infected with HIV is the responsibility to ascertain and respect patients' wishes about terminal care. This obligation extends to the provision of a variety of settings such as hospices in which AIDS patients can spend their final days.

Health Care Costs Resulting from HIV Infection

The direct health care costs resulting from HIV infection include those for pre-test and post-test counseling associated with serologic testing, detection and confirmation of infection by serologic testing, monitoring of asymptomatic infected individuals, and treatment of the broad range of HIV-associated conditions.

Most studies to date have focused on the direct health care costs for AIDS patients arising from care in and out of the hospital. As estimated by these studies, the average total costs for inpatient care from the time of diagnosis until death range from about $50,000 to $150,000. The difference in the figures derives largely from differences in the numbers of hospital days used.

Several factors—including hospital readmission, length of stay, and type of care—have been identified as making the costs of treating AIDS patients higher than those for treating other patients. These costs also vary with the type of AIDS patient—IV drug user, homosexual male, infant—because the disease manifestations can differ accordingly.

The Public Health Service has estimated that the direct cost of care for the 174,000 AIDS patients projected to be alive during the year 1991 will be $8 billion to $16 billion in that year alone. Because this estimate does not include the care of ARC patients and seropositive individuals, and because it does not take into account the costs associated with experimental therapies or lengthened survival times, it significantly underestimates the total annual direct costs for HIV infection in that year.

The costs for care of ARC patients and seropositive persons—of whom there are many more than there are AIDS patients—also need consideration. These patients will incur costs for a longer period of time, and care for HIV-related conditions such as dementia is extremely costly. The committee found no attempts to estimate the future magnitude of the direct health care costs associated with ARC patients and seropositive individuals, but believes they will be substantial.

There are also large *indirect* costs associated with HIV-related conditions including AIDS. Some of these indirect costs are the loss of wages for sick persons, the loss of future earnings for persons who are permanently incapacitated or die because of illness, and the cost of infection control in the course of other health services, such as dental care.

For urban areas handling a large number of AIDS cases, the strain on available resources will be especially great. Large numbers of infected IV drug users in certain cities will seriously encumber their municipal hospital facilities. In New York City, AIDS patients who are IV drug users may occupy more than 10 percent of municipal hospital beds by 1991.

Having studied the projected course of the epidemic and its implications for health care costs, **the committee believes** that more information must be gathered on all aspects of the costs of care for persons with HIV-related conditions, especially AIDS. Such data should permit calculation of the direct lifetime health care costs resulting from HIV infection and the indirect costs associated with the disease. It is essential to determine which are the most cost-effective approaches to providing care for patients with AIDS and other HIV-related conditions. Thus, **the committee recommends** that all demonstration projects be designed to facilitate comparison of patients, their health outcomes (e.g., longevity, quality of life), the effectiveness of care, and the costs associated with its provision.

The Financing of Health Care for HIV-Related Conditions

The financing of care for patients with AIDS and other HIV-related illness now depends on the same variety of public and private plans that apply to patients with other diseases. Most of the public funds for care of AIDS patients come through the Medicaid program, which is estimated to cover about 40 percent of such patients. Medicare serves only a small percentage of AIDS patients, because its two-year time-to-eligibility for individuals below the age of 65 is longer than the remaining life of most AIDS victims (although this may change if survival increases). Private plans cover a substantial proportion of AIDS patient care, as would be expected from the fact that at least 85 percent of Americans have health insurance, much of it through their jobs.

Despite the fact that most Americans have health insurance, an estimated 80 million have inadequate coverage or none, mostly because they have no jobs, they have no fringe benefits in their jobs, or they are poor health risks. Their plight is indicative of many shortcomings in health care financing, most of which are underscored in the case of HIV-related conditions. In addition, AIDS poses such potentially large expenditures for care that some insurance companies and employers are already wary of offering coverage or employment to persons at high risk of exposure to HIV.

The committee believes that all persons with AIDS or other HIV-related conditions are entitled to adequate care and that mechanisms equitable both to recipients and to providers should be found for financing this care. It is preferable that solution of the problems arising from the financing of care for AIDS and other HIV-related conditions be achieved within a mechanism that ameliorates problems existing in general for the financing of care for other serious illnesses. Measures could include national health insurance for catastrophic illnesses or state-based pools for persons medically at high risk.

The Public Health Service has proposed the establishment of a commission to evaluate the problems of financing the costs of care associated with HIV-related conditions. Finding the optimal mechanism for financing the care of HIV-infected patients, especially those not now covered, should become the first order of business of such a commission.

FUTURE RESEARCH NEEDS

Basic Research

Since the identification of HIV as the cause of AIDS, analyses of the virus have characterized its entire genetic structure and have enabled the identification of many, if not all, of its genes. At the same time, increased knowledge of how the virus is transmitted has helped in the design of public health and education programs. Such insights, however, provide only the first milestone on what promises to be a long and difficult path toward effective therapy to minimize the effects of HIV infection and toward vaccines to limit the spread of the virus.

Developing an effective vaccine or acceptable drugs will depend on a better understanding of the basic biological processes and consequences of HIV infection. The characteristics of viral proteins and their interactions with cellular proteins and processes must be determined. And the design of strategies to prevent the clinical manifestations of HIV infection will require a greatly improved understanding of the normal functioning of the human immune system.

The same types of basic research that have generated the progress of the past few years can also be expected to yield valuable insights into ways to limit the establishment and progression of HIV infection. Thus, basic research in virology and immunology should be considered an important part of the AIDS research effort and should be fortified in the years ahead.

The Natural History of HIV Infection

Much remains to be learned about the natural history of HIV infection—how the virus establishes and maintains infection and how it leads to the immunologic deficits and pathologic consequences associated with ARC and AIDS. For instance, it is not known what factors activate the provirus; what influences the ability to isolate the virus from an infected person; whether the virus is transmitted as free virus, as cell-associated virus, or in both forms; or what proportion of infected individuals will become sick. In the study of HIV infections in human beings, there should be a greater emphasis on defining the introduction and spread of HIV *in vivo*, on identifying the *in vivo* reservoirs of infected cells, and on studying the effects of HIV on the immune and central nervous systems throughout the course of infection.

In addition, drug development efforts, epidemiologic studies, and public health measures all require more comprehensive immunologic and virologic analyses than are presently available. Such analyses could resolve questions about the efficiency with which infected persons infect others, the existence and extent of a virus-positive but antibody-negative population, the relevance of host or environmental cofactors in the development of AIDS, and the efficiency of heterosexual transmission.

Epidemiologic Approaches

Since AIDS was first identified in 1981, much has been learned from epidemiologic research about how HIV is transmitted and about how the virus affects people who are infected with it. But more must be discovered. For instance, epidemiologic studies could provide much of the information needed to fashion improved models of the future course of the epidemic.

Reporting of AIDS should be continued and augmented by the selective reporting of other stages of HIV infection. In addition, active surveillance is needed of groups of particular epidemiologic importance, such as heterosexuals and non-IV drug users in high-incidence areas, IV drug users and homosexual men in low-incidence cities, spouses of infected individuals, pregnant women, newborn children of infected mothers, prostitutes throughout the country, and recipients of blood products. Better information is also needed to quantify the number of persons infected with HIV.

Epidemiologic studies of the immunologic effects and pathologic manifestations of HIV infection can contribute to knowledge of the natural history of infection. Prospective cohort studies should be continued and expanded, and studies should be undertaken to determine differences in the characteristics of infection and disease among different populations.

Natural history and epidemiologic studies would be facilitated by better tests for antibodies to HIV and by simpler, quantitative ways of detecting virus. Tests for both virus antigen and infectious particles are necessary. In addition, viral isolation procedures need to be refined so that a standard is available for evaluating other techniques.

Animal Models

Animal models that reproduce or mimic the consequences of HIV infection in human beings can play a crucial role in improving the understanding of disease pathogenesis and in the development and testing of antiviral drugs and vaccines. However, no completely analogous animal model for HIV infection and disease is now available.

The most relevant and promising animal models are provided by nonhuman primates. Therefore, the nation's primate centers should be improved to permit the expansion of the primate populations available for AIDS-related research, the development of appropriate biocontainment facilities, and the education of appropriately trained investigators.

The committee believes that available supplies of test animals, especially chimpanzees, will be insufficient for future research needs, and that the plans for the conservation, expansion, and optimal use of these animals appear inadequate. Populations of primate models need to be expanded as rapidly as possible to meet the future needs of research and testing. Furthermore, a national system should be set up to facilitate appropriate access to test animals for valid experimentation by qualified investigators, regardless of institutional affiliation.

Chimpanzees in particular must be treated as an endangered national resource that will be irreplaceable if squandered. Thus, mechanisms should be developed to ensure that AIDS-related experiments with chimpanzees proceed only if there is a broad consensus among the interested scientific community that the proposed experiment is critically important to the development of vaccines or antiviral agents and cannot be conducted in any other species or by any other means.

Antiviral Agents

The development of acceptably safe and effective antiviral agents for the treatment of HIV infection is likely to be a long, hard job with no certainty of success. The ideal AIDS drug must fulfill a number of requirements: it must be conveniently administered, preferably orally; it must be sufficiently nontoxic to be used for prolonged periods, perhaps for a lifetime; and it must be active not only in peripheral immune system cells but in the central nervous system, because HIV may infect the nervous system early in the disease process. Several drugs are under clinical evaluation, but thus far no drug meeting these criteria has been identified.

Until an agent effective against HIV and reasonably safe for prolonged administration is identified, the committee believes that the quickest, most efficient, and least-biased way to identify and validate the efficacy and safety of treatments for HIV infection is by means of randomized clinical trials in which control groups receive a placebo. When an effective and acceptably safe agent is found, newer candidate drugs should be compared against it.

Shortly before the publication of this report, data were released by the National Institutes of Health and the Burroughs Wellcome Company from a study of azidothymidine (AZT) administered for 20 weeks to a group of approximately 140 AIDS patients while a similar group received a placebo. The patients were selected for having had no more than one bout of *Pneumocystis carinii* pneumonia. There was 1 death in the AZT group compared with 16 deaths in the placebo group. Because of the time at which this information became available, the committee was not able to analyze the data from this study in enough detail to judge the risks and benefits of this drug. Further evaluation will be needed to fully determine the side effects of AZT treatment and its long-term efficacy and safety for various categories of patients.

Decisions on the design of studies to test new drugs for HIV infection must be made on a case-by-case basis. Such decisions should take into account the results of further studies on the efficacy and toxicity of AZT, the category of patients to whom the drug under consideration would be given, and preliminary information on the safety and efficacy of the drug.

It is essential that mechanisms for the efficient testing of candidate drugs be established. Efforts should be undertaken now to ensure that organizational and financial support will be sufficient to permit the expeditious evaluation of promising therapeutic agents for HIV infection.

Success in the development of antiviral agents will be much more likely if the expertise resident in the industrial, governmental, and academic research communities can be engaged and coordinated.

Vaccines

The development of a vaccine against viruses like HIV has never been seriously attempted, much less achieved. Except for a vaccine used in cats, no vaccine against such viruses is available. The properties of viruses related to HIV suggest that developing a vaccine will be difficult. It is also likely that a subunit vaccine, rather than a whole-virus vaccine, will be needed, and these have additional problems of efficacy. Moreover, even if the scientific obstacles were surmounted, legal, social, and ethical factors could delay or limit the availability of a vaccine. For these reasons, the committee does not believe that a vaccine is likely to be developed for at least five years and probably longer.

Because HIV attacks the immune system itself, a successful vaccine development program will require a greatly expanded knowledge base.

The urgency of the problem calls for the active and cooperative participation of scientists in government, academia, and industrial laboratories.

Much of the expertise in vaccine development is in the industrial sector. However, contributions of industry to the development of an HIV vaccine are inhibited by the substantial developmental costs in the absence of a significant probability of financial return and by apprehension over potential liability incurred in the course of vaccine distribution. Creative options for the governmental support of industrial research, guarantees of vaccine purchase, and the assumption of reasonable liability should, therefore, be actively explored and encouraged.

The committee finds that the federal coordination of vaccine development has been inadequate. The National Institutes of Health has recently reorganized its efforts on AIDS, and **the committee encourages** the appointment of strong leadership to the vaccine program with the authority and responsibility to develop a strategy for a broad-ranging vaccine development program.

Social Science Research Needs

Social science research can help develop effective education programs to encourage changes in behavior that will break the chain of HIV transmission. It can contribute to the design of policies that reduce the public's fear of AIDS and that help eliminate discriminatory practices toward AIDS patients. And it can shape the establishment of health care and social services for AIDS patients.

A major research need is for studies that will improve understanding of all aspects of sexual behavior and drug use and the factors that influence them. There has been little social science research specifically focusing on HIV infection and AIDS. Demographic features and social dynamics related to HIV infection should be thoroughly studied in order to develop effective means to reach people at risk, to delineate the obstacles to behavioral change, and to determine effective language and styles of communication among various population groups.

Different approaches to achieving behavioral change in the various groups at risk of HIV infection should be monitored. Wherever feasible, educational programs should have an evaluation component.

Treatment, social service programs, and hospital management practices should be assessed to determine which practices work best and are most cost-effective. Experiments based on different models of patient care should be evaluated with regard to their applicability to other areas, providing a foundation on which to build locally relevant programs.

Funding for Research on AIDS and HIV

Confronting the AIDS epidemic will require new and substantially increased financial support for basic biomedical and social science research activities. The rapid and effective application of the insights provided by basic research will also require the significant expansion of applied research activities. In addition, funds are needed to provide researchers with adequate equipment and facilities, to attract high-caliber individuals into the field, and to support the training of future investigators.

The Public Health Service's request to the U.S. Department of Health and Human Services for AIDS-related research in FY 1988 was $471 million. If appropriated, this budget would represent a doubling of funds from FY 1986 to FY 1988. The National Science Foundation spends just over $50 million annually on social science research, but presently a very small amount of this is on studies related to AIDS.

The committee believes that there are sufficient areas of need and opportunity to double research funding again by 1990, leading to an approximately $1 billion budget in that year. These funds must be new appropriations, not a reallocation of existing Public Health Service funds. Areas of clear need include high-containment facilities for primate research, better containment facilities for universities and research institutes, training funds, construction and renovation funds, equipment funds, social science and behavioral research funding, vaccine and drug development efforts, international studies, basic research efforts, and epidemiologic studies. In addition, funds diverted from NIH programs to support the AIDS effort should be returned.

In recent years there has been a steady decline in the proportion of NIH funds spent on grants for investigator-initiated research on AIDS and an increasing proportion expended on contracts for NIH-designed studies. A more balanced growth of support is desirable in coming funding cycles to promote the involvement of the nonfederal basic research community to a greater extent. The level of funding for investigator-initiated studies in all areas (including non-AIDS studies) must be adequate to continue to attract the most able younger scientists to clinical, social science, and basic biomedical research, or the quality and productivity of the scientific enterprise will suffer.

INTERNATIONAL ASPECTS OF AIDS AND HIV INFECTION

More than half the countries of the world have reported cases of AIDS. Although reporting may not be reliable in many countries, it has been estimated, based on studies in specific areas, on the number of identified cases, and on the U.S. ratio of cases to seropositive persons, that up to 10 million people worldwide may be infected with HIV. A substantial proportion of these are in sub-Saharan Africa, particularly central Africa.

It is likely that millions of infected adults will progress to AIDS in the next decade, and that tens of thousands of infants will contract the syndrome perinatally. In response to this situation, many developed and developing countries are initiating research and prevention programs, and the World Health Organization is initiating a global program for the control of AIDS.

Rationale for U.S. International Involvement

The United States has actively promoted the technological development of less developed countries for economic, altruistic, and political reasons. Because AIDS most often occurs in young adults, it imposes a particularly severe burden on development efforts in these nations by draining off intellectual and economic assets—namely, productive individuals.

U.S. technical assistance programs have often included major contributions to efforts in improving health through programs in immunization and nutrition. The burden of AIDS and other HIV-related conditions added to the lengthy existing agenda of health problems in developing countries may negate the hard-won gains made by these programs.

New knowledge critical to prevention and treatment of HIV infection may be more readily obtained outside of the United States. For instance, the extent of perinatal and heterosexual transmission in central Africa offers opportunities for U.S. research resources to complement local expertise in mutually beneficial investigations.

Certain federal agencies have special international responsibilities or may be able to make contributions to the global effort to control the AIDS epidemic through support of activities in the United States. These agencies include the Agency for International Development, the Food and Drug Administration, and the Centers for Disease Control. There is also need for U.S. involvement in AIDS internationally because the operations of many federal agencies and other organizations require that their personnel visit or live in countries where HIV infection may be relatively prevalent. Such personnel may be at risk of infection or need appropriate care.

Risks of Infection Outside the United States

Sexual transmission probably accounts for the largest proportion of transmission of HIV outside of the United States. Bidirectional heterosexual transmission is the dominant mode of HIV transmission in sub-Saharan Africa. HIV infection is also becoming a major problem among female prostitutes in many areas.

HIV transmission between homosexual men must be presumed to be possible wherever behavior involving risk of infection is practiced. Knowledge of the frequency with which homosexual behavior occurs in different countries and cultures is incomplete, however, and existing information may not be reliable.

Transfusion of blood poses a substantial risk of HIV infection in many countries of the world that have not adopted procedures necessary to prevent such transmission and that lack the laboratories, finances, or personnel needed to institute such measures.

Application of currently available serologic tests will be possible only in some situations. **The committee concludes** that simpler serologic tests that give sensitive and specific results rapidly and reliably are essential before widespread efforts to control HIV transmission via the blood supply in developing countries will be practicable.

Transmission of HIV through the sharing of needles and syringes used to inject IV drugs is well documented in countries where IV drug use is common. However, some evidence suggests that in Africa injections administered for medical purposes with unsterile needles and syringes may be a route of HIV transmission.

There is no evidence to support the hypothesis that HIV is transmitted through insect vectors or casual contact. Studies in Africa of household contacts of infected persons and the age distribution of AIDS and HIV infection suggest that transmission by casual contact is very infrequent or nonexistent. The relative ineffectiveness of needlestick transmission in health professionals and the age distribution of AIDS and HIV infection also suggest that mechanical transmission by insects is unlikely.

International Research Opportunities

The United States has contributed greatly to the understanding of AIDS and HIV infection through its investment in domestic research. The international efforts undertaken to date illustrate the reasons and opportunities for the United States to contribute to multinational and bilateral efforts.

As is appropriate, some of the United States' support for international efforts on AIDS and HIV is committed for use exclusively through the World Health Organization (WHO). The committee believes that additional bilateral or multinational activities involving the United States outside of the WHO program will be essential to enhancing the prospects for achieving rapid control over the disease.

The WHO program is in the early phases of organization, but the need for action in some countries is urgent. The focus of the WHO program is prevention and control of AIDS and HIV infection rather than research opportunities, and links of U.S. investigators or institutions with affected countries could provide a means of rapid response to their needs.

The committee recommends that the United States be a full participant in international efforts against AIDS and HIV infection. U.S. involvement should be both through support of WHO programs and through bilateral arrangements in response to the needs and opportunities in individual countries. These arrangements should be pursued in a fashion that is acceptable to host governments.

The magnitude of the problem internationally and the variety of reasons warranting U.S. participation in international efforts convince the committee that the United States should make clear its commitment to global prevention and control of AIDS and HIV infection.

The following are feasible goals: (1) the total amount of U.S. funding going to international efforts in AIDS-related research and prevention should reach $50 million per year by 1990 (this is approximately 2.5 percent of the amount recommended by the committee for use in the United States for these purposes); (2) increased funding should be provided to the WHO program on the basis of demonstrated capacity to use such funds productively; and (3) increased funds to bilateral research or technical assistance programs or projects abroad should be provided on the basis of review procedures involving persons familiar with the local conditions under which such projects are undertaken.

The committee found information to be lacking on the extent and kinds of work on HIV-related conditions by U.S. investigators in other countries or on their collaborations with foreign researchers. **The committee recommends** that an evaluation be initiated immediately to identify all work under way and to assess and coordinate the roles and responses of the various U.S. federal agencies, private voluntary groups, and foundations interested in international efforts on AIDS and HIV.

GUIDANCE FOR THE NATION'S EFFORTS

No single approach—whether education and other public health measures, vaccination, or therapy—is likely to be wholly successful in combating all the problems posed by HIV infection. Similarly, neither the public sector, the private sector, nor any particular agency, organization, or group can be expected by itself to provide the solution to the diverse problems posed by the disease. Federal agencies (notably the National Institutes of Health, the Centers for Disease Control, and the Food and Drug Administration) have contributed enormously to the rapid acquisition of knowledge about AIDS and HIV or to techniques to help in its control. They should continue their efforts, but greater involvement of the academic and private sectors should now be encouraged.

All of these approaches and entities must be organized in a national effort, integrated and coordinated so that participants are working toward common goals and are aware of each other's activities. Such coordination does not imply management by a centralized directorate. However, monitoring of the many activities in the effort is necessary to ensure that important matters are not overlooked and that periodic review can be conducted for the adjustment of priorities and general directions.

What Is Needed?

The committee found gaps in the efforts being directed against the AIDS epidemic and in the employment of the nation's resources. It also identified as a major concern a lack of cohesiveness and strategic planning throughout the national effort. A body is needed to identify necessary actions and to mobilize underused resources in meeting the challenge of the epidemic. Therefore, **the committee recommends** that a new entity—a National Commission on AIDS—be established to meet the need for guidance of the national efforts against HIV.

The commission would monitor the course of the epidemic; evaluate research, health care, and public health needs; encourage federal, state, philanthropic, industrial, and other entities to participate; stimulate the strongest possible involvement of the academic scientific community; encourage greater U.S. contribution to international efforts by relevant government agencies and other organizations; make recommendations for altering the directions or intensity of health care, public health, and research efforts as the problem evolves; monitor and advise on related legal and ethical issues; and report to the American public.

The commission should achieve its purposes by assuming an advisory role and by acting catalytically in bringing together disparate groups. It should not dispense funds but should be provided with sufficient resources to undertake its mission effectively.

Establishment of the Commission

To oversee and marshal the nation's resources effectively, the proposed commission should have certain attributes. It should be able to engage all of the diverse public and private resources that can be brought to bear on HIV-associated problems. It must be sufficiently independent to give critical advice to participants in these efforts. It should have sufficient national and international stature and credibility for its advice to command the attention of participants.

The advantages and disadvantages of various institutional locations for the commission were evaluated by the committee. The requirement for spanning both public and private sectors implies that it should not be created within the administrative structure of the federal executive branch. However, the desirability of affirming a national commitment to the control of AIDS and HIV suggests that the commission should be endorsed at the highest levels of government. Accordingly,

• **The committee recommends** that the proposed National Commission on AIDS be created as a presidential or joint presidential-congressional commission.

• **The committee recommends** that the President take a strong leadership role in the effort against AIDS and HIV, designating control of AIDS as a major national goal and ensuring that the financial, human, and institutional resources needed to combat HIV infection and to care for AIDS patients are provided.

• **The committee urges** all cabinet secretaries and other ranking executive branch officials to determine how AIDS and HIV relate to their responsibilities and to encourage the units within their purview to work collaboratively toward responding to the epidemic on a national and international level.

• **The committee recommends** that the U.S. Congress maintain its strong interest in the control of AIDS and HIV infection and increase research appropriations toward a level of $1 billion annually by 1990. In addition, it recommends that by 1990 there be significant federal contributions toward the $1 billion annually required for the total costs of education and public health measures.

MAJOR RECOMMENDATIONS

In summary, the committee recommends that two major actions be undertaken to confront the epidemic of HIV infection and AIDS. They are as follows:

1. Undertake a massive media, educational, and public health campaign to curb the spread of HIV infection.

2. Begin substantial, long-term, and comprehensive programs of research in the biomedical and social sciences intended to prevent HIV infection and to treat the diseases caused by it.

Within a few years these two major areas of action should each be supported with expenditures of $1 billion a year in newly available funds not taken from other health or research budgets. The federal government should bear the responsibility for the $1 billion in research funding and is also the only possible majority funding source for expenditures of the magnitude seen necessary for education and public health.

Furthermore, to promote and integrate public and private sector efforts against HIV infection, a National Commission on AIDS should be created. Such a commission would advise on needed actions and report to the American people.

Curbing the spread of HIV infection will entail many actions, including the following:

• Expand the availability of serologic testing, particularly among persons in high-risk groups. Encourage testing by keeping it voluntary and ensuring confidentiality.

• Expand treatment and prevention programs against IV drug use. Experiment with making clean needles and syringes more freely available to reduce sharing of contaminated equipment.

The care of HIV patients can be greatly improved by applying the results of health services research. In the meantime, the following actions should be taken:

• Begin planning and training now for an increasing case load of patients with HIV infection. Emphasize care in the community, keeping hospitalization at a minimum.

• Find the best ways to collect demographic, health, and cost data on patients to identify cost-effective approaches to care.

• Devise methods of financing care that will provide appropriate and adequate funding.

The recommended research efforts should include the following actions:

• Enhance the knowledge needed for vaccine and drug development through basic research in virology, immunology, and viral protein structure.

• Improve understanding of the natural history and pathogenesis of AIDS, and trace the spread of HIV infection by means of epidemiologic and clinical research.

• Study sexual behavior and IV drug use to find ways to reduce the risk of infection.

• Encourage participation of academic scientists in research against AIDS, in part by increasing the funding for investigator-initiated research proposals.

• Solicit participation of industry in collaboration with federal and academic research programs.

• Expand experimental animal resources, working especially to conserve chimpanzee stocks, and develop new animal models of HIV infection.

Because AIDS and HIV infection are major and mounting health problems worldwide:

• The United States should be a full participant in international efforts against the epidemic.

• United States involvement should include both support of World Health Organization programs and bilateral efforts.

B

CDC Classification System for HIV Infections and Revised Case Definition for AIDS

CDC Classification System for HIV Infections*

INTRODUCTION

Persons infected with the etiologic retrovirus of acquired immunodeficiency syndrome (AIDS) (1-4)* may present with a variety of manifestations ranging from asymptomatic infection to severe immunodeficiency and life-threatening secondary infectious diseases or cancers. The rapid growth of knowledge about human T-lymphotropic virus type III/lymphadenopathy-associated virus (HTLV-III/LAV) has resulted in an increasing need for a system of classifying patients within this spectrum of clinical and laboratory findings attributable to HTLV-III/LAV infection (5-7).

Various means are now used to describe and assess patients with manifestations of HTLV-III/LAV infection and to describe their signs, symptoms, and laboratory findings. The surveillance definition of AIDS has proven to be extremely valuable and quite reliable for some epidemiologic studies and clinical assessment of patients with the more severe manifestations of disease. However, more inclusive definitions and classifications of HTLV-III/LAV infection are needed for optimum patient care, health planning, and public health control strategies, as well as for epidemiologic studies and special surveys. A broadly applicable, easily understood classification system should also facilitate and clarify communication about this disease.

In an attempt to formulate the most appropriate classification system, CDC has sought the advice of a panel of expert consultants[†] to assist in defining the manifestations of HTLV-III/LAV infection.

GOALS AND OBJECTIVES OF THE CLASSIFICATION SYSTEM

The classification system presented in this report is primarily applicable to public health purposes, including disease reporting and surveillance, epidemiologic studies, prevention and control activities, and public health policy and planning.

---

*The AIDS virus has been variously termed human T-lymphotropic virus type III (HTLV-III), lymphadenopathy-associated virus (LAV), AIDS-associated retrovirus (ARV), or human immunodeficiency virus (HIV). The designation human immunodeficiency virus (HIV) has recently been proposed by a subcommittee of the International Committee for the Taxonomy of Viruses as the appropriate name for the retrovirus that has been implicated as the causative agent of AIDS (4).

[†]The following persons served on the review panel: DS Burke, MD, RR Redfield, MD, Walter Reed Army Institute of Research, Washington, DC; J Chin, MD, State Epidemiologist, California Department of Health Services; LZ Cooper, MD, St Luke's-Roosevelt Hospital Center, New York City; JP Davis, MD, State Epidemiologist, Wisconsin Division of Health; MA Fischl, MD, University of Miami School of Medicine, Miami, Florida; G Friedland, MD, Albert Einstein College of Medicine, New York City; MA Johnson, MD, DI Abrams, MD, San Francisco General Hospital; D Mildvan, MD, Beth Israel Medical Center, New York City; CU Tuazon, MD, George Washington University School of Medicine, Washington, DC; RW Price, MD, Memorial Sloan-Kettering Cancer Center, New York City; C Konigsberg, MD, Broward County Public Health Unit, Fort Lauderdale, Florida; MS Gottlieb, MD, University of California—Los Angeles Medical Center; representatives of the National Institute of Allergy and Infectious Diseases, National Cancer Institute, National Institutes of Health; Center for Infectious Diseases, CDC.

SOURCE: Reprinted from *Morbidity and Mortality Weekly Report* 35 (May 23, 1986):334–339.

Immediate applications of such a system include the classification of infected persons for reporting of cases to state and local public health agencies, and use in various disease coding and recording systems, such as the forthcoming 10th revision of the International Classification of Diseases.

DEFINITION OF HTLV-III/LAV INFECTION

The most specific diagnosis of HTLV-III/LAV infection is by direct identification of the virus in host tissues by virus isolation; however, the techniques for isolating HTLV-III/LAV currently lack sensitivity for detecting infection and are not readily available. For public health purposes, patients with repeatedly reactive screening tests for HTLV-III/LAV antibody (e.g., enzyme-linked immunosorbent assay) in whom antibody is also identified by the use of supplemental tests (e.g., Western blot, immunofluorescence assay) should be considered both infected and infective (8-10).

Although HTLV-III/LAV infection is identified by isolation of the virus or, indirectly, by the presence of antibody to the virus, a presumptive clinical diagnosis of HTLV-III/LAV infection has been made in some situations in the absence of positive virologic or serologic test results. There is a very strong correlation between the clinical manifestations of AIDS as defined by CDC and the presence of HTLV-III/LAV antibody (11-14). Most persons whose clinical illness fulfills the CDC surveillance definition for AIDS will have been infected with the virus (12-14).

CLASSIFICATION SYSTEM

This system classifies the manifestations of HTLV-III/LAV infection into four mutually exclusive groups, designated by Roman numerals I through IV (Table 5). *The classification system applies only to patients diagnosed as having HTLV-III/LAV infection (see previous section,* **DEFINITION OF HTLV-III/LAV INFECTION**). Classification in a particular group is not explicitly intended to have prognostic significance, nor to designate severity of illness. However, classification in the four principal groups, I-IV, is hierarchical in that persons classified in a particular group should not be reclassified in a preceding group if clinical findings resolve, since clinical improvement may not accurately reflect changes in the severity of the underlying disease.

Group I includes patients with transient signs and symptoms that appear at the time of, or shortly after, initial infection with HTLV-III/LAV as identified by laboratory studies. All patients in Group I will be reclassified in another group following resolution of this acute syndrome.

TABLE 5. Summary of classification system for human T-lymphotropic virus type III/ lymphadenopathy-associated virus

Group I.	Acute infection
Group II.	Asymptomatic infection*
Group III.	Persistent generalized lymphadenopathy*
Group IV.	Other disease
Subgroup A.	Constitutional disease
Subgroup B.	Neurologic disease
Subgroup C.	Secondary infectious diseases
Category C-1.	Specified secondary infectious diseases listed in the CDC surveillance definition for AIDS[†]
Category C-2.	Other specified secondary infectious diseases
Subgroup D.	Secondary cancers[†]
Subgroup E.	Other conditions

*Patients in Groups II and III may be subclassified on the basis of a laboratory evaluation.
[†]Includes those patients whose clinical presentation fulfills the definition of AIDS used by CDC for national reporting.

Group II includes patients who have no signs or symptoms of HTLV-III/LAV infection. Patients in this category may be subclassified based on whether hematologic and/or immunologic laboratory studies have been done and whether results are abnormal in a manner consistent with the effects of HTLV-III/LAV infection.

Group III includes patients with persistent generalized lymphadenopathy, but without findings that would lead to classification in Group IV. Patients in this category may be subclassified based on the results of laboratory studies in the same manner as patients in Group II.

Group IV includes patients with clinical symptoms and signs of HTLV-III/LAV infection other than or in addition to lymphadenopathy. Patients in this group are assigned to *one or more* subgroups based on clinical findings. These subgroups are: A. constitutional disease; B. neurologic disease; C. secondary infectious diseases; D. secondary cancers; and E. other conditions resulting from HTLV-III/LAV infection. There is no *a priori* hierarchy of severity among subgroups A through E, and these subgroups are not mutually exclusive.

Definitions of the groups and subgroups are as follows:

Group I. Acute HTLV-III/LAV Infection. Defined as a mononucleosis-like syndrome, with or without aseptic meningitis, associated with seroconversion for HTLV-III/LAV antibody (*15-16*). Antibody seroconversion is required as evidence of initial infection; current viral isolation procedures are not adequately sensitive to be relied on for demonstrating the onset of infection.

Group II. Asymptomatic HTLV-III/LAV Infection. Defined as the absence of signs or symptoms of HTLV-III/LAV infection. To be classified in Group II, patients must have had no previous signs or symptoms that would have led to classification in Groups III or IV. Patients whose clinical findings caused them to be classified in Groups III or IV should not be reclassified in Group II if those clinical findings resolve.

Patients in this group may be subclassified on the basis of a laboratory evaluation. Laboratory studies commonly indicated for patients with HTLV-III/LAV infection include, but are not limited to, a complete blood count (including differential white blood cell count) and a platelet count. Immunologic tests, especially T-lymphocyte helper and suppressor cell counts, are also an important part of the overall evaluation. Patients whose test results are within normal limits, as well as those for whom a laboratory evaluation has not yet been completed, should be differentiated from patients whose test results are consistent with defects associated with HTLV-III/LAV infection (e.g., lymphopenia, thrombocytopenia, decreased number of helper [T_4] T-lymphocytes).

Group III. Persistent Generalized Lymphadenopathy (PGL). Defined as palpable lymphadenopathy (lymph node enlargement of 1 cm or greater) at two or more extra-inguinal sites persisting for more than 3 months in the absence of a concurrent illness or condition other than HTLV-III/LAV infection to explain the findings. Patients in this group may also be subclassified on the basis of a laboratory evaluation, as is done for asymptomatic patients in Group II (see above). Patients with PGL whose clinical findings caused them to be classified in Group IV should not be reclassified in Group III if those other clinical findings resolve.

Group IV. Other HTLV-III/LAV Disease. The clinical manifestations of patients in this group may be designated by assignment to one or more subgroups (A-E) listed below. Within Group IV, subgroup classification is independent of the presence or absence of lymphadenopathy. Each subgroup may include patients who are minimally symptomatic, as well as patients who are severely ill. Increased specificity for manifestations of HTLV-III/LAV infection, if needed for clinical purposes or research purposes or for disability determinations, may be achieved by creating additional divisions within each subgroup.

Subgroup A. Constitutional disease. Defined as one or more of the following: fever persisting more than 1 month, involuntary weight loss of greater than 10% of baseline, or diarrhea persisting more than 1 month; and the absence of a concurrent illness or condition other than HTLV-III/LAV infection to explain the findings.

Subgroup B. Neurologic disease. Defined as one or more of the following: dementia, myelopathy, or peripheral neuropathy; and the absence of a concurrent illness or condition other than HTLV-III/LAV infection to explain the findings.

Subgroup C. Secondary infectious diseases. Defined as the diagnosis of an infectious disease associated with HTLV-III/LAV infection and/or at least moderately indicative of a defect in cell-mediated immunity. Patients in this subgroup are divided further into two categories:

Category C-1. Includes patients with symptomatic or invasive disease due to one of 12 specified secondary infectious diseases listed in the surveillance definition of AIDS[§]: *Pneumocystis carinii* pneumonia, chronic cryptosporidiosis, toxoplasmosis, extraintestinal strongyloidiasis, isosporiasis, candidiasis (esophageal, bronchial, or pulmonary), cryptococcosis, histoplasmosis, mycobacterial infection with *Mycobacterium avium* complex or *M. kansasii*, cytomegalovirus infection, chronic mucocutaneous or disseminated herpes simplex virus infection, and progressive multifocal leukoencephalopathy.

Category C-2. Includes patients with symptomatic or invasive disease due to one of six other specified secondary infectious diseases: oral hairy leukoplakia, multidermatomal herpes zoster, recurrent *Salmonella* bacteremia, nocardiosis, tuberculosis, or oral candidiasis (thrush).

Subgroup D. Secondary cancers. Defined as the diagnosis of one or more kinds of cancer known to be associated with HTLV-III/LAV infection as listed in the surveillance definition of AIDS and at least moderately indicative of a defect in cell-mediated immunity[¶]: Kaposi's sarcoma, non-Hodgkin's lymphoma (small, noncleaved lymphoma or immunoblastic sarcoma), or primary lymphoma of the brain.

Subgroup E. Other conditions in HTLV-III/LAV infection. Defined as the presence of other clinical findings or diseases, not classifiable above, that may be attributed to HTLV-III/LAV infection and/or may be indicative of a defect in cell-mediated immunity. Included are patients with chronic lymphoid interstitial pneumonitis. Also included are those patients whose signs or symptoms could be attributed either to HTLV-III/LAV infection or to another coexisting disease not classified elsewhere, and patients with other clinical illnesses, the course or management of which may be complicated or altered by HTLV-III/LAV infection. Examples include: patients with constitutional symptoms not meeting the criteria for subgroup IV-A; patients with infectious diseases not listed in subgroup IV-C; and patients with neoplasms not listed in subgroup IV-D.

Reported by Center for Infectious Diseases, CDC.

Editorial Note: The classification system is meant to provide a means of grouping patients infected with HTLV-III/LAV according to the clinical expression of disease. It will require periodic revision as warranted by new information about HTLV-III/LAV infection. The defini-

---

[§]This subgroup includes patients with one or more of the specified infectious diseases listed whose clinical presentation fulfills the definition of AIDS as used by CDC for national reporting.

[¶]This subgroup includes those patients with one or more of the specified cancers listed whose clinical presentation fulfills the definition of AIDS as used by CDC for national reporting.

tion of particular syndromes will evolve with increasing knowledge of the significance of certain clinical findings and laboratory tests. New diagnostic techniques, such as the detection of specific HTLV-III/LAV antigens or antibodies, may add specificity to the assessment of patients infected with HTLV-III/LAV.

The classification system defines a limited number of specified clinical presentations. Patients whose signs and symptoms do not meet the criteria for other groups and subgroups, but whose findings are attributable to HTLV-III/LAV infection, should be classified in subgroup IV-E. As the classification system is revised and updated, certain subsets of patients in subgroup IV-E may be identified as having related groups of clinical findings that should be separately classified as distinct syndromes. This could be accomplished either by creating additional subgroups within Group IV or by broadening the definitions of the existing subgroups.

Persons currently using other classification systems *(6-7)* or nomenclatures (e.g., AIDS-related complex, lymphadenopathy syndrome) can find equivalences with those systems and terminologies and the classification presented in this report. Because this classification system has only four principal groups based on chronology, presence or absence of signs and symptoms, and the type of clinical findings present, comparisons with other classifications based either on clinical findings or on laboratory assessment are easily accomplished.

This classification system does not imply any change in the definition of AIDS used by CDC since 1981 for national reporting. Patients whose clinical presentations fulfill the surveillance definition of AIDS are classified in Group IV. However, not every case in Group IV will meet the surveillance definition.

Persons wishing to comment on this material are encouraged to send comments in writing to the AIDS Program, Center for Infectious Diseases, CDC.

References

1. Gallo RC, Salahuddin SZ, Popovic M, et al. Frequent detection and isolation of cytopathic retroviruses (HTLV-III) from patients with AIDS and at risk for AIDS. Science 1984;224:500-3.
2. Barré-Sinoussi F, Chermann JC, Rey F, et al. Isolation of a T-lymphotropic retrovirus from a patient at risk for acquired immune deficiency syndrome (AIDS). Science 1983;220:868-71.
3. Levy JA, Hoffman AD, Kramer SM, Landis JA, Shimabukuro JM, Oshiro LS. Isolation of lymphocytopathic retroviruses from San Francisco patients with AIDS. Science 1984;225:840-2.
4. Coffin J, Haase A, Levy JA, et al. Human immunodeficiency viruses [Letter]. Science 1986;232:697.
5. CDC. Revision of the case definition of acquired immunodeficiency syndrome for national reporting—United States. MMWR 1985;34:373-5.
6. Haverkos HW, Gottlieb MS, Killen JY, Edelman R. Classification of HTLV-III/LAV-related diseases [Letter]. J Infect Dis 1985;152:1095.
7. Redfield RR, Wright DC, Tramont EC. The Walter Reed staging classification for HTLV-III/LAV infection. N Engl J Med 1986;314:131-2.
8. CDC. Antibodies to a retrovirus etiologically associated with acquired immunodeficiency syndrome (AIDS) in populations with increased incidences of the syndrome. MMWR 1984;33:377-9.
9. CDC. Update: Public Health Service Workshop on Human T-Lymphotropic Virus Type III Antibody Testing—United States. MMWR 1985;34:477-8.
10. CDC. Additional recommendations to reduce sexual and drug abuse-related transmission of human T-lymphotropic virus type III/lymphadenopathy-associated virus. MMWR 1986;35:152-5.
11. Selik RM, Haverkos HW, Curran JW. Acquired immune deficiency syndrome (AIDS) trends in the United States, 1978-1982. Am J Med 1984;76:493-500.
12. Sarngadharan MG, Popovic M, Bruch L, Schüpbach J, Gallo RC. Antibodies reactive with human T-lymphotropic retroviruses (HTLV-III) in the serum of patients with AIDS. Science 1984;224:506-8.
13. Safai B, Sarngadharan MG, Groopman JE, et al. Seroepidemiological studies of human T-lymphotropic retrovirus type III in acquired immunodeficiency syndrome. Lancet 1984;I:1438-40.
14. Laurence J, Brun-Vezinet F, Schutzer SE, et al. Lymphadenopathy associated viral antibody in AIDS. Immune correlations and definition of a carrier state. N Engl J Med 1984;311:1269-73.
15. Ho DD, Sarngadharan MG, Resnick L, Dimarzo-Veronese F, Rota TR, Hirsch MS. Primary human T-lymphotropic virus type III infection. Ann Intern Med 1985;103:880-3.
16. Cooper DA, Gold J, Maclean P, et al. Acute AIDS retrovirus infection. Definition of a clinical illness associated with seroconversion. Lancet 1985;I:537-40.

Revision of the CDC Surveillance Case Definition for AIDS*

INTRODUCTION

The following revised case definition for surveillance of acquired immunodeficiency syndrome (AIDS) was developed by CDC in collaboration with public health and clinical specialists. The Council of State and Territorial Epidemiologists (CSTE) has officially recommended adoption of the revised definition for national reporting of AIDS. The objectives of the revision are a) to track more effectively the severe disabling morbidity associated with infection with human immunodeficiency virus (HIV) (including HIV-1 and HIV-2); b) to simplify reporting of AIDS cases; c) to increase the sensitivity and specificity of the definition through greater diagnostic application of laboratory evidence for HIV infection; and d) to be consistent with current diagnostic practice, which in some cases includes presumptive, i.e., without confirmatory laboratory evidence, diagnosis of AIDS-indicative diseases (e.g., *Pneumocystis carinii* pneumonia, Kaposi's sarcoma).

The definition is organized into three sections that depend on the status of laboratory evidence of HIV infection (e.g., HIV antibody) (Figure 1). The major proposed changes apply to patients with laboratory evidence for HIV infection: a) inclusion of HIV encephalopathy, HIV wasting syndrome, and a broader range of specific AIDS-indicative diseases (Section II.A); b) inclusion of AIDS patients whose indicator diseases are diagnosed presumptively (Section II.B); and c) elimination of exclusions due to other causes of immunodeficiency (Section I.A).

Application of the definition for children differs from that for adults in two ways. First, multiple or recurrent serious bacterial infections and lymphoid interstitial pneumonia/pulmonary lymphoid hyperplasia are accepted as indicative of AIDS among children but not among adults. Second, for children<15 months of age whose mothers are thought to have had HIV infection during the child's perinatal period, the laboratory criteria for HIV infection are more stringent, since the presence of HIV antibody in the child is, by itself, insufficient evidence for HIV infection because of the persistence of passively acquired maternal antibodies < 15 months after birth.

The new definition is effective immediately. State and local health departments are requested to apply the new definition henceforth to patients reported to them. The initiation of the actual reporting of cases that meet the new definition is targeted for September 1, 1987, when modified computer software and report forms should be in place to accommodate the changes. CSTE has recommended retrospective application of the revised definition to patients already reported to health departments. The new definition follows:

---

*Reported by Council of State and Territorial Epidemiologists; AIDS Program, Center for Infectious Diseases, CDC.

SOURCE: Reprinted from *Morbidity and Mortality Weekly Report* 36, suppl. 1S (August 14, 1987):3S–15S.

1987 REVISION OF CASE DEFINITION FOR AIDS FOR SURVEILLANCE PURPOSES

For national reporting, a case of AIDS is defined as an illness characterized by one or more of the following "indicator" diseases, depending on the status of laboratory evidence of HIV infection, as shown below.

I. Without Laboratory Evidence Regarding HIV Infection

If laboratory tests for HIV were not performed or gave inconclusive results (*See* Appendix I) and the patient had no other cause of immunodeficiency listed in Section I.A below, then any disease listed in Section I.B indicates AIDS if it was diagnosed by a definitive method (*See* Appendix II).

A. Causes of immunodeficiency that disqualify diseases as indicators of AIDS in the absence of laboratory evidence for HIV infection

1. high-dose or long-term systemic corticosteroid therapy or other immuno-suppressive/cytotoxic therapy ≤3 months before the onset of the indicator disease
2. any of the following diseases diagnosed ≤3 months after diagnosis of the indicator disease: Hodgkin's disease, non-Hodgkin's lymphoma (other than primary brain lymphoma), lymphocytic leukemia, multiple myeloma, any other cancer of lymphoreticular or histiocytic tissue, or angioimmunoblastic lymphadenopathy
3. a genetic (congenital) immunodeficiency syndrome or an acquired immunodeficiency syndrome atypical of HIV infection, such as one involving hypogammaglobulinemia

B. Indicator diseases diagnosed definitively (*See* Appendix II)

1. candidiasis of the esophagus, trachea, bronchi, or lungs
2. cryptococcosis, extrapulmonary
3. cryptosporidiosis with diarrhea persisting >1 month
4. cytomegalovirus disease of an organ other than liver, spleen, or lymph nodes in a patient >1 month of age
5. herpes simplex virus infection causing a mucocutaneous ulcer that persists longer than 1 month; or bronchitis, pneumonitis, or esophagitis for any duration affecting a patient >1 month of age
6. Kaposi's sarcoma affecting a patient < 60 years of age
7. lymphoma of the brain (primary) affecting a patient < 60 years of age
8. lymphoid interstitial pneumonia and/or pulmonary lymphoid hyperplasia (LIP/PLH complex) affecting a child <13 years of age
9. *Mycobacterium avium* complex or *M. kansasii* disease, disseminated (at a site other than or in addition to lungs, skin, or cervical or hilar lymph nodes)
10. *Pneumocystis carinii* pneumonia
11. progressive multifocal leukoencephalopathy
12. toxoplasmosis of the brain affecting a patient >1 month of age

II. With Laboratory Evidence for HIV Infection

Regardless of the presence of other causes of immunodeficiency (I.A), in the presence of laboratory evidence for HIV infection (*See* Appendix I), any disease listed above (I.B) or below (II.A or II.B) indicates a diagnosis of AIDS.

A. Indicator diseases diagnosed definitively (*See* Appendix II)

1. bacterial infections, multiple or recurrent (any combination of at least two within a 2-year period), of the following types affecting a child < 13 years of age:

   septicemia, pneumonia, meningitis, bone or joint infection, or abscess of an internal organ or body cavity (excluding otitis media or superficial skin or mucosal abscesses), caused by *Haemophilus, Streptococcus* (including pneumococcus), or other pyogenic bacteria

2. coccidioidomycosis, disseminated (at a site other than or in addition to lungs or cervical or hilar lymph nodes)

3. HIV encephalopathy (also called "HIV dementia," "AIDS dementia," or "subacute encephalitis due to HIV") (*See* Appendix II for description)

4. histoplasmosis, disseminated (at a site other than or in addition to lungs or cervical or hilar lymph nodes)

5. isosporiasis with diarrhea persisting >1 month

6. Kaposi's sarcoma at any age

7. lymphoma of the brain (primary) at any age

8. other non-Hodgkin's lymphoma of B-cell or unknown immunologic phenotype and the following histologic types:

   a. small noncleaved lymphoma (either Burkitt or non-Burkitt type) (*See* Appendix IV for equivalent terms and numeric codes used in the *International Classification of Diseases*, Ninth Revision, Clinical Modification)

   b. immunoblastic sarcoma (equivalent to any of the following, although not necessarily all in combination: immunoblastic lymphoma, large-cell lymphoma, diffuse histiocytic lymphoma, diffuse undifferentiated lymphoma, or high-grade lymphoma) (*See* Appendix IV for equivalent terms and numeric codes used in the *International Classification of Diseases*, Ninth Revision, Clinical Modification)

   Note: Lymphomas are not included here if they are of T-cell immunologic phenotype or their histologic type is not described or is described as "lymphocytic," "lymphoblastic," "small cleaved," or "plasmacytoid lymphocytic"

9. any mycobacterial disease caused by mycobacteria other than *M. tuberculosis*, disseminated (at a site other than or in addition to lungs, skin, or cervical or hilar lymph nodes)

10. disease caused by *M. tuberculosis*, extrapulmonary (involving at least one site outside the lungs, regardless of whether there is concurrent pulmonary involvement)

11. *Salmonella* (nontyphoid) septicemia, recurrent

12. HIV wasting syndrome (emaciation, "slim disease") (*See* Appendix II for description)

B. Indicator diseases diagnosed presumptively (by a method other than those in Appendix II)

Note: Given the seriousness of diseases indicative of AIDS, it is generally important to diagnose them definitively, especially when therapy that would be used may have serious side effects or when definitive diagnosis is needed for eligibility for antiretroviral therapy. Nonetheless, in some situations, a patient's condition will not permit the performance of definitive tests. In other situations, accepted clinical practice may be to diagnose presumptively based on the presence of characteristic clinical and laboratory abnormalities. Guidelines for presumptive diagnoses are suggested in Appendix III.

1. candidiasis of the esophagus
2. cytomegalovirus retinitis with loss of vision
3. Kaposi's sarcoma
4. lymphoid interstitial pneumonia and/or pulmonary lymphoid hyperplasia (LIP/PLH complex) affecting a child <13 years of age
5. mycobacterial disease (acid-fast bacilli with species not identified by culture), disseminated (involving at least one site other than or in addition to lungs, skin, or cervical or hilar lymph nodes)
6. *Pneumocystis carinii* pneumonia
7. toxoplasmosis of the brain affecting a patient >1 month of age

III. With Laboratory Evidence Against HIV Infection

With laboratory test results negative for HIV infection (*See* Appendix I), a diagnosis of AIDS for surveillance purposes is ruled out *unless*:

A. all the other causes of immunodeficiency listed above in Section I.A are excluded; **AND**
B. the patient has had either:
    1. *Pneumocystis carinii* pneumonia diagnosed by a definitive method (*See* Appendix II); **OR**
    2. a. any of the other diseases indicative of AIDS listed above in Section I.B diagnosed by a definitive method (*See* Appendix II); **AND**
        b. a T-helper/inducer (CD4) lymphocyte count <400/mm^3.

COMMENTARY

The surveillance of severe disease associated with HIV infection remains an essential, though not the only, indicator of the course of the HIV epidemic. The number of AIDS cases and the relative distribution of cases by demographic, geographic, and behavioral risk variables are the oldest indices of the epidemic, which began in 1981 and for which data are available retrospectively back to 1978. The original surveillance case definition, based on then-available knowledge, provided useful epidemiologic data on severe HIV disease (1). To ensure a reasonable predictive value for underlying immunodeficiency caused by what was then an unknown agent, the indicators of AIDS in the old case definition were restricted to particular opportunistic diseases diagnosed by reliable methods in patients without specific known causes of immunodeficiency. After HIV was discovered to be the cause of AIDS, however, and highly sensitive and specific HIV-antibody tests became available, the spectrum of manifestations of HIV infection became better defined, and classification systems for HIV infection were developed (2-5). It became apparent that some progressive, seriously disabling, and even fatal conditions (e.g., encephalopathy, wasting syndrome) affecting a substantial number of HIV-infected patients were not subject to epidemiologic surveillance, as they were not included in the AIDS case definition. For reporting purposes, the revision adds to the definition most of those severe non-infectious, non-cancerous HIV-associated conditions that are categorized in the CDC clinical classification systems for HIV infection among adults and children (*4,5*).

Another limitation of the old definition was that AIDS-indicative diseases are diagnosed presumptively (i.e., without confirmation by methods required by the old definition) in 10%-15% of patients diagnosed with such diseases; thus, an appreciable proportion of AIDS cases were missed for reporting purposes (*6,7*). This proportion may be increasing, which would compromise the old case definition's usefulness as a tool for monitoring trends. The revised case definition permits the reporting of these clinically diagnosed cases as long as there is laboratory evidence of HIV infection.

The effectiveness of the revision will depend on how extensively HIV-antibody tests are used. Approximately one third of AIDS patients in the United States have been from New York City and San Francisco, where, since 1985, < 7% have been reported with HIV-antibody test results, compared with > 60% in other areas. The impact of the revision on the reported numbers of AIDS cases will also depend on the proportion of AIDS patients in whom indicator diseases are diagnosed presumptively rather than definitively. The use of presumptive diagnostic criteria varies geographically, being more common in certain rural areas and in urban areas with many indigent AIDS patients.

To avoid confusion about what should be reported to health departments, the term "AIDS" should refer only to conditions meeting the surveillance definition. This definition is intended only to provide consistent statistical data for public health purposes. Clinicians will not rely on this definition alone to diagnose serious disease caused by HIV infection in individual patients because there may be additional information that would lead to a more accurate diagnosis. For example, patients who are not reportable under the definition because they have either a negative HIV-antibody test or, in the presence of HIV antibody, an opportunistic disease not listed in the definition as an indicator of AIDS nonetheless may be diagnosed as having serious HIV disease on consideration of other clinical or laboratory characteristics of HIV infection or a history of exposure to HIV.

Conversely, the AIDS surveillance definition may rarely misclassify other patients as having serious HIV disease if they have no HIV-antibody test but have an AIDS-indicative disease with a background incidence unrelated to HIV infection, such as cryptococcal meningitis.

The diagnostic criteria accepted by the AIDS surveillance case definition should not be interpreted as the standard of good medical practice. Presumptive diagnoses are accepted in the definition because not to count them would be to ignore substantial morbidity resulting from HIV infection. Likewise, the definition accepts a reactive screening test for HIV antibody without confirmation by a supplemental test because a repeatedly reactive screening test result, in combination with an indicator disease, is highly indicative of true HIV disease. For national surveillance purposes, the tiny proportion of possibly false-positive screening tests in persons with AIDS-indicative diseases is of little consequence. For the individual patient, however, a correct diagnosis is critically important. The use of supplemental tests is, therefore, strongly endorsed. An increase in the diagnostic use of HIV-antibody tests could improve both the quality of medical care and the function of the new case definition, as well as assist in providing counselling to prevent transmission of HIV.

FIGURE I. Flow diagram for revised CDC case definition of AIDS, September 1, 1987

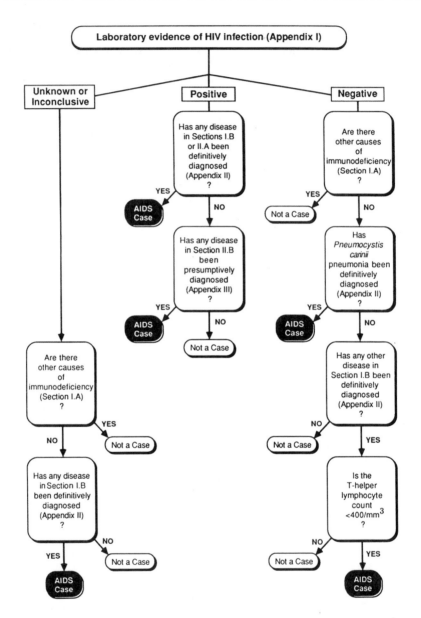

References

1. World Health Organization. Acquired immunodeficiency syndrome (AIDS): WHO/CDC case definition for AIDS. WHO Wkly Epidemiol Rec 1986;61:69-72.
2. Haverkos HW, Gottlieb MS, Killen JY, Edelman R. Classification of HTLV-III/LAV-related diseases [Letter]. J Infect Dis 1985;152:1095.
3. Redfield RR, Wright DC, Tramont EC. The Walter Reed staging classification of HTLV-III infection. N Engl J Med 1986;314:131-2.
4. CDC. Classification system for human T-lymphotropic virus type III/lymphadenopathy-associated virus infections. MMWR 1986;35:334-9.
5. CDC. Classification system for human immunodeficiency virus (HIV) infection in children under 13 years of age. MMWR 1987;36:225-30,235.
6. Hardy AM, Starcher ET, Morgan WM, et al. Review of death certificates to assess completeness of AIDS case reporting. Pub Hlth Rep 1987;102(4):386-91.
7. Starcher ET, Biel JK, Rivera-Castano R, Day JM, Hopkins SG, Miller JW. The impact of presumptively diagnosed opportunistic infections and cancers on national reporting of AIDS [Abstract]. Washington, DC : III International Conference on AIDS, June 1-5, 1987.

APPENDIX I

Laboratory Evidence For or Against HIV Infection

1. For Infection:

When a patient has disease consistent with AIDS:

a. a serum specimen from a patient ≥15 months of age, or from a child <15 months of age whose mother is not thought to have had HIV infection during the child's perinatal period, that is repeatedly reactive for HIV antibody by a screening test (e.g., enzyme-linked immunosorbent assay [ELISA]), as long as subsequent HIV-antibody tests (e.g., Western blot, immunofluorescence assay), if done, are positive; **OR**

b. a serum specimen from a child < 15 months of age, whose mother is thought to have had HIV infection during the child's perinatal period, that is repeatedly reactive for HIV antibody by a screening test (e.g., ELISA), plus increased serum immunoglobulin levels and at least one of the following abnormal immunologic test results: reduced absolute lymphocyte count, depressed CD4 (T-helper) lymphocyte count, or decreased CD4/CD8 (helper/suppressor) ratio, as long as subsequent antibody tests (e.g., Western blot, immunofluorescence assay), if done, are positive; **OR**

c. a positive test for HIV serum antigen; **OR**

d. a positive HIV culture confirmed by both reverse transcriptase detection and a specific HIV-antigen test or in situ hybridization using a nucleic acid probe; **OR**

e. a positive result on any other highly specific test for HIV (e.g., nucleic acid probe of peripheral blood lymphocytes).

2. Against Infection:

A nonreactive screening test for serum antibody to HIV (e.g., ELISA) without a reactive or positive result on any other test for HIV infection (e.g., antibody, antigen, culture), if done.

3. **Inconclusive (Neither For nor Against Infection)**:
   a. a repeatedly reactive screening test for serum antibody to HIV (e.g., ELISA) followed by a negative or inconclusive supplemental test (e.g., Western blot, immunofluorescence assay) without a positive HIV culture or serum antigen test, if done; **OR**
   b. a serum specimen from a child < 15 months of age, whose mother is thought to have had HIV infection during the child's perinatal period, that is repeatedly reactive for HIV antibody by a screening test, even if positive by a supplemental test, without additional evidence for immunodeficiency as described above (in 1.b) and without a positive HIV culture or serum antigen test, if done.

APPENDIX II

Definitive Diagnostic Methods for Diseases Indicative of AIDS

Diseases	Definitive Diagnostic Methods

cryptosporidiosis
cytomegalovirus
isosporiasis
Kaposi's sarcoma
lymphoma
lymphoid pneumonia
  or hyperplasia
Pneumocystis carinii
  pneumonia
progressive multifocal
  leukoencephalopathy
toxoplasmosis
	microscopy (histology or cytology).

candidiasis	gross inspection by endoscopy or autopsy or by microscopy (histology or cytology) on a specimen obtained directly from the tissues affected (including scrapings from the mucosal surface), not from a culture.
coccidioidomycosis cryptococcosis herpes simplex virus histoplasmosis	microscopy (histology or cytology), culture, or detection of antigen in a specimen obtained directly from the tissues affected or a fluid from those tissues.
tuberculosis other mycobacteriosis salmonellosis other bacterial infection	culture.

HIV encephalopathy*
(dementia)
} clinical findings of disabling cognitive and/or motor dysfunction interfering with occupation or activities of daily living, or loss of behavioral developmental milestones affecting a child, progressing over weeks to months, in the absence of a concurrent illness or condition other than HIV infection that could explain the findings. Methods to rule out such concurrent illnesses and conditions must include cerebrospinal fluid examination and either brain imaging (computed tomography or magnetic resonance) or autopsy.

HIV wasting syndrome*
} findings of profound involuntary weight loss >10% of baseline body weight plus either chronic diarrhea (at least two loose stools per day for ≥ 30 days) or chronic weakness and documented fever (for ≥ 30 days, intermittent or constant) in the absence of a concurrent illness or condition other than HIV infection that could explain the findings (e.g., cancer, tuberculosis, cryptosporidiosis, or other specific enteritis).

*For HIV encephalopathy and HIV wasting syndrome, the methods of diagnosis described here are not truly definitive, but are sufficiently rigorous for surveillance purposes.

APPENDIX III

Suggested Guidelines for Presumptive Diagnosis of Diseases Indicative of AIDS

Diseases

Presumptive Diagnostic Criteria

candidiasis of esophagus

a. recent onset of retrosternal pain on swallowing; **AND**
b. oral candidiasis diagnosed by the gross appearance of white patches or plaques on an erythematous base or by the microscopic appearance of fungal mycelial filaments in an uncultured specimen scraped from the oral mucosa.

cytomegalovirus retinitis

a characteristic appearance on serial ophthalmoscopic examinations (e.g., discrete patches of retinal whitening with distinct borders, spreading in a centrifugal manner, following blood vessels, progressing over several months, frequently associated with retinal vasculitis, hemorrhage, and necrosis). Resolution of active disease leaves retinal scarring and atrophy with retinal pigment epithelial mottling.

mycobacteriosis	microscopy of a specimen from stool or normally sterile body fluids or tissue from a site other than lungs, skin, or cervical or hilar lymph nodes, showing acid-fast bacilli of a species not identified by culture.
Kaposi's sarcoma	a characteristic gross appearance of an erythematous or violaceous plaque-like lesion on skin or mucous membrane. **(Note:** Presumptive diagnosis of Kaposi's sarcoma should not be made by clinicians who have seen few cases of it.)
lymphoid interstitial pneumonia	bilateral reticulonodular interstitial pulmonary infiltrates present on chest X ray for ≥2 months with no pathogen identified and no response to antibiotic treatment.
Pneumocystis carinii pneumonia	a. a history of dyspnea on exertion or nonproductive cough of recent onset (within the past 3 months); **AND** b. chest X-ray evidence of diffuse bilateral interstitial infiltrates or gallium scan evidence of diffuse bilateral pulmonary disease; **AND** c. arterial blood gas analysis showing an arterial pO_2 of <70 mm Hg or a low respiratory diffusing capacity (<80% of predicted values) or an increase in the alveolar-arterial oxygen tension gradient; **AND** d. no evidence of a bacterial pneumonia.
toxoplasmosis of the brain	a. recent onset of a focal neurologic abnormality consistent with intracranial disease or a reduced level of consciousness; **AND** b. brain imaging evidence of a lesion having a mass effect (on computed tomography or nuclear magnetic resonance) or the radiographic appearance of which is enhanced by injection of contrast medium; **AND** c. serum antibody to toxoplasmosis or successful response to therapy for toxoplasmosis.

APPENDIX IV

Equivalent Terms and International Classification of Disease (ICD) Codes for AIDS-Indicative Lymphomas

The following terms and codes describe lymphomas indicative of AIDS in patients with antibody evidence for HIV infection (Section II.A.8 of the AIDS case definition). Many of these terms are obsolete or equivalent to one another.

ICD-9-CM (1978)

Codes	Terms
200.0	**Reticulosarcoma** lymphoma (malignant): histiocytic (diffuse) reticulum cell sarcoma: pleomorphic cell type or not otherwise specified
200.2	**Burkitt's tumor or lymphoma** malignant lymphoma, Burkitt's type

ICD-O (Oncologic Histologic Types 1976)

Codes	Terms
9600/3	**Malignant lymphoma, undifferentiated cell type** non-Burkitt's or not otherwise specified
9601/3	**Malignant lymphoma, stem cell type** stem cell lymphoma
9612/3	**Malignant lymphoma, immunoblastic type** immunoblastic sarcoma, immunoblastic lymphoma, or immunoblastic lymphosarcoma
9632/3	**Malignant lymphoma, centroblastic type** diffuse or not otherwise specified, or germinoblastic sarcoma: diffuse or not otherwise specified
9633/3	**Malignant lymphoma, follicular center cell, non-cleaved** diffuse or not otherwise specified
9640/3	**Reticulosarcoma, not otherwise specified** malignant lymphoma, histiocytic: diffuse or not otherwise specified reticulum cell sarcoma, not otherwise specified malignant lymphoma, reticulum cell type
9641/3	**Reticulosarcoma, pleomorphic cell type** malignant lymphoma, histiocytic, pleomorphic cell type reticulum cell sarcoma, pleomorphic cell type
9750/3	**Burkitt's lymphoma or Burkitt's tumor** malignant lymphoma, undifferentiated, Burkitt's type malignant lymphoma, lymphoblastic, Burkitt's type

C

Correspondents

KAREN AUDITORE-HARGREAVES, Program for Appropriate Technology in Health, Seattle, Wash.

LEWELLYS F. BARKER, American Red Cross, Washington, D.C.

DAVID W. BARRY, Burroughs Wellcome Company, Research Triangle Park, N.C.

RONALD BAYER, The Hastings Center, Briarcliff Manor, N.Y.

SAMUEL BRODER, National Institutes of Health, Bethesda, Md.

ANN F. BRUNSWICK, Columbia University, New York City

DONALD S. BURKE, Walter Reed Army Medical Center, Washington, D.C.

JAMES CHIN, World Health Organization, Geneva, Switzerland

MOLLY COOKE, San Francisco General Hospital, San Francisco

DEBORAH COTTON, Beth Israel Hospital, Boston, Mass.

JAMES W. CURRAN, Centers for Disease Control, Atlanta, Ga.

WILLIAM J. CURRAN, Harvard Medical School, Boston, Mass.

WILLIAM W. DARROW, Centers for Disease Control, Atlanta, Ga.

DON C. DES JARLAIS, New York State Division of Substance Abuse Services, New York City

RONALD C. DESROSIERS, New England Regional Primate Research Center, Southborough, Mass.

DONALD P. FRANCIS, Department of Health Services, State of California, Berkeley

DAVID W. FRASER, Swarthmore College, Swarthmore, Pa.

GERALD FRIEDLAND, Albert Einstein College of Medicine, Bronx, N.Y.

218

PATRICIA N. FULTZ, Yerkes Regional Primate Research Center, Emory University, Atlanta, Ga.

ROBERT C. GALLO, National Institutes of Health, Bethesda, Md.

MURRAY B. GARDNER, University of California, Davis

BARRY D. GINGELL, Gay Men's Health Crisis, New York City

JAMES J. GOEDERT, National Institutes of Health, Bethesda, Md.

LARRY GOSTIN, American Society of Law and Medicine, Boston, Mass.

JESSE GREEN, New York University Medical Center, New York City

MARK GURNEY, The University of Chicago, Chicago, Ill.

MARGARET C. HEAGARTY, Columbia University, New York City

PEGGY HEINE, National Hemophilia Foundation, New York City

BETTY HOLM, Bank of America, San Francisco

KING K. HOLMES, University of Washington, Seattle

HARRY F. HULL, New Mexico Health and Environment Department, Santa Fe

RICHARD T. JOHNSON, The Johns Hopkins Medical Institutions, Baltimore, Md.

STEPHEN C. JOSEPH, New York City Department of Health

PHYLLIS J. KANKI, Harvard School of Public Health, Boston, Mass.

RONALD C. KENNEDY, Southwest Foundation for Biomedical Research, San Antonio, Texas

CHARLES C. LEIGHTON, Merck Sharp & Dohme Research Laboratories, West Point, Pa.

NORMAN L. LETVIN, New England Regional Primate Research Center, Southborough, Mass.

JEFFREY LEVI, National Gay and Lesbian Task Force, Washington, D.C.

JAY A. LEVY, University of California, San Francisco

JOHN L. MARTIN, Columbia University, New York City

JAMES O. MASON, Centers for Disease Control, Atlanta, Ga.

GENE W. MATTHEWS, Centers for Disease Control, Atlanta, Ga.

J. STEVEN McDOUGAL, Centers for Disease Control, Atlanta, Ga.

LEON McKUSICK, University of California, San Francisco

JOHN A. NEWMEYER, Haight-Ashbury Free Medical Clinic, San Francisco

JUNE E. OSBORN, University of Michigan, Ann Arbor

PETER L. PERINE, Uniformed Services University of the Health Sciences, Bethesda, Md.

PHYLLIS T. PIOTROW, The Johns Hopkins University, Baltimore, Md.

RICHARD W. PRICE, Memorial Sloan-Kettering Cancer Center, New York City

JONAS SALK, The Salk Institute for Biological Studies, San Diego

ANNE SCITOVSKY, Palo Alto Medical Foundation, Palo Alto, Calif.
GENE M. SHEARER, National Institutes of Health, Bethesda, Md.
MICHAEL STOTO, Institute of Medicine, Washington, D.C.
THOMAS M. VERNON, Colorado Department of Health, Denver
HANS WIGZELL, Karolinska Institutet, Stockholm, Sweden
CATHERINE M. WILFERT, Duke University Medical Center, Durham, N.C.
WARREN WINKELSTEIN, JR., University of California, Berkeley
CONSTANCE B. WOFSY, San Francisco General Hospital

D

Biographical Notes on Committee Members

STUART H. ALTMAN, dean of the Heller Graduate School for Social Policy, Brandeis University, and Sol C. Chaikin Professor of National Health Policy, is in his second term as chairman of the congressionally legislated Prospective Payment Assessment Commission, which oversees the Medicare hospital payment system. Between 1971 and 1976, Dean Altman was deputy assistant secretary for planning and evaluation/health in the Department of Health, Education, and Welfare. As deputy assistant secretary, he was one of the principal contributors to the development and advancement of the administration's national health insurance proposal. From 1973 to 1974, he served as deputy director for health of the President's Cost-of-Living Council and was responsible for developing the council's program on health care cost containment. Dean Altman has testified before various congressional committees on the problems of rising health care costs and the need to mandate a minimum benefits package for all full-time workers. He holds a Ph.D. in economics from the University of California, Los Angeles, and has taught at Brown University and the University of California, Berkeley.

DAVID BALTIMORE is director of the Whitehead Institute for Biomedical Research and professor of biology at the Massachusetts Institute of Technology. From 1974 until 1982, when he was named director of the institute, he was with the Center for Cancer Research of the Massachusetts Institute of Technology. He has taught in the Department of Biology at the Massachusetts Institute of Technology since being appointed to the faculty in 1968. In 1975 he received the Nobel Prize, together with Howard Temin and Renato Dulbecco, for the discovery of reverse transcriptase retroviruses. That same year he was an organizer of the Asilomar Conference in California, which focused attention on the development of genetic engineering, and he was later a member of the National Institutes of Health Recombinant DNA Advisory Committee. His present research focuses on molecular immunology, virology, AIDS, and cancer. Dr. Baltimore received his B.A. degree in chemistry from Swarthmore College and his Ph.D. in biology from Rockefeller University.

THEODORE COOPER is chairman of the board and chief executive officer of The Upjohn Company, Kalamazoo, Michigan. Prior to joining Upjohn in 1980, Dr. Cooper was dean of the Cornell University Medical College. He was appointed to that position in 1977. From 1975 until 1977, he served as assistant secretary for health in the Department of Health, Education, and Welfare. Dr. Cooper has also directed the Heart and Lung Institute of the National Institutes of Health and has held academic appointments at St. Louis University, the University of New Mexico, Cornell University Medical College, and Rockefeller University. He is the author or coauthor of more than 150 scientific papers and is a member of the American College of Cardiology, the American Physiological Society, the American Society for Clinical Investigation, and the American Society for Pharmacology and Experimental Therapeutics. Dr. Cooper is also a member of the Director's Advisory Committee of the National Institutes of Health, the Army Science Board, and the Advisory Council on Hazardous Substances Research and Training.

KRISTINE GEBBIE is the administrator of the Oregon Health Division, a position she has held since 1978. She has taught nursing studies at St. Louis University and the University of California, Los Angeles, and is an adjunct associate professor of nursing at the Oregon Health Sciences University School of Nursing. She is presently a member of the Presidential Commission on the Human Immunodeficiency Virus Epidemic. Ms. Gebbie is past president of the Association of State and Territorial Health Officials and chairs the Oregon AIDS Task Force. She received a B.S. degree in nursing from St. Olaf College, Minnesota, and an M.N. in community mental health nursing from the University of California School of Nursing in Los Angeles.

DONALD R. HOPKINS is a senior consultant to Global 2000 Inc. and the Task Force for Child Survival of the Carter Presidential Center in Atlanta, Georgia. From 1984 to 1987, he was deputy director of the

Centers for Disease Control; he served as assistant director for international health at CDC from 1978 to 1984. Dr. Hopkins taught tropical public health at the Harvard School of Public Health from 1974 to 1977 and directed the smallpox eradication program in Sierra Leone from 1967 to 1969. He has also authored an authoritative text on the history of smallpox, *Princes and Peasants: Smallpox in History.* Dr. Hopkins received his B.S. degree from Morehouse College, the M.D. degree from the University of Chicago, an M.P.H. from Harvard University, and an honorary D.Sc. from Morehouse College. He is a member of the Institute of Medicine.

KENNETH PREWITT, a political scientist, came to the Rockefeller Foundation in 1985 from the presidency (1979–1985) of the Social Science Research Council. From 1965 to 1982 he was a faculty member of the University of Chicago, becoming chairman of its Department of Political Science in 1975 and the following year, director of the National Opinion Research Center. Dr. Prewitt has had extensive first-hand experience in Africa, first as a visiting lecturer (1965–1966) at the University of East Africa and Makarere, Uganda, and subsequently (1970–1973) as a Rockefeller Foundation Visiting Research Fellow at the University of Nairobi in Kenya. Dr. Prewitt received his B.A. degree from Southern Methodist University, an M.A. degree from Washington University, and his Ph.D. from Stanford University. He is a director of (among other organizations) the Center for Advanced Study in the Behavioral Sciences at Washington University and the author or coauthor of a dozen books. He is also a member of the advisory bodies of several universities, foundations, and academic councils. Dr. Prewitt is a member of the American Academy of Arts and Sciences and the recipient of a Guggenheim fellowship.

HOWARD M. TEMIN is American Cancer Society Professor of Viral Oncology, Harold P. Rusch Professor of Cancer Research, and Steenbock Professor of Biological Sciences at the University of Wisconsin School of Medicine, Madison, where he has been since 1960. He has worked on retroviruses continuously since 1956, when he was a graduate student at the California Institute of Technology. In 1975 he received the Nobel Prize, together with David Baltimore and Renato Dulbecco, for some of this work. He is a member of the National Academy of Sciences and has served on the National Institutes of Health Virology Study Section and on the editorial board of several virology journals. He was also a member of the committee that wrote *Confronting AIDS.*

PAUL VOLBERDING is associate professor of medicine at the University of California, San Francisco, and chief of the Medical Oncology

Division and the AIDS Program at San Francisco General Hospital. During the past several years he has served on a variety of local, national, and international AIDS committees. He was a member of the steering committee of the IOM/ NAS panel that wrote *Confronting AIDS* and is on the executive committee of the AIDS Clinical Trials Group of the National Institute of Allergy and Infectious Diseases. Dr. Volberding is actively involved in the provision of care to AIDS patients and undertakes clinical research in the treatment of HIV infection and Kaposi's sarcoma. He received an A.B. degree from the University of Chicago and an M.D. from the University of Minnesota.

Index

Index

A

Acquired immune deficiency syndrome (AIDS)
  age trends, 4–5, 36
  animal models of, 18, 124; *see also* Animal models/experiments
  budget for, 22, 88
  cases by risk group, 34, 51–52
  clinical manifestations, 3, 36, 203–206, 214–216
  definition/defining, 2–3, 36–37, 81, 105, 173, 207–217
  demographic impact, 52, 109
  diagnosis, 71, 214–216
  disease presentation, 106
  economic costs in U.S., 16, 104–105, 108
  etiologic agent, 2, 33–35; *see also* Human immunodeficiency virus
  geographic differences in clinical manifestations, 106
  incidence, 36
  incubation period, 29, 61, 66, 83
  infectiousness, 5, 29, 61
  international scope of, 22–23, 159–160, 195
  mortality, 29, 52
  parallels and contrasts with past epidemics, 1, 27–28
  patterns of spread, 23, 33, 40, 70, 159–160
  progression from HIV infection to, 2, 34, 35–36, 37–38, 52, 127, 159, 173
  projected cases and deaths, 57, 108, 171
  reporting of cases, 159
  social response to, 2, 29; *see also* Discrimination
  as a special case, 1, 29–30
  worldwide cases, 22–23, 159
  see also Cofactors in AIDS; HIV infection; Human immunodeficiency virus; Pediatric AIDS
Africa
  AIDS cofactors in, 40
  blood supply contamination, 40
  heterosexual transmission of HIV in, 3, 40
  parenteral transmission in, 40
  seroprevalence in, 174
AIDS-associated retrovirus, *see* Human immunodeficiency virus
AIDS Federal Policy Bill, 11, 81
AIDS patients
  costs of care for, 104–106
  health care needs of specific populations, 13–14, 94–96, 106
  life expectancy, 108
  minorities, 15, 27, 98–99

227